A History of Urban America

A History of
URBAN
AMERICA

Charles N. Glaab
A. Theodore Brown
The University of Wisconsin–Milwaukee

The Macmillan Company
Collier-Macmillan Limited, London

PRINTING   111213   YEAR   3456789

Library of Congress catalog card number: 67–15198

THE MACMILLAN COMPANY
866 THIRD AVENUE, NEW YORK, NEW YORK 10022
COLLIER-MACMILLAN CANADA, LTD., TORONTO, ONTARIO

Printed in the United States of America

To the memory of
R. Richard Wohl

Preface

The word *urban* has come in our day to have almost the value of a talisman in academic as well as political life. It lends an air of serious and informed concern to discourse in which it appears. And yet, other than the fact that *urban* has somehow to do with cities, there is little agreement in ordinary discussion on what it means. Sociologists, geographers, political scientists, and economists have in recent years subjected city and metropolitan phenomena to intensive examination from many points of view and are endeavoring to make analytical tools of such concepts as urbanization. Historians, although not characteristically seeking generalizations and definitions, have contributed substantially to our knowledge of cities. Still, there has been almost no effort to synthesize the historical evidence which has been discovered—to use urban growth as the organizing theme in a study of the American past and to try to discover the historical meaning of that useful but elusive adjective, *urban*.

This book is an attempt to do just that. Many themes relevant to American urban history have not been examined here. Nevertheless, the book reflects our views of the subject's coherence, developed during a combined experience of twenty years' teaching and research in urban history. Particularly, we have avoided subordination of the subject to the periodization and other conventional categories of national history; readers will find little mention of the Revolution and Early National Period, the Civil War and Reconstruction, or the Progressive Era. We feel strongly that more is learned about the social process of urbanization when it is regarded as an "independent variable," when it is allowed to reveal its own phases and is not stretched to a Procrustean framework which was constructed long before scholars took urban history seriously.

We have made no effort to treat developments since the Second World War in any comprehensive way. The rapidly proliferating data on recent urban expansion, which the nation's scholars, journalists, and administrators amass in their growing attention to the city and the metropolis, cannot yet be viewed synthetically. We believe also that there is a point—impossible to locate exactly—as our studies approach the present day, at which the usefulness of historians' work diminishes relative to the usefulness of contributions by other social scientists.

While much that appears on the following pages rests upon our own conclusions developed during close study of original material, in a work of this kind the necessity for unsparing appropriation of the scholarship of others is obvious. Our colleagues will understand that adequate acknowledgment has not been possible, although we have tried to indicate those works from which our borrowing has been the heaviest.

We accept joint responsibility for the entire book. We wish to acknowledge special assistance generously extended by Lyle W. Dorsett, Catherine Goldsmith, and Eric E. Lampard, Shirley Darling and members of our departmental typing pool, and several graduate students in the Urban Affairs and Urban History programs at The University of Wisconsin–Milwaukee.

C. N. G.
A. T. B.

Contents

5

I

The Colonial Matrix

There is irony in the fact that the British Crown, from a very early date in the colonization of North America, encouraged its subjects in "the plantations" to organize towns and to arrange their farming and other extractive industries around these towns. In the seventeenth century colonial governors were often instructed, as in one actual case, "to draw tradesmen and handicraftmen into towns." One of the governors of Virginia told the colonial assembly in 1680 to pass measures facilitating the organization of towns; the King, he said, "is resolved as soon as storehouses and conveniences can be provided, to prohibit ships trading here to land or unload but at certain fixed places." The imperial rulers saw advantages to themselves in fostering the Americans' dependence upon their colonial towns. In the view of these rulers, the American colonies were like all other colonies: sources of English wealth and sources also of administrative problems. Colonies were supposed to function so as to profit the Empire —or at least to profit the relatively small group which ran the Empire—and for this purpose they had to be controlled; the doings of the energetic colonists had to be overseen. This task of control could best be carried out if colonial life, and especially colonial economic life, was channeled through a limited number of focal points. At these points the imperial authorities could regulate trade and check illicit businesses. So the Crown encouraged, even required, the laying out and chartering of towns in its American possessions—as in the case of Burlington, in what is now New Jersey, late in the seventeenth century: "Not any thing being of greater efficiency to promote trade and business . . . than the indult of such privileges as may invite active and ingenious men to resort thither and coinhabit therein and adventure their stocks and estates upon the issue of Providence in the way of trade. . . ." Or, a few decades later on, in the case of Suffolk, Virginia: "Great numbers of people have lately settled themselves at and near a place called Constances warehouse . . . and . . . in case a town was laid out there, trade would be greatly encouraged." Irony lay in the process by which town life, originally promoted partly in the interest of royal authority and imperial control, became the matrix of self-sustaining cultural life, business ambition, and political training in the colonies, all of which culminated in their secession from the British Empire. But that process occupied the better part of a century and three-quarters; people in the colonies were not generally aware of what was happening to them as their towns and later their cities flourished. Settlements designed originally to serve the needs of a mercantilist empire became agencies in its dissolution.*

To an extent, of course, the colonists needed no encouragement

---

* *Mercantilism* signifies, broadly, the political economy of the early nationalist era. Although the term never represented a thoroughly consistent, agreed-upon theory, its leading propositions were that a country's economic power should be systematically mobilized in the interest of national (usually imperial) security, and that this was best accomplished by strictly controlling productive activity and trade to the end that hard money (gold and silver) would flow into the country rather than out of it. Colonies were sought as sources of raw materials and colonists were restricted in their access to finished products to the mother country.

in starting town settlements. The civilization which shaped them and which they represented when they reached the shore of the wilderness was far past the stage where subsistence agriculture could play any significant part in it. The Virginia and New England pioneers came from an England whose political, social, and economic life depended upon connections and inter-actions which focused on London and the provincial cities. There, in the cities, goods were exchanged and ideas clashed; there wealth accumulated, power resided, and decisions were made. In their American enterprise the colonists would begin with closely-knit communities which would soon become towns. These towns would serve as markets, temples (in the sense that religious life would gather around them), and centers of political organization and control. The towns were essential to colonial life from the beginning. They were not called into existence by an earlier development of farming, but rather constituted the necessary positions from which agriculture and other activities, such as the fur trade, could spread inland without losing connection with the great world. Thus, the roots of American urbanization go back to the day of the first permanent settlement.

The Winthrops, Byrds, Livingstons, and those who accompanied them westward across the Atlantic Ocean, brought along notions of what towns were for and how people should live in them which still bore traces of the thought and custom of medieval Europe. Towns had appeared on the largely rural landscape of the Dark Ages and had grown at first almost as cracks in the social edifice of serfdom, manor, vassalage, and fealty. Although they were obviously very useful economically, and increasingly so as Western Europe arose from the patchwork efforts at organization which succeeded the fall of Rome, towns and townsfolk fitted uncomfortably into the localized and hierarchical arrangements of the earlier middle ages. Bit by bit, usually in the face of noble or clerical hostility, the people in the towns were able to defend their claims to varying measures of self-government and to such privileges of trading as they thought would be profitable. Thus, in a legal sense, towns became "bundles of privileges," or concessions which had been wrung from traditional authorities. This characteristic was carried over into the period when national states

3

dominated political life; that is, the towns and cities of England, France, and other countries in Western Europe were groups of people, living close together, to whom the sovereign granted the privilege of holding a market, establishing a municipal court or constabulary, and other similar functions. In the sixteenth and seventeenth centuries, as the principles of English mercantilism became clarified, the "privileges" were dispensed more in the interests of control than of benevolence.

There was another good reason for the organization of towns, which also reflected the need to impose authority upon the doings of people who lived close together. Social disorder usually attended such assemblages of people and the force of police and legal regulation of behavior had to be made available to the more responsible inhabitants of an area. The Mayflower Compact is an example of what was necessary; the leaders of the Pilgrim expedition formally agreed "to covenant and combine ourselves together into a civil Body Politick, for our better Ordering and Preservation . . . ." Before leaving London, the migrants had picked up as volunteers what one of their principal men called "an undesirable lot," and hence they wanted to provide themselves with some kind of seemingly authoritative means of making and enforcing laws. This could be done on a voluntary basis, as among the settlers of New England (and many other Americans after them) or the necessary stamp of legitimacy could come from the Crown. Thus, Elizabeth, New Jersey, was chartered in mid-eighteenth century, among other things, "for the promotion of good order and the establishment of a firm, certain, and peaceable government." Schenectady, New York, a bit later, reveals the same motive: "to prevent disorders and excesses because of the influx of so many strangers to this rapidly growing trading center."

While the building of towns was a crucial feature of American colonization, the towns were to be thought of as instruments of control—not as laboratories of democracy or experiments in individual freedom. Economic life was strictly regulated. Externally, the lines of trade were prescribed: it could be carried on only in English ships, which included English colonists' ships, and its most important components could be shipped only between the colonies (hinterland) and the mother country (metropolis). Internally the

4

price and quality of goods was subject to public regulation, as were wages, profits, and the time and place of marketing—as well as who would be eligible to sell certain kinds of goods.

Regulations bore heavily on idleness. Individuals were legally responsible to work on public projects and even on private projects which were felt to be in the interest of the community. When, in 1644, three New Haven entrepreneurs proposed to deepen the channel of a creek, the authorities gave them four days of work from each male resident between the ages of sixteen and sixty. On another occasion, Newark offered three days of work from every able-bodied resident to assist anyone who undertook to set up a corn mill.

Social life was regulated similarly and sometimes as explicitly. When street plans for colonial towns were laid out on paper it was always understood that some of the future inhabitants would be wealthier and of higher social rank than others, and different areas were provided for spacious estates and more modest accommodations. In at least one case (Swansea, Massachusetts), the original plan specified areas for three denominated ranks. "Not only did this action receive the sanction of the townsmen," writes Thomas J. Wertenbaker, "but in after years committees were appointed to perpetuate these distinctions, or to promote and degrade persons from one rank to another." Laws provided that clothing must reflect the status of the person wearing it. Gentlemen and their ladies were allowed to wear lace, gold, and silver ornaments and items made of silk, which were forbidden to those in lower classes. The assignment of seats in churches was almost everywhere made on the basis of sharp and explicit class distinction, and anyone who tried to claim a seat not befitting his status was likely to be punished severely.

In this omnipresence of the regulating hand of government, the colonial towns mirrored arrangements in the mother country. But there were circumstances of colonial life, in this early period at least, which reinforced the idea that a high degree of social control was desirable. These towns, as colonial and European writers often stressed, were placed on the edge of a wilderness of uncalculated extent. Separated by thousands of miles of dangerous ocean from their only source of outside assistance, the colonists confronted the unknown strength of Indians and competing empires as well as the threatening and all-encompassing forest which dwarfed their tiny settlements. John Winthrop of Massachusetts Bay, often charged with undue preference for authoritarianism in the governing of his colony, explained the need for social control. "It is to be feared," he wrote, "that many [creep] out at a broken wall. For such as come together into a wilderness, where are nothing but wild beasts and beast-like men, and there confederate together in civil and church estate, whereby they do—implicitly at least—bind themselves to support each other and all of them that society . . . whereof they are members, how they can break from this . . . is hard to find . . . Ask thy conscience if thou wouldst have plucked up thy estates and brought thy family three thousand miles, if thou hadst expected that all, or most, would [forsake] thee there?" In a much different environment, Captain John Smith had already found it necessary to impose the severest kind of dictatorial control on his infant Jamestown settlement in the simple interest of its survival.

Physical necessity, then, along with the political and military nature of mercantilism, helps explain the closely regulated character of life in the first generation or two of most of the colonial cities. But beyond these considerations, certain values of urbane life were believed to inhere in the regulating, the planning, of communities. William Penn planned carefully for the growth of his Philadelphia project which he laid out in 1682. From the very choice of its classical name, utopian impulses guided his thoughts as he designed the city which was to cap and serve a colony of prosperous Quaker farmers. Streets were to form a gridiron pattern but five spacious squares interrupted the monotony, providing pleasure grounds and space for civic and religious centers. Residential streets were fifty feet wide and stately trees arose along them soon after the turn of the century. One great artery (later called Market Street), one hundred feet wide, traversed the city and ended at the Delaware River. Everything was planned to assure comfortably compact settlement of which even the physical layout would encourage social organization and a vital community life. Penn could not abide the passionate land hunger which increasingly dispersed American settlements all over the landscape

6

—land hunger (an important part of which was coming to be real estate hunger) which increasingly supported individualistic attitudes largely foreign to the seventeenth century. It might be added that the hunger and the attitudes also made it difficult for Penn to collect rents which were supposed to accrue to him from his colony project.

The importance of all this is not simply in Penn's physical vision of a "city beautiful." Cities, if properly built, represented the possibility of realizing important social values and Penn had these clearly in mind. A German pastor who led his flock to Pennsylvania shortly after the colony had begun to flourish, remarked that Penn "will not give any man his portion separately, but all must dwell together in townships and towns, and this not without weighty reasons . . . the children can be kept at school and much more conveniently brought up well. Neighbors also can better offer each other loving and helpful hands and with united mouth can in public assemblies praise and extol the greatness of God." This insight into the notion of a city as a social organism to be carefully nourished and guided in its development for the benefit of the parts that made it up was more clearly expressed in Penn's plan for Philadelphia than elsewhere, but it was not really peculiar to him.

All of the colonial cities and towns were planned communities in origin; the idea that their growth might be shaped by individuals' interests in real estate speculation was to emerge only slowly. New Haven's street plan was set out on a scale almost as impressive as Philadelphia's: there was a common 825 feet square in the center of town with provision of space for meeting house, jail, school, and courthouse. Surrounding this square were eight others of the same dimensions, in which residential neighborhoods could be built. Much of the seeming confusion of Boston's streets, which can still frustrate the tourist, was actually due to careful planning: the first proprietors took pains to follow the local topography when they sketched their plan and then stuck to it.

The most impressive example of city planning after Philadelphia came with the establishment of Savannah, Georgia. Early in the eighteenth century, a well-to-do Englishman named James Oglethorpe became interested in prison reform. He began planning a New World colony where formerly imprisoned debtors might start life anew. In 1732 he and some associates got a charter from the King for the colony of Georgia. The first party was led by Oglethorpe himself, and it began by plotting out Savannah. On a good level site, about ten miles upstream from the mouth of the Savannah River, the founders outlined the town's limits in a large rectangle. Within the rectangle, house lots were grouped in square wards of forty each; a gridiron of main streets seventy-five feet wide and others with half that width divided the wards. Squares where the lines of the main streets intersected were mostly to be given over to churches and other public buildings. Around the outside of the rectangle there was a common, as the language of the plan has it, "for Convenience of Air"; around this common, the next area was to be divided into five-acre garden plots and outside the garden plots it was to be divided into forty-four-acre farms. It is not surprising that Savannah, thus imaginatively and painstakingly founded, grew steadily; its population reached 3,000 by the 1770's, although the philanthropic impulse in Oglethorpe's plans had by then dropped out of view.

This widespread and often imaginative concern for city planning reflects the assumption, common to Britons and Americans in the seventeenth and eighteenth centuries, that civilized life is urban life and that personal development in any full sense is possible only to people who live in or near towns. Thus the main proprietor of the Carolinas, communicating with his agents in the colony in 1671, stressed the value of "the Planting of People in Townes;" this was "the Cheife thing that hath given New England soe much the advantage over Virginia." Five years later he repeated the admonition: "for wee must assure you," he wrote on behalf of his associates, "that it is your and our Concerne very much to have some very good Towns in your Plantations for other wise you will not longe continue civilized or ever bee considerable or secure." The authors of the pamphlet *The Present State of Virginia,* printed in 1727, lamented the colony's failure to progress as rapidly as it might have, owing to "want of towns, markets, and money." An earlier Virginia writer, arguing the need for towns, referred to "well ordered Schools, in well governed Towns," "nurseries of learning and piety," and at one point postulated that "Christians (if they have Liberty) ought to live together in visible united societies, in

8

cities, towns, or villages." A Massachusetts preacher in 1705 excoriated the impulse which led people to leave the city and move into the country. "By that means," he said, such individuals "bid defiance, not only to Religion, but to Civility itself." There was little doubt among the colonists that the city was man's proper habitat.

To whatever extent their development was guided by planning, and whatever they may have owed to British protection and British commerce, many communities in the American colonies were developing rapidly by the eighteenth century and several of them deserved the title of "city" by any reasonable usage current at that time. These were the important seaports, and their impressive growth testified to the vitality of the imperial partnership and to the role of these cities as channels of commerce governed according to mercantilist considerations. Boston, the first of them, numbered about 13,000 inhabitants by 1730. New York, which had amounted to very little as the Dutch outpost of New Amsterdam, had grown to something more than 8,000 once under the aegis of the British Empire, and there were already more than 11,000 Philadelphians even though that community was less than half a century old. Norfolk, Charleston, and Providence also flourished around their busy ports. Some of the interior settlements showed signs of growth, but American colonial civilization continued to be mostly a maritime phenomenon; its cities arose on the shores of the ocean and faced outward, across the water toward the metropolitan mother country. Until a very late period in their development, these colonies each had more communication and connection with Britain than they had among themselves.

Still, within the process of growth itself, there were seeds of conflict. The leading colonial cities grew beyond a point, wherever it lay, at which they could still function—or could still be made to function—as key pieces in the structure of a mercantilist empire. This came about for two reasons, and both are closely related in turn to social development in the cities. In the first place, ships owned and based in the colonial ports began searching out profitable trade areas outside of those permitted them by the Navigation Laws—mercantilism's operating code, as those laws may be called. Tentative and on a small scale at first, this kind of smuggling grew in importance until it had become almost systematized by the middle of the eighteenth century. In the second place, business might also be done in the other direction: westward. Here, in the unmapped expanse of continent which lay just over the back doorsteps, so to speak, of American city dwellers in the colonial period, was the source of highly profitable trade in furs. Later on, it occurred to some enterprising men that the land in the interior could be converted into real estate: the colonists (perhaps in partnership with homeland English) could themselves plant colonies out there for the greater glory of the empire and also for sizeable accretions to their own bank accounts. In other words, while the colonies radiated outwards from urban centers which faced east toward the empire as it existed in the seventeenth and eighteenth centuries, there was no obvious reason why they should restrict themselves to that direction. They could also face westward and capitalize upon resources to which the imagination of no man could set any limit.

These two developments both reached significant stages by the mid-eighteenth century, and both had come about because growth had complicated society in the colonial cities. Local elites had appeared in each of them: groups of merchants and land owners with fortunes which were considerable for the day, with ambitions which outran those fortunes, with increasing political and administrative experience, and with the firm conviction that they possessed the same rights and perquisites, the same claims to status and deference, as their counterparts in the mother country. In short, born in the hinterland of a mercantilist empire, these communities bred groups of men who began to think of themselves as imperialists in their own right, and of their communities as nascent metropolitan centers which might command hinterlands of their own. That such prospects absolutely contradicted the major propositions which the imperial rulers in London simply assumed as the basis for all their policy and action was true enough, although for a long time this was not evident to the colonists. When it did become evident, their only reaction was to question the validity of those propositions.

By that time, the colonial leaders had grown used not only to directing private business ventures on a large scale, whatever officials in England might think of their legality, but also to administering an increasingly complicated and challenging public life. As the colonial cities had grown on their expanding economic bases, their social and political characteristics had become more elaborate and the problems which had to be met if large numbers of people were to live together closely were more and more demanding. Public problems, in other words, were precipitated by growth; in dealing with them the colonists accumulated an impressive fund of administrative (or, more broadly, *political*) experience. In the same measure, their political ambitions extended.

The growth of each successful colonial town was nourished by one or more basic economic activities. The cluster of settlements in Plymouth and Massachusetts Bay colonies, for example, quickly found that fishing in the North Atlantic gave them a surplus product which they could trade (especially in the West Indies and later in southern Europe) for cash as well as articles which they needed —or which someone else needed—and would trade for, thus adding another transaction to what became a rather complicated pattern of commercial triangles. It led to shipbuilding in Marblehead, Salem, Boston, and other places in the area, both for the fishing fleets and the wider-flung maritime trade. This base industry required others to support it: rope-walks, foundries and forges, sail-making shops, and so on. The people who worked in all these establishments needed others to furnish food and clothing, cabinet work, and other carpentry. Growth in these circumstances took place rapidly. In 1650 when Boston was only twenty years old, an observer called it a "City-like towne," and wrote admiringly of the many buildings which were going up, "whose continuall enlargement presages some sumptuous city. The wonder of this Moderne Age that a few yeares should bring forth such great matters by so meane a handfulle. But now behold, in these very places where at their first landing the hideous Thickets in this place were such that Wolfes and Beares nurst up their young . . . the streets are full of Girles and Boies sporting up and downe."

New York City began as New Amsterdam, a fur trading post for the Dutch West India Company. Although it was situated at the finest natural harbor on the Atlantic coast, it was not especially profitable to the company and no effort was made to develop it. (The French, who had spotted and investigated the harbor before

11

the Dutch, never showed any constructive interest in it at all.)
The British took over the port in 1674, and shortly it began to
grow. The fur trade interest remained and even increased, but it
was joined by other activities as New York began to look like a
growing colonial city. Flour milling especially became important
in the local economy; New York began to export flour to the West
Indies, and by the same token New Yorkers became increasingly
interested in pushing out a wheat-growing hinterland around the
city.

Norfolk, Virginia is another example of a city rising upon an
economic base activity. Its municipal beginnings date from the
1720's, when it was organized as a result of the Crown's policy of
trying to channel all commercial activity in the colonies through
specified towns. Its first significant income derived from the export
of naval stores—tar, pitch, and turpentine—to England. Then, as
the neighboring colony of North Carolina began to attract farmers,
residents of Norfolk discovered that their town could serve as the
most convenient port for the newcomers: much of the Carolina
coast was lined by sea islands so that ocean-going vessels could
not reach it; produce was loaded onto special low-draft vessels and
sent to Norfolk, at the southern end of Chesapeake Bay, there to be
trans-shipped. (Norfolk merchants demonstrated a dramatic interest in this hinterland by helping to capture the pirate Blackbeard,
who had made a hiding place out of the shallow water between the
islands and the coast of North Carolina.) By the outbreak of the
Revolution, Norfolk had flourished mostly on this business to the
extent that 6,000 people made their homes there.

Baltimore was perhaps the most spectacular example of the
same process, and can be called the first "boom town" in America,
although that phrase was not used until much later. In 1729 the
colonial legislature granted a charter to a group of men who wanted
to put a town on some land belonging to the powerful and wealthy
Carroll family. This enterprise suffered the fate of most of the
"towns" that were chartered in Maryland and Virginia primarily
for the purpose of controlling the shipment of tobacco. The heavily
indented Chesapeake Bay coast, with its many inlets and rivers
which were simply narrow arms of the sea, made it easy for
tobacco ships to sail directly to the wharves of the large plantations,

thus escaping regulation in the towns. Early Baltimore languished; by mid-century only a very few ships had picked up any tobacco at the wharf, and there were not more than twenty-five houses scattered around on the town's land. At about this time, however, a pair of Scots, brothers named Stevenson, arrived on the scene. They saw what appeared to them to be good wheat-raising country in back of the town, which was being exploited very lightly. They wrote to a friend in Ireland to send over a ship to load flour; then they went around the countryside buying up all the wheat they could get—it was cheap, for no one knew of a market extending beyond the few people in Baltimore and the surrounding tobacco farms. A flour mill was hastily erected; the ship from Ireland arrived in due time, picked up its cargo presumably for market in the West Indies, and the Stevensons had made a killing. Others were attracted by their success, and it was not long before other mills appeared, wheat-farming extended farther and farther into the hinterland, a new wharf was built, and population began to grow. In 1763, Charles Carroll recognized the drift of events when he shifted 10,000 acres of his land to wheat growing, and by 1790 there were 13,000 people living where only a hundred or a hundred and fifty could have been found forty years earlier.

The economic bases of most of the colonial cities were secure by the end of the seventeenth century. Commerce was the most important element in each case, and it was at the outset a commerce closely related to imperial need and profit: masts and ships from New England towns, furs from New York and Philadelphia, pitch and turpentine from Norfolk and Charleston. Later, reaching large proportion in the eighteenth century, came the ominous African slave trade and the various exchanges which arose out of it—rum from New England ports to the African Gold Coast, slaves from there to the West Indies (or Sugar Islands, as they were called), and sugar from there back to New England. There were other patterns of maritime commerce; as the Sugar Islands developed their kind of monoculture, they had to be supplied from abroad with food which came increasingly from the middle colonies, later from Norfolk, and still later from Maryland as the city of Baltimore grew up after 1750.

Along with perfectly legal and highly profitable maritime trade, there developed more and more illegal, and also highly profitable, trade. The Navigation Acts would have been difficult to enforce in any case, the colonists needed money with which to buy British-made goods, and it put a strain on human nature to serve paying customers in the British Sugar Islands while ignoring potential paying customers in the islands belonging to France. Coupled with this was the fact that the British authorities made very little effort to enforce their trade regulations until the early 1760's. Some of the British understood that the illegal trade carried on by the colonists performed an economic function in supporting at least the northern colonies. Some of them felt, like Robert Walpole, that it was best not to stir up a hornet's nest by trying to enforce the trade laws.

That the Americans were smuggling at an increasing rate was generally known. As early as 1672, a complaint was made to the Privy Council that Massachusetts traders "boldly employ two or three hundred Sail of ships yearly, trading to and fro . . . and this without being under the restrictions of such laws as put our Merchants to vast charges." The complaint averred that by ignoring the Navigation Acts colonial shippers were able to undersell their British counterparts, a state of affairs which would, if not checked, provide "an infallible bait to all our Manufacturers to remove thither, where people trade with such advantage over their fellow subjects." Far from being checked, smuggling continued to flourish, reaching its most profitable proportions during wars, when many colonial merchants traded brazenly with the French enemy. In 1759 Thomas Penn reported to the Prime Minister the appearance of several new Philadelphia fortunes. These arose from illegal trade with the French West Indies. Philadelphia, Penn continued, was full of "shallops unloading these illegal cargoes . . . besides carrying provisions and ready money to the enemy." The people in this nefarious business included, in Penn's words, "a very great part of the principal merchants" of the City of Brotherly Love. In 1764, a colonial official said of New York City's merchants that "many of them have rose suddenly from the lowest rank of the People to considerable Fortunes, and chiefly by illicit Trade in the last War. They abhor every limitation of Trade . . . and therefore gladly go into every measure whereby they hope to have Trade free." The

14

same sort of thing was going on elsewhere; John Hancock, one of Boston's "principal merchants," when he signed the Declaration of Independence owed the British customs authorities thousands of pounds sterling in unpaid tariffs and imposts. The important point is that by the 1760's, an important part of the mercantile elite groups, which governed the colonial cities, depended upon smuggling for their continued prosperity. Even though the number of colonists directly involved in trade of any kind was small, still colonial life at its urban focal points was dependent to a significant degree on smuggling.

Townspeople could also find opportunities in the other direction: inland. This began in a small way at an early date. By the time Boston was a generation old, Carl Bridenbaugh has written, "it had begun to extend its control into the back country, and to develop a metropolitan form of economy that was essentially modern." The other ports quickly developed interest in their surrounding areas, and each began to appear as the small metropolitan center of its own hinterland. Concern for the hinterland could go much farther than this. By the middle of the eighteenth century Philadelphians (and Virginians) were examining the possibility of planting large colonies, in the nature of real estate investments, west of the Appalachian mountain chain. Had they been able to carry any of these ideas through to fruition, the entire character of the imperial structure in North America would have changed. Benjamin Franklin understood this, and suggested (in an unguarded moment) that developing the American interior along these lines might make it desirable at some future date to move the capital of the British Empire across the ocean. As the British authorities also came to understand the implications of the colonists' developing western hinterlands, they looked with more and more suspicion upon the whole idea.

The opportunities which led American colonial merchants to look outside the Navigation Acts for trade, and to look beyond the confines of imperial land policy for real estate profits, thus placing more and more of them in opposition to the whole tenor of mercantilist imperial regulations, were rooted in city growth. The internal consequences of this growth were equally important to the development of autonomous community life in the colonies. As local populations grew, the problems of sanitation, fire protection, police, schooling, and—from a very early day—poverty arose. It was in their confrontation with these problems that the colonial cities developed political and administrative techniques which were fairly sophisticated in the world of the seventeenth and eighteenth centuries. Local leadership began to emerge from the problem-solving process, and the knowledge and experience were accumulated which would later make reasonable the demand for more freedom from metropolitan (British) regulation, and which would sustain political independence when the colonists reluctantly concluded that this was the only way they could escape the onerous regulations on which the mercantilist empire rested.

The story of fire protection illustrates a fairly consistent pattern in the genesis of community enterprises. The colonists brought with them from Europe community responsibility laws relating to the prevention of fire damage. These laws required each property holder to turn out on a fire signal and help quench the blaze. As towns grew into cities this arrangement became less and less adequate, and came to be largely replaced by volunteer fire companies. Bostonians led the way: in 1717, twenty leading citizens got together and agreed to attend every fire that broke out in the city, bringing with them sand, buckets, and other equipment to put it out. They called themselves the Boston Fire Society, and their idea spread rapidly to other towns and cities with former Bostonian Benjamin Franklin organizing a volunteer company in his adopted Philadelphia. It is not surprising to find leading property owners in the forefront of this kind of work; their own monetary interests were served by it. Sometimes the wealthier among them supplied the companies with water pumping equipment. In 1736 the richest man in Newport, Rhode Island, bought the best fire engine available at the time in England, had it shipped across the Atlantic, and gave it to the city outright. By the time of the Revolution, there were at least six volunteer fire companies in Philadelphia, several in Boston, and all of the leading communities had at least one.

The story is similar in the case of police protection. The traditional night watch, dating back to medieval times, was not sufficient security for life and property in a growing seaport. Here again, men of wealth made their own arrangements; sometimes they started out by taking turns at a night-time police patrol themselves. It was not long, in any case, until they found it better to contribute money to a common fund out of which other men could be paid to do the patrolling. Here again, private interest and the community's general welfare overlapped. This curious mixture between public and private enterprise came to be a recurrent characteristic of American municipal development.

The problem of poverty also called forth responses which mingled public and private initiatives. That communities were collectively responsible for the poor who lived within their boundaries was an old proposition in English public law, formalized in the famous Statute of Artificers of 1562 and the Poor Law of 1601. The principle was that the poor had to be maintained out of local tax money; the burden might be lightened by requiring the recipients of this relief to work at publicly set wages, usually in private enterprises. The colonies either adopted these English laws or drew up others for themselves, which closely resembled the earlier models in the homeland. In some cases public workhouses were established; Plymouth Colony had one by 1658 and within a century they were to be found in all the large colonial towns. Binding out (requiring the poor to work for enterprisers on contract) was another possibility. Both practices could be carried on together as in Boston, after its workhouse was put up in 1685. During the same period, towns and provincial authorities passed strict laws regulating immigration, in the hope of minimizing the tax burden which "sturdy beggars" represented, especially in bad times. Thus Bostonians were forbidden in 1636 to house strangers without official permission; three years later it was provided that any newcomers had to be able to name a permanent inhabitant as a kind of bond if he wished to remain in the city; in 1647 legislation forbade any inhabitant to sell or rent a dwelling or shop without official permission. In New Amsterdam-New York, in the seventeenth century, laws were promulgated to assure that the town authorities knew the name and the whereabouts of everyone who came into the city. In Newport bond had to be posted for all newcomers before they could be admitted to the city. Beginning in 1705, Philadelphia adopted a set of regulations similar to those of New York City.

17

These restrictive provisions were not peculiar to the British North American colonies during the mercantilistic period; neither was it peculiar that here the practices began to break down as time passed. The erosion of mercantilistic restrictions in the colonies, however, is of considerable importance. It testifies to the growth of the colonial communities—to their success as communities—which went beyond any seventeenth century expectations and which ultimately made it impossible for them to find satisfactory places within imperial structure as it then existed. The prevailing labor shortage and the availability of land in all of the colonies, as Richard Morris has noted, made it certain both that the system of strict internal regulation would be tried and also that it would not be as successful as in the mother country. Adam Smith estimated that, around the time of the Revolution, average standards of living in the colonies were three times as high as in Britain itself. This made migration attractive to many people, and presented a problem to the imperial rulers. After about 1700 they began to try to restrict the migration of skilled workers, but they knew also that some kinds of workmen (those familiar with naval stores, for example) had to be provided in the colonies. At about the same time, the authorities in the colonial cities started having second thoughts about the policy of exclusion. They found it more and more desirable to encourage the growth of local labor forces and made efforts to attract foreign workers.

This change represented a serious breach in the structure of mercantilist social control. At the same time a kind of society began to emerge in the colonies which was markedly different from the parent society in Britain. While the colonists were by no means thorough-going egalitarians, and while vast distinctions continued to separate the highest social ranks from the lowest, labor (including the lower paid kinds of what would today be called "white collar" employment) had more respectability—which naturally accompanied more opportunity to rise economically—in the colonies. The common assumption of polite society in Europe and England, as Carl Bridenbaugh has pointed out, was that labor, usually called "the mechanic arts," was mean or base. Plenty of colonists shared this assumption; but, as one of them had to concede in 1744, the lower house of the New Jersey colonial legislature "was chiefly composed of mechanicks and ignorant wretches; obstinate to the last degree." In Philadelphia, a commentator noted in 1772 that "the poorest labourer . . . thinks himself entitled to deliver his sentiments in matters of religion or politics with as much freedom as the gentleman or the scholar." He concluded that "there is less distinction among the citizens of Philadelphia than among those of any civilized city in the world . . . For every man expects one day to be upon a footing with his wealthiest neighbor." Bridenbaugh has found that in New York between 1700 and 1776, two fifths of those granted "the freedom of the city" were craftsmen such as leather workers and woodworkers. In Philadelphia in 1774 thirty per cent of those who had assessable property (real estate, slaves, servants, and livestock) were listed as craftsmen. These figures reflect a high degree of social mobility, judged by the standards of European civilization at the time.

Commercial growth tended also to disintegrate religious orthodoxy, at least as a means of social control. This was apparent even in 1663 to the Netherlands authorities in charge of New Amsterdam. Noting that the town had recently exiled a Quaker, they advised local officials to take great care in these matters: "although it is our cordial desire that similar and other sectarians might not be found there, yet as the contrary seems to be the case, we doubt very much if rigorous proceedings against them ought not to be discontinued except you intend to check and destroy your population, which however in the youth of your existence ought rather to be encouraged by all possible means." A few years earlier, a pious Bostonian protested that the city's merchants "would willingly have . . . the Commonwealth tolerate divers kinds of sinful opinions to intice men to come and sit down among us, that their purses might be filled with coyn, the civil Government with contention, and the Church of our Lord Christ with errors."

The spread of printing establishments and newspapers in the colonial cities suggests a cultural aspect of the growth that was sapping the basis of the mercantilist empire. The first printing press in British America was set up in Boston in 1639. It remained the only one for many years, but there were five presses in that city by 1715 and at least nine booksellers. By 1776 seven newspapers were published in Philadelphia, four in Boston, and at least one in every other colonial city. There are records of more than forty printers in Philadelphia between 1740 and 1776. Their significant social role has been described by Bridenbaugh: "Skilled craftsmen, they belonged by interest and training with the mechanics and artisans. The superior education that practice of their profession required made them important members of the growing middle class, and the widening market for their wares occasioned by the increasing literacy of their times brought them material prosperity that often placed them economically at the head of it."

Printing and the circulation of books and newspapers provide evidence of an intellectually vigorous culture growing up in the cities, and they were also associated with another important development: the rise of an inter-colonial culture. It continued to be true for more than a century after the planting of the colonies that each of the cities had more connection with the mother country than with its sister cities in the colonies. In 1704, a quick (and difficult) trip from Boston to New York took six days. But the printers and the newspaper editors, with Franklin playing a prominent part, led in a long series of agitations to improve communication, especially through the mails. This, along with the coasting trade which was promoted especially by Philadelphia merchants, was essential to the emergence of any feeling of community between, say, residents of Boston and residents of Charleston. Here, in the relationships between the colonial cities, lay the seeds of a sense of nationality.

The cities had been called "nurseries of learning" and it is not surprising to find schools of various kinds proliferating in the commercial centers. Some of the founders of the colonies were, of course, profoundly interested in making education widely available for religious reasons. After 1647 each town in Massachusetts was required to have an elementary school. Penn tried to have the municipal government in Philadelphia provide for an educational system, but was unsuccessful. Another significant impulse which helped produce an impressive educational establishment in the colonial cities was commerce. This introduced a strong vocational element into the teaching which distinguished American education from the classical studies of the English upper classes. "The City," one man wrote of New York in 1713, "is so conveniently Situated for Trade and the Genius of the people are so inclined to merchandise, that they seek no other Education for their children than writing and Arithmetick." The practical approach of which this writer did not fully approve was quite consciously defended by others. "Thus instructed," wrote a Philadelphian about a proposal which emphasized subjects necessary for success in a mercantile calling, "youth will come out of this School fitted for learning any business, calling, or profession, except wherein [Latin and Greek] are required." The exceptions would have included law, the ministry, and very little else.

During the passing years of commercial prosperity and economic and cultural growth, urban society in the colonies developed a variety of forms of organization. The cities were not simply collections of individuals; instead, they were made up of groups which were interconnected in many ways, and this gave city life somewhat the character of a finely woven web of social and personal relationships. It meant that for almost any given purpose, the energies and talents of many people could be quickly combined and concentrated in the desired direction. A century's growth of voluntary associations, for example, gave the cities a degree of social versatility. From an early period in the 1700's, travelers commented on the plethora of clubs which they found: in New York the Hum Drum Club, in Philadelphia the Beefsteak Club, in Newport the Philosophical Club, in Annapolis the Tuesday Club, in Charleston the French Club—and many more in each of the cities. There are records of about fifty in Philadelphia during the twenty-five years before the Revolution. Some were devoted to special activities such as singing, debating, or discussion of shared hobbies or interests. New York City had a chamber of commerce from 1768; Charleston organized one before the Revolution. Other associations were purely social, the members perhaps having dinner together once a month.

Even the purely social clubs were related to community interests, whether consciously or not: one traveler in 1744 was royally entertained at Newport's Philosophical Club, but observed that philosophy was not discussed: "they talked of privateering and the building of vessels." In most places the volunteer fire societies, of which there were six or seven in Philadelphia and eleven in New

York City, added social functions to their practical ones; in Philadelphia some of the fire societies sponsored regular debates of public issues. Effective and quickly organized resistance to imperial policies after 1763 was made possible by just this kind of experience. Associational life also served to crystallize and mobilize public opinion. Philadelphia's delegates to the First Continental Congress, for example, called upon representatives of most of the clubs in the city to assist their deliberations on propositions to be submitted to the Congress.

We are not here concerned with the Revolution itself. The cities' experiences during the years 1775–1783 were various: Boston remained in American hands from the moment near the beginning of the war when General Gage abandoned it. New York was captured by the British in the same year Boston was evacuated by them, and it remained an occupied city until the end of the war. Philadelphia was captured, abandoned, re-captured, and abandoned yet again. Norfolk was held by the Americans, but their way of holding it was to make it useless to the British by burning it to the ground.

The particular fortunes of particular communities are less important than the changed environment of independence and how this change affected American urbanization. The change had no immediate effect upon that process. Certain restrictions upon business enterprise were removed; certain opportunities were opened. But the legal opportunity to colonize the West did not of itself produce colonization; and the legal opportunity to trade outside the limitations of the Navigation Acts did not necessarily make up for Americans' having lost their partnership in the world's most profitable empire. The demographic and technological forces which were beginning to accelerate the urbanization of the western world were not affected by the Revolution. How the histories of communities on the American shore would be shaped by these forces rested on many contingencies.

New York City, for example, with its aggressive and already well organized business community, managed actually to capitalize on its occupation by the British during the Revolution. The presence of British troops meant that more hard money circulated there than anywhere else in the colonies. When the troops left in 1783, many American loyalists went with them from New York, and had to sell most of their possessions at sacrifice prices. It was not long before old enterprises revived and new ones joined them. Banking flourished at the southern end of Manhattan Island by the 1790's; merchants with large views were already risking their money in what would prove to be a lucrative trade from New York to Canton, China. Soon New Yorkers would be looking westward toward the vast interior of a continent, and planning to reach it with a canal to the Great Lakes, as their city came to surpass even Philadelphia in size and wealth.

Norfolk, Virginia exemplifies a different fate. Its wealth had come to be built on supplying the West Indies with food. After the Revolution, Britain's commercial regulations kept Americans—like other foreigners—out of the islands, or from time to time allowed them to trade there only under heavy and inconvenient restrictions. Norfolk's merchants dedicated themselves to the task of regaining the commerce which had been lost; they agitated at the nation's capital for diplomatic negotiations to secure re-entry of American ships into the ports of the Sugar Islands. As these almost continuous negotiations waxed and waned, the spirits of the Norfolk business community rose and fell. Finally, in 1830, the negotiations were successful, but by that time Norfolk could gain but little from the outcome; the Sugar Islands trade was no longer important. Meanwhile, other projects had been slighted; only belatedly did the Chesapeake port rally in support of railroad projects to connect with the interior, and then it was found that other interests had arisen in Richmond and Petersburg to prevent the realization of a unified transportation scheme radiating from Norfolk. Baltimore had seized much of what might have been Norfolk's hinterland, and the older city languished throughout the nineteenth century.

But, if the consequences of independence were problematic for particular cities, still the bearing of urban growth on American independence was obvious enough. The cities nurtured economic life so successfully as to feed economic ambition. The cities offered problems for solution by associated effort, thus stimulating the colonists to accumulate political experience—and political ambition. The cities were focal points for the development of a colonial culture, in which the life of the mind or spirit shaped itself to an

American rather than to an imperial environment. In doing these things, the colonial cities were simply functioning as cities classically functioned: they were both matrix and evidence for the appearance of a civilization.

2

Cities in the New Nation

The story of American urbanization as outlined by the statistics of growth has an interesting dialectical feature about it. The first settlements were, of course, towns, which made possible the subsequent growth of agricultural (and increasingly commercial) hinterlands. Consequently, in the early decades, town-dwellers made up a *decreasing* percentage of the total population. The urban percentage continued to decrease for a longer period than might be supposed. As late as 1690, between nine and ten per cent of the American colonists could have been classified as urban. A century later, the first federal census revealed twenty-four places with more than 2,500 people living in them, but these people accounted for only 5.1 per cent of the population. For the next thirty years the proportion remained fairly stable, rising almost imperceptibly to about six per cent in 1800, to 7.3 in 1810, and then apparently dropping to 7.2 in 1820. (The figures in these

25

early censuses are more convenient than those derived by the kind of guesswork required for the colonial period, but it should be kept in mind that they are not reliable enough to support any very sophisticated statistical operations.) After 1820, the figure begins to rise significantly, as it has continued to do ever since; by 1830, it was back to where it had been 140 years earlier.

In other words, during the eighteenth century and the first two decades of the nineteenth, urbanization barely kept pace with the diffusion of hundred of thousands of settlers into the back country. To the extent that city growth represents specialization and there-fore increasing productivity, the fall and leveling off of our figure suggests that no very important rise in average living standards took place during that period. One or two economists have con-cluded that the average American standard of living actually fell in the early 1800's, as westward-migrating throngs spread the country's stock of resources more and more thinly over a wide expanse of territory.

Leaving aside (and open) the question of how much generaliz-ing the rather paltry handful of available statistics really allows, we can see, in the decrease-increase curve, urbanization extending the territory which could be exploited by Western European—including American—commercial agencies, and then beginning to gather momentum as the results of commercial expansion began to accumulate. Total population continued to grow rapidly, increas-ing by about one third during every decade between 1810 and 1860. But the urban population grew three times as fast as the total; by the later year about one fifth of all Americans were living in places of 2,500 or more.

The percentage not only rose, but new and larger urban centers were appearing rapidly. In 1820, when one American in fourteen could be called an urbanite, one third of these people lived in New York City and Philadelphia; the country contained only twelve cities with populations larger than 10,000, and these twelve ac-counted for over two thirds of the city-dwelling total. By 1860, however, there were 101 such cities, including eight which had passed the 100,000 mark and one (New York plus its large suburb of Brooklyn) which exceeded a million.

How had this happened? In large part it was the local reflection

26

of a world trend. Rapid and sustained urbanization is a recent phenomenon, reflecting technological progress and changes in forms of social organization: the steam engine, agricultural machinery, the nation-state, the joint-stock company and its descendant the corporation, developments in medical and sanitary practices which slowly cut away at the death rate, and so on. In 1800, it is estimated that perhaps three per cent of the world's inhabitants lived in places of more than 5,000 inhabitants. In the next century and a half, world population went up by 250 per cent, but the urban component went up by 2,600 per cent, so that the earlier three per cent has now become over thirty per cent. Great Britain, northwestern Europe, Japan, the United States, and more recently the Soviet Union—those places which have industrialized earliest—have simply been at the front of this world wide trend.

The figures tell only part of the story, and for our purposes it is not necessarily the most important part. As cities grew, their natures and functions in many cases changed. At the beginning of the nineteenth century, the sizeable cities of the United States were strung out along the coast; they were ports and reflected what George R. Taylor calls the "extractive–commercial" character of the American economy at that time. "The streets of every large city," in Taylor's apt phrase, "led down past the warehouses to the piers." These cities faced the sea and the maritime trade which had nurtured them. By the time of the Civil War, however, this could no longer be said. Maritime trade, indeed, was still directly or indirectly an important element in the life of the cities, but new cities had appeared deep in the continental interior and the older ones, the great seaports, had engaged in great metropolitan rivalries with one another to secure as much as possible of the commerce which came from the interior. Manufacturing had begun to influence the shape of many of the cities, accounting for the activities of ten per cent of the people in New York and Philadelphia, about seventeen per cent of those in Cincinnati, twenty-six per cent of those in Newark—not to mention a group of smaller New England river towns which lived entirely by manufacturing. Horse-drawn buses dating from the 1830's, commuter train service from the 1840's, and street railways (still horse-drawn for another quarter-century) from the 1850's enabled the cities to encompass

27

larger areas and to generate residential suburbs. Widespread town promoting and urban ambition had become characteristic of the optimistic, progress-minded culture which foreigners and natives alike often identified as "American."

Nor did American urbanization come unexpectedly upon a surprised people. Commercial journals such as *Niles' Weekly Register* in Baltimore, *Hunt's Merchants Magazine* in New York, and later *De Bow's Review* in New Orleans had national circulation and constantly bemused their readers with glowing accounts of city growth, buttressed with endless statistics. A Bostonian writing in 1816 described at length the types of cities that were growing up in the young nation and analyzed quite accurately the rivalry between the port cities for commercial control over portions of the hinterland. New Orleans seemed to him certain to flourish with the settlement of the Mississippi Valley. Baltimore was "struggling with Philadelphia to obtain the preference of the western country." Philadelphia had begun to lose some of its business to New York, and had turned its attention to "the increase of the western country" and to a variety of manufacturing projects. New York, already anticipating its canal between the Hudson River and the Great Lakes, was "probably destined to become the greatest commercial emporium in the United States." Boston could profitably encourage the vigorous development of the New England region which was tributary to it. The writer's obvious enthusiasm for the metropolitan drama he described was by no means unusual in early America.

American growth is usually, and correctly, associated with the westward retreat of the "frontier," which represented not, as in Europe, a line marking the limit of opportunity within a country but rather a vast reservoir of unexploited resources. Only recently, however, has it been made clear that this very westward movement was made possible by urban impulses and, in Richard C. Wade's metaphor, "spearheaded" by townsmen hoping to convert strategic positions in the continental wilderness into cities, putting down checkerboarded streets with hotels and public buildings where Indian trails had run irregularly through the forest.

It is important to discard the image of expanding agricultural settlement bringing towns along behind it. In the first English settlement of the country, towns were the necessary bases from which the farmers could move out and begin to subdue the new land to their purposes. Pittsburgh, St. Louis, Louisville, and Cincinnati were all founded before there was any significant farming in their respective areas. In the cases of all these except St. Louis, Indians and the problem of military security alone would have dictated some kind of concentrated settlement before agricultural development could safely begin. George Washington noted the spot where the Allegheny and Monongahela Rivers join to form the Ohio as an ideal one for a fort; he also belonged to a company of land-speculating Virginians who proposed for a time to put a town near the site. It was to be laid off, in the words of one of the group's agents, "in squares of two acres each, every square to be divided into four lots so that every lot may front two streets, if the ground will so admit, and . . . all the streets [should] be of convenient width." French and British authorities alike agreed with Washington on the military evaluation, and it was first as Fort Duquesne and later as Fort Pitt, during the early stages of the French and Indian War (1756–1763), that the settlement which became Pittsburgh first took shape. The settlement which was to become Louisville began similarly, in 1778, as a military base set up by George Rogers Clark. Cincinnati, while it was not originally a military post of any kind, became the site of a temporarily important fort three years after its founding. Another example is the town of Lexington, Kentucky, which began as a stockade against the Indians in 1779, and rose by 1800 to become the biggest of these interior places with a population of 1,500 and a reputation as "the Philadelphia of Kentucky."

St. Louis was a somewhat special case among what were to become the main inland cities, in that its original auspices were French. Early in the 1760's, the most powerful fur traders in New Orleans began to explore the possibility of establishing a central sub-station on the Mississippi River to co-ordinate and supply their enterprises. They already had some up-river posts, but they were about to lose the best two of these (Kaskaskia and Cahokia, both of which had come to number over 1,500 inhabitants) because the French had surrendered to the British all claims to the east bank of the great river, on which these posts were located. Their one

29

substantial post on the west bank, Ste. Genevieve, was not entirely satisfactory owing to the erratic behavior of the river around its site. Several miles below the point where the Missouri River enters the Mississippi, a party of men sent out by the New Orleans traders found a limestone bluff which offered excellent possibilities, a place which, as the chief of the party said, "might become, hereafter, one of the finest cities in America." The following year, 1764, the construction of St. Louis began. The settlement did not grow rapidly—but no one particularly wanted it to—until a much later date. Nevertheless, here in the middle of an almost unpopulated continent there were by 1800 about a thousand people. St. Louis was an administrative headquarters for the governing authorities, as well as a key point in the widespread fur trading business.

Many, although by no means all, western towns began as forts but at an early stage they became speculative enterprises, and the decisive questions in each case were whether or not the speculative enterprise would pay off, and whether in the process of paying off it would work itself into a growing regional economy. The answers depended partly on forces beyond the control of local residents. Once founded, the futures of places like Pittsburgh and Cincinnati depended upon the agricultural and commercial development of the areas that became the states of Kentucky, Ohio, and Indiana. This development, in turn, was critically affected by the Indian policy of the federal government, the land disposal policies of the same government, arrangements for political organization of the territory (provided by the Northwest Ordinance of 1787), and finally military success against the Indians during the War of 1812. The future of the interior towns depended also on the kind of use which could be made of the rivers which ran right past most of them. Thus Robert Fulton's successful development of the steamboat and its adaptation to inland river navigation (long before it was of any importance on the ocean) lifted the horizons for western city growth far above the level which slower means of transportation could have sustained.

There were ways, however, by which local enterprise or its absence could determine the success or failure of a town promotion scheme. In the pre-steamboat period, endeavors in Pittsburgh,

Cincinnati, and other towns to design and build more efficient river craft were examples of local efforts to serve hinterlands better and therefore more profitably. Between 1801 and 1816, the value of western goods shipped down-stream to New Orleans rose from $3,700,000 to $8,000,000, partly because of such efforts.

Pittsburgh merchants, admirably situated to supply the rising tide of westward migration along the Ohio River, tried to furnish everything migrants needed. At first, the merchants brought these goods in from eastern seaports, especially Philadelphia and Baltimore. Increasingly, they began to manufacture many of them; foundries, nail and glass factories, and machine shops appeared; Pittsburgh was soon known as "the Birmingham of America." Here and in the other river towns merchants tried to supply credit to their customers, without which trade could not move in an area always short of hard cash, and trading companies often became fledgling banks. Townsites needed advertising, so local boosters imported presses and sometimes editors in order to establish newspapers— not for local information, but rather with an eye to eastern readers. Hotels had to be provided for the temporary accommodation of prospective investors and settlers. Fire and police protection, street grading, market and wharf supervision, and many other urban services were necessary and on a rising scale, as the successful town enterprises grew.

Clearly, in addition to their private business activities, the promoters had to see to it that public authority functioned as efficiently as possible. It is not surprising, then, to find the leading merchants of a young city prominent in efforts to get legislative authorization from the state, in the form of charters, and, generally, to find these men directing political life. The day of the professional city politician was still far off. "Throughout the West," says Richard C. Wade, "the pattern was everywhere the same, with city-council lists reading like the local business directory."

Location, the course of events in the world outside, decisions made in eastern cities, and local ability and energy all went to determine whether a particular speculative town project would grow. Most projects did not. Hundreds of New Athenses, New Lisbons, Palermos—as well as a fantasy called the Town of America, expected to raise shimmering towers at the junction of the Ohio and Mississippi Rivers—remained little or nothing more than paper speculations. Sometimes they were designed simply to defraud the unwary; sometimes their surprised proprietors were bankrupted along with the others. One western observer during this period remarked that most town projects came to nothing and added that "it requires the united influence of many individuals and various interests and the concurrence of a diversity of circumstances, to give impulse to the healthy growth of a town." The American scenes in Charles Dickens's *Martin Chuzzlewit* give sharp, if satirical, insight into what happened more often than not in the course of town promotion.

The failure of Lexington is illustrative, for here was a place which progressed far beyond the merely speculative stage and which for several years had more of urbanity about it than any other place in the west. After the Indian threat subsided, a group of men got a land grant from the Virginia legislature (Kentucky was the western part of that State until 1791) for the purpose of putting up a town. They laid it out carefully in a gridiron pattern, reserving some sites for public purposes, and proceeded to advertise it. The rapid development of Tennessee and western Kentucky in the 1790's gave Lexington a solid economic base, outfitting the migrants who travelled overland. Farmers prospered in the surrounding Blue Grass region, marketing their surplus through Lexington. The town began to flourish culturally as well as in a business way; at the beginning of the nineteenth century its people, numbering just under 2,000, enjoyed a variety of amenities, including Transylvania, the first institution of higher learning west of the mountains. There were at least two newspapers, a monthly literary journal, a library, musical and debating societies, as well as several churches. The wealthier residents offered lavish hospitality.

Lexington continued to grow through the period of the War of 1812, its population reaching 5,200 in 1820. It added the profits of hemp manufacture to its commercial income, as other western towns began processing the raw produce of their immediate hinterlands. A branch of the Second Bank of the United States was located there. The local real estate market became livelier and land prices rose with each passing year. But continued success for

Lexington was not in the cards. Depression hit there, as it hit the entire country, shortly after the war when the resumption of imports from Britain bankrupted thousands of American manufacturers and the inflation of real estate values reached a point as high as it could go. Lexington declined, just as a new force which was to benefit other western towns—the steamboat—came upon the scene. Its inland location now a serious competitive disadvantage, Lexington stopped growing and began to slide downhill economically, as business sought the river towns, especially Louisville. Projects for connecting with the river, first by turnpike and then by railroad, and a program designed to make Lexington a permanently great cultural center, all failed to arrest the decline. A visitor to the town in 1829 who had known its former prosperity wrote that "it has degenerated beyond measure. . . . Where was once the dwelling of gayety and friendship, with every good and noble sentiment, was now a rusty and moss-grown mansion of ill nature and repulsive indifference." City building was obviously a risky, uncertain business.

Still, as more and more river steamboats carried the West's rapidly increasing commerce, other towns of course did grow: the basis for urban life and function in Pittsburgh, Louisville, Cincinnati, Memphis, New Orleans, and other places, was apparently permanent. Increasing population meant that new states were carved out of the Northwest Territory; they needed state capitals, and Columbus, Indianapolis, and Jacksonville—later Springfield— were planted in the retreating wilderness to fulfill this need. To these were added the many county seats. A few town projects had initiated the attack upon the wilderness and their success had made the area accessible to thousands upon thousands of westward-moving farmers. This incursion, in turn, sustained a further expansion of urban civilization in the interior. In 1828 one observer caught the spirit of taming frontiers, reporting that "the stranger views here with wonder, the rapidity with which cities spring up in the forests; and with which barbarism retreats before the approach of art and civilization."

Urbanization also accompanied the American westward movement in the South, where slavery and the cotton plantation gave somewhat different characteristics to social and political life. Balti-

33

more, Norfolk, and Charleston, of course, were English settlements antedating the Revolution. Baltimore continued its high rate of growth and indeed in the early decades of the nineteenth century hoped to surpass Philadelphia. Norfolk had not fulfilled expectations and grew only very slowly in the pre-Civil War period. Charleston, similarly, lost most of its earlier momentum, and while its population rose from 20,000 in 1820 to 40,000 in 1860, its rank among American cities dropped from fifth to twenty-second. Efforts by the city's business leaders to maintain a vital connection with a moving cotton hinterland were occasionally energetic and imaginative: early in the 1830's the longest railroad in the world ran between Charleston and Augusta. But these efforts were unavailing, and some of the more articulate residents developed a marked nostalgia for past greatness.

Far to the west, commanding the Mississippi River's delta, was the most spectacular urban success of the cotton South. New Orleans, from its founding by the French in 1718, had been a hot, sleepy, and somewhat unhealthy administrative center, to which the magnates of the fur trade added their homes and offices. The period of its rapid growth came after the War of 1812, as northern family farms and southern cotton plantations moved west and as towns along the Ohio River grew and funneled more and more produce down the great system of rivers. American names and American projects moved into New Orleans to crowd its hitherto French, and rather leisurely, culture. Warehousing and maritime shipping displaced the once important fur trade. Between 1810 and 1860, New Orleans's population grew from 17,000 to 168,000. In the 1840's, New Orleans's metropolitan position—which had obviously rested on the river trade—was threatened by railroads, which ultimately did divert much of the river trade into a west-to-east direction. Even so, concerned businessmen wanted to launch a railroad program of their own. They managed to have the Louisiana constitution changed so as to make financial subsidies to railroads easier, and also to remodel the city's charter in such a way as to improve greatly its credit rating—so, of course, that it, too, could help finance the railroad program. The lines were begun, and New Orleans remained the greatest city in the South. While Charlestonians may have mourned their city's disappearing grandeur, people in New Orleans experienced, as a native later reminisced, "an overweening confidence in the ability of the city to become speedily and without exertion the metropolis of America, if not eventually of the world."

Mobile was another southern port started by the French early in the eighteenth century which began to grow in response to dynamic business impulses initiated later by Americans. Its population, insignificant until 1819 when the United States bought the land in which it was located, came to 12,000 twenty years later and the population continued to grow with the flourishing cotton trade. Savannah became another growing southern city after the War of 1812. Sharply competitive commercial policies—at first maritime and later involving railroads—enabled it to command a profitable hinterland, to grow from 7,500 in 1820 to 11,000 in 1840, and to attract praise from a Northerner who found in Savannah "a spirit of enterprise that could honor any place in this country." Savannah's growth continued to be guided by the original plan set down by James Oglethorpe almost a century earlier. Consequently, it was probably the best example of urban design to be found in the United States during the first half of the nineteenth century. A British visitor not predisposed in favor of American city life favorably noted "no less than eighteen large squares, with grass-plots and trees, in the very heart of the city, disposed at equal distances from each other in the greatest order; while every principal street is lined on each side with rows of trees, and some of the broader streets have also an avenue of trees running down their centre." Richmond, Virginia was yet another impressive southern city, with 38,000 residents by 1860. Here the manufacturing spirit was as prominent as in any northern city of comparable size: a large iron-making establishment and many tobacco factories early gave Richmond, like Pittsburgh, the appearance of a phenomenon of the Industrial Revolution.

But even if the myth of the agrarian South must be discarded, as it obviously must be, still urbanization proceeded there in a less fruitful environment than elsewhere in the country. The relationship between slavery and urban-industrial growth cannot yet be clearly described, but it is certain that city life tended to disintegrate the peculiar institution. Slaves could more easily learn trades in the towns, they could congregate together to exchange news or plans or teach one another to read, they could and did hire themselves out to labor, absenting themselves for long periods from their owners. The extent to which southern thought attached itself to slavery, then—and this increased noticeably after 1815—would tend to mark an ill-defined limit to the South's enthusiasm for urbanization. Certainly the artisans and mechanics, so necessary to growing cities, found in the South, and often expressed, a grievance in the threat to their own well-being which slave and free Negro competition offered. Similarly, it is not seriously disputed that while businessmen of all kinds flourished in the cotton South, they were never given as high a rank in the popular culture there— never became representative symbols of virtue, so to speak, held up to the young for emulation—as they were in northern and western cities. The battle over the cultural value of "enterprise" had only begun in the pre-Civil War south; in the northern cities it was won by the entrepreneurs even before it began.

In the early nineteenth century western urbanization was one important index of national growth; another index was the dramatic growth of the metropolitan centers of the east coast. Between 1790, the year of the first federal census, and 1860 New York City's population went from 33,000 to about one million (this figure includes Brooklyn, which was actually a great suburb but still politically independent), Philadelphia's increased from 42,000 to slightly over half a million, Baltimore's from 13,500 to 212,000, and Boston's from 18,000 to 177,840. It is useful to think of the entire country as an expanding hinterland with the great seaports encouraging the expansion and trying individually and competitively to draw to themselves as much as possible of the trade yielded by the hinterland. Abstractly, one might imagine each of the port cities carving out as large a part of the hinterland for itself as it could; the only trouble with this abstraction is that the sub-hinterlands of the several seaports overlapped geographically, with the rough exception of New England which remained commercially subordinate to Boston. In fact, by mid-century, it is in a broad way accurate to say that, with the same exception, the entire country was the hinterland of New York City, with Philadelphia and Baltimore competing for that business which New York was simply not big enough to handle. The story of this metropolitan growth can best be organized around the roles of luck and enterprise in the sudden rise of New York, and around varying responses to this rise in the other cities.

In the first twenty years of United States history, Philadelphia and New York were, in that order, the two biggest cities in the country; among the eight or ten largest, Baltimore was growing most rapidly, but was far behind the leaders. By the end of the second twenty years, New York was unchallenged as the biggest, and Philadelphia *was* being seriously challenged by Baltimore for second place. What lay behind these developments was, as has been suggested, the interplay of chance and policy.

New York's and Philadelphia's populations were about equal at the time of the War of 1812; the war injured both cities by disrupting their maritime trade. Its effects, and the commercial restrictions which preceded it, also encouraged manufacturing in some parts of the country, notably along the seaboard. Behind the protective wall of commercial exclusion and then war, Americans began to manufacture things which they had been importing from Britain. The war, however, had no sooner broken out than negotiations were begun to end it, and during its two and a half year duration British manufacturers anxiously planned how to regain their lucrative American market. They resolved, quite deliberately, to sell their products for a time at a loss, if necessary, and as the hour for a peace treaty drew near they loaded ships with goods for the American market. When the negotiations were over and the peace was ratified, these ships sailed, most of them, into New York's harbor where the goods were unloaded and "dumped" on the market at unusually low prices. This policy succeeded admirably in bankrupting many American manufacturers. It also made New York particularly attractive to buyers from inland towns, who now went there in larger numbers, giving that port an obvious and fortuitous, if temporary, advantage over the others.

This was in 1815 and 1816, and the advantage could have been lost, had not certain other decisions made their effects felt. Some New Yorkers had been interested for years in cutting a water connection between the Hudson River and the Great Lakes; nature favored the Empire State with a combination of river courses and

37

valleys which made possible something close to "the water level route" which a later railroad company has advertised. The whole matter was a political issue in the State, its fortunes identified with those of DeWitt Clinton. As Governor, Clinton pushed the canal project through the legislature with strong New York City backing. The State undertook what was for the period a staggering bond program, and in 1817 the digging began. The success story of the Erie Canal is well known. Some sections of the canal were in profitable operation even before 1825 when the whole route was opened; within a few years after that, canal tolls had paid off the entire original cost and were financing improvements along the line to handle business, which continued steadily to rise.

The success of the canal struck contemporaries so forcefully that canal programs were begun in many parts of the country where they proved to be much too expensive, even bringing some states close to financial disaster. It has struck later observers when they have tried in retrospect to account for the supremacy of New York City. This is understandable, but it has also, according to one careful scholar, obscured much of the real explanation. Robert G. Albion has pointed out that in the first place, the full effect of the Erie Canal was not felt until after 1825 by which time New York had already taken a commanding lead over Philadelphia. In the second place, the canal stimulated exports more than imports, whereas the latter were more important for metropolitan supremacy than the former; New Orleans' ante-bellum export trade was often close to New York's in volume and value, and for a few years actually surpassed it, but New Orleans never threatened New York's commercial dominance. In the third place, a number of significant business decisions were taken at about the time construction of the Erie Canal was started, which were less spectacular but which, taken together, perhaps played a larger part in the long-run achievement.

One important policy had to do with the auction sale of merchandise. Instead of selling his goods to a British exporter who then sold them to an American importer, the British manufacturer could consign his shipment to an auctioneer on this side of the water, keeping title to them until they were sold here. Two middlemen were thus eliminated, and auction prices were usually the lowest a buyer could find. This irritated many of the importers, and in Philadelphia and Boston they managed to have certain legal inconveniences put in the way of auctions. In New York, however, legislation favorable to that mode of sale was secured in 1817 and 1818, in the hope that, as one leading auctioneer put it, "all the Atlantic cities [would] become tributary to New York." Again, the western storekeepers were encouraged to do their trading in the Empire City.

At almost the same time, another entrepreneurial innovation added to New York's commercial attractions: the institution of regularly scheduled shipping service (called "packet service") across the Atlantic Ocean. No one on either side of the ocean had done this before 1817, when four local Quaker merchants determined to try it. To many, it looked foolhardy to announce a sailing schedule months in advance, and to stick to it whether the ships had cargo or not. Nevertheless, late in December, New York papers announced that the Black Ball Line would begin trans-Atlantic packet service—both ways—in January. The advantages of regularity and dependability were apparent to shippers and importers, and the line succeeded, very quickly receiving the homage of extensive imitation. New Yorkers also developed their coastwise packet service all the way round to New Orleans.

They were still seeking out new trading areas, as in earlier days when China had beckoned to a few adventurous merchants. In the 1820's, Latin American countries, especially after they gained independence from Spain and Brazil, and also Cuba which remained in the Spanish Empire, attracted the attention of New Yorkers. Resident agents were sent into these countries. They made credit extensively available; the Latins were encouraged to borrow from them. New Yorkers were doing the same thing in the American south, travelling into the cotton country, establishing branch offices in southern cities, providing maritime insurance, and through the advantages which volume, European connections, and the profitability of their other enterprises gave them, establishing general financial control over much of the trade which went to other cities, especially New Orleans. By the 1840's and 1850's, when southern chambers of commerce began to seek escape from northern commercial power and to urge that the cotton trade go directly between their ports and Europe, it was too late for this to be anything more than a dream, a kind of business romanticism. A Norfolk editor summed up what had happened; in 1834 he wrote that "instead of being what its geographical position entitles it to be . . . [Norfolk] is reduced to the humiliating condition of waiting on the pampered aristocracy of New York." Norfolk's hopes of becoming a great port were gone, along with those of many another southern port, and "now, since the concentration of capital in the North, she has become a hewer of wood and drawer of water to the lordly merchants of the northern city." New York was at one corner of every trading triangle which touched the United States, and her metropolitan supremacy could have been destroyed only by a properly located earthquake.

The other main seaports gradually gave up the notion of over-taking New York City, but in a hinterland the size of the United States there was considerable trade left over for which they could compete. Philadelphians had experienced the troublesome competition of Baltimore from the first days after the Revolution, when Baltimore interests began building roads up into the Susquehanna Valley—cutting in behind Philadelphia and taking away some trade that had gone to that city. The Philadelphians responded with a road of their own, the Lancaster Turnpike, and then discovered that their rivals were considering a combination of canals and improvements to the Susquehanna River which would carry Pennsylvania trade south to Chesapeake Bay. Accordingly, Philadelphia began to develop a canal program of its own.

By the mid-1820's, however, the Erie Canal and New York's dramatic growth posed a more serious threat to Philadelphia's western connections, and plans were drawn up to meet it. One concerned resident wrote, "we observe our population daily diverging from our State. . . . We have beheld our markets neglected. . . . We have found that while we slept our *locks* have been shorn." About the same time, forty or fifty local business men, led by the economist and publicist Matthew Carey, organized the Pennsylvania Society for the Promotion of Internal Improvements in the Commonwealth. The Society began public agitation for a response to the Erie Canal; its members collected and circulated technical and financial data on transportation facilities—roads, canals, and railroads. As it happened, the British had just experimented successfully with the world's first commercial steam railroad line, the Stockton and Darlington. Interest arose in some quarters in the United States, and Philadelphians found themselves divided into a canal party and a railroad party on the question of how they should improve their connections with the trans-Appalachian west.

After lengthy and sometimes bitter public debate, in journals and newspapers, at meetings, in the city council and the state legislature, the canal party won. On their side was the great, if conservative, argument from experience: the Erie Canal seemed to prove the superiority of canals in general, while the value of railroads was speculative and "theoretic." What was wanted, one typical proponent of this view urged, was "something solid, the usefulness of which is not doubted, but tested by experience; such undertakings will always have *public confidence* to promote them."

Perhaps due to the quiet tempo of its Quaker-dominated business life, perhaps due in part to its defensive responses to Baltimore's commercial aggressiveness, Philadelphia had already the reputation of a rather conservative community. Whether or not the designation was accurate, the city (in this instance supplying leadership for the entire state) now deliberately rejected an innovation—the railroad —and proceeded to tie its hopes to a canal connection with Pittsburgh. There were, of course, the mountains to be dealt with; these were conquered by a series of winch-drawn cable cars on inclined planes. This fantastic combination of devices took seven years to build, cost more than $12,000,000 (almost double the cost of the Erie Canal), and never began to fulfill the hopes which had accompanied its progress. Within four years of its completion, a movement arose to replace it with a railroad, and in 1846 the Pennsylvania Railroad was chartered for precisely this purpose; it received large amounts of public aid as its construction advanced across the state. The whole experience was disappointing. The project not only lost money but delayed Philadelphia's western rail connections. One businessman wrote in 1852 that many of his associates had become disheartened, and "some of our most astute and enterprising merchants removed to New York."

In Baltimore the story was quite different. Interest in the Stockton and Darlington experiment arose very early, and a project to build a railroad was carefully and quietly organized by a few of the city's leading men. When matured, the proposal was presented to the public in urgent terms: "whilst the Cities of Philadelphia and New York are making such great and efficient exertion to draw to themselves the trade of the West, . . . Baltimore must soon lose the comparatively small portion which remains to her . . . should she remain inactive." After a favorable eye-witness account of the British railroad, this small group of men decided quickly against a canal, formed a committee to get a charter for a Baltimore and Ohio Railroad company, organized the company, and began construction—with both state and municipal aid—all within about two years. Significantly, the Baltimore group knew it was taking a risk. In its own words, "the stock of information upon the general subject of railroads . . . is admitted to be not very extensive," but the risk was accepted. The Baltimore and Ohio Railroad did not, indeed, push Baltimore ahead of Philadelphia, but it did narrow the gap between them and rivet the city into third place which it held until Chicago edged it out after the Civil War.

Boston's response was different again. Bostonians were urged in familiar terms to do something: "if we sleep much longer, Boston will sink, in a commercial view, into comparative oblivion." How could the city cut through the hills of western Massachusetts and connect with the Erie Canal at Albany, thus tapping at least some of the rich canal trade that was going on down to New York? The business community began considering the problem at the same time as this happened in Philadelphia and Baltimore, in 1825 and 1826. Time passed; a few experiments were made with short railroads; and finally, after ten years of consideration, a railroad across Massachusetts was begun. There was much less rush about the project, and apparently less anxiety about the relative advantages of other cities.

For one thing Bostonians were doing well enough superintending the industrialization of New England. This process had its tentative beginnings in the years just before the War of 1812, as already noted. The westward movement took its toll from New England, as its citizens moved west toward better farming land or else moved into growing cities while some areas experienced urban as well as agricultural decline. At the end of the Revolution, Connecticut had

42

nine towns with populations of over six thousand, but by 1820 only three—New Haven, Hartford, and Bridgeport—had as many as five thousand inhabitants. This decline probably reflected a concentration of population in the new factory towns, as those who did not move west sought jobs in the factories. As late as 1860, half the product of American industry came from a rectangular area on the map whose corners were Hartford, Lowell, New York City, and Wilmington.

Boston capitalists did not, of course, found all of the mills and factories which dotted the New England landscape by mid-century, but they were very active, and frequently helped finance enterprises in which they did not otherwise participate. One group, calling itself the Boston Associates, which by 1850 controlled about half the city's banking and insurance capital and about a third of the railroad mileage in Massachusetts, had for several decades put much of its money into industrial enterprises. They went about looking for water-power sites, buying them up, and erecting mills of various kinds. Thus, in 1823, the Boston and Springfield Manufacturing Company, a Boston Associates concern, bought a waterfall site where it began to manufacture both textiles and textile machinery; the town of Chicopee, Massachusetts grew up around the mills. Again, in the later 1840's, the Associates paid $300,000 for land and water rights where a railroad had been built along one of Massachusetts' many turbulent streams. In 1851, their first mills were opened here and the factory town of Holyoke appeared on the map.

During the earlier stages in the growth of these new towns, the Boston Associates endeavored to put up housing for employees, as well as retail stores, churches, and schools. The most famous project along these lines was the provision at Lowell, Massachusetts of a complete set of social institutions (and regulations) for the young New England girls who were recruited to work in the mills there. The backers had to do this in order to attract employees, but it fitted in well enough with ideas about well-regulated communities which they derived in part from older New England traditions of orderly social life. In the later nineteenth century the opprobrious term "company town" would have been applied to these projects, but in their historical context they did reflect an effort to control the development of the industrial revolution in the interests of community life. It was hoped that the establishment of manufacturing communities in rural settings would make it possible for Americans to avoid the abuses of the European industrial cities, which had horrified Francis Lowell on his travel abroad. When the protecting, if paternalistic, hand was withdrawn it is highly questionable that the factory towns became better places to live.

Beginning in the late 1840's, and continuing in subsequent years, the labor force for these mills came to be recruited increasingly among poverty-stricken French Canadians rather than New England farmers' daughters. Barriers of language and religion between these workers and the factory owners perhaps diluted the latters' sense of responsibility for their operatives. A flood of Irish immigration, providing abundant cheap labor, combined with financial reverses in the late 1850's to complete the destruction of the planned social control systems in the factory towns. But the mills remained and the towns continued to grow. They confronted Americans for the first time with large urban concentrations made up mostly of industrial workers.

The Bostonians—to return to their position during the years of New York's surge forward—were also profiting from the China trade and from the western railroad projects in which some of them became increasingly interested. They seemed to be less concerned than their Philadelphia contemporaries about "losing out." One of them, in fact, noted in his diary that "some think the city is large enough and do not want to increase it."

In the competition between the seaports for western hinterlands some suggestive points emerge. There was the more or less conscious adoption of metropolitan goals: the delineation of hoped-for trading areas and the elaboration of strategies to gain them. In this process some kind of public consensus had to be achieved if only because the transportation schemes required considerable public financing and other legislation. Consequently, notions of the "general interest" emerged in debates about the proper competitive course to pursue; the railroad or the canal was desired, or was talked about as desired, not just by this or that group of aggressive Baltimore or Philadelphia businessmen but by "Baltimore" or "Philadelphia." In this way, the cities acquired public images in-

44

dicating that they possessed one or another set of individual characteristics. Philadelphia was frequently characterized as conservative; its business leaders, one English traveler asserted, "do not conduct their business in the same *dashing* style which is done in some commercial cities, but confine themselves within bonds and secure what they gain." New Yorkers, on the other hand, were said (by a Baltimorean) to "*deserve* success for their enterprise. There is a good spirit among the citizens to advance the business of New York. Let it be imitated—not envied."

This kind of city rivalry was to be repeated many times and in every part of the country; it always took the same forms and was expressed in the same sort of community personification. The community's general interest crystallized around a project conceived to stimulate growth, and the community's character was cast in terms of the success of its businessmen. Much of the pushing, aggressive spirit that attracted the attention of every observant foreign traveller in the United States during the nineteenth century stemmed from these efforts to foster city growth in thousands of places from New York to San Francisco.

As the great seaports sought more and more western trade, their activities speeded western development. Baltimore's railroad, Philadelphia's misfortune with the "main line" to Pittsburgh and later its railroad, and New York's Erie Canal (and later *its* railroad as well) all made it possible for western agriculture to expand and necessitated more urban establishments in the interior. The Erie Canal, especially, opened up a whole new region tributary to the Great Lakes and triggered the growth of a new urban complex on the shores of the lakes. Beginning with Buffalo and continuing westward to Duluth, from the later 1820's on, the cities of the Great Lakes region grew faster than the older river towns and came to eclipse them in size.

Just as on the Ohio Valley frontier, towns were established around the Great Lakes far in advance of any agricultural development in the area, although their growth, of course, had to proceed along with that development. This process—towns, followed by exploitation of an area's agricultural (or mineral) resources, and this in turn accompanied by rapid urban expansion—was repeated from east to west along the lakes about a generation after it had

45

been exhibited in the rise of the river towns. Those towns had established themselves between the 1790's and the 1820's. In the lake region, the period ran from the 1820's into the 1850's, the second phase in the growth of what later Americans would call the Middle West.

Cleveland, Ohio is one example, although it was laid out as a town much earlier than most of the lake cities. In 1796, shortly after a company had been organized in Connecticut to dispose of lands reserved for that state and located in the Northwest Territory, and also shortly after the Indians in the Ohio country had been defeated in the battle of Fallen Timbers, a party representing the company and led by Moses Cleaveland chose the site of the future town. At the mouth of the Cuyahoga River they found high and level ground on either bank and a shoreline offering a fine potential harbor. Cleaveland chose the heights on the Cuyahoga's east bank, and saw that a plan was drawn up. The plan centered around a commodious public square, from which wide thoroughfares led off through rectangles of numbered lots to the limits of the projected town. Although changes were made in the layout on a few later occasions, its form, by now somewhat shadowy, can be discerned on any street map of the present-day city.

Time passed and little happened. In 1810, the fourteen-year-old town's population was just fifty-seven; in 1815 it was not over a hundred and fifty, and only two of the ten streets originally on the plan were actually cleared. Then a road was completed linking Cleveland with the Ohio River; in 1818 the first Great Lakes steamboat called at the little port; in the late 1820's the harbor was improved at federal government expense, and a canal between Cleveland and the Ohio River was built. By 1830 there were about a thousand Clevelanders, and they had among them two newspapers, a school house, a church, a courthouse and a steam sawmill.

The effect of the Erie Canal's completion now began to be felt; ships became more numerous in the harbor and population mounted to 6,000 in 1840, and to 17,000 in 1850. The next year, the first railroad entered Cleveland, from the south, and marked the beginning of even more rapid growth. Cleveland businessmen began to build up an iron industry; at first they used relatively low grade ores which could be found in Ohio, but by the 1850's they

46

were looking as far afield as northern Wisconsin, and several of them were vitally concerned in the events which led to the cutting of the Soo Canal between Lakes Michigan and Superior in 1855. Cleveland had already become an industrial city.

Detroit was officially older than Cleveland; like New Orleans and St. Louis, its founding dated from the days when Frenchmen still hoped to dominate North America. By the end of the eighteenth century, about 2,500 people lived in Detroit and were legally under the American flag. In all important respects, however, the place was still a rather sizeable fur trade settlement, the inhabitants of which felt much closer to Canada than to the United States. With the creation of Michigan Territory in 1805, Detroit became a political center, but in the same year it was almost completely destroyed by fire. This proved to be a watershed in its history; it was rebuilt according to a completely new plan, which probably borrowed some features from L'Enfant's proposals for the nation's capital, and began to become an American city in its leading social, cultural, and political characteristics.

Still, the land around it was not popular with settlers and did not fill up; early maps printed the words "interminable swamp" across the southern part of Michigan Territory. Life in the city suffered another disaster when British forces defeated the Americans in the area in 1813, and during the rest of the War of 1812 Detroit was garrisoned by the British. Not until after the war was over and after the Erie Canal was completed did the city's urban prospects begin to seem at all impressive. Then, as lake commerce began to grow, Detroit's location along the narrow connection between Erie and Huron began to return dividends. Detroiters could outfit the migrants who now began to interest themselves in Michigan land; they also sent Michigan's growing agricultural surplus back east in lake ships. Detroit's population, which was 1,400 in 1820 and still only 2,200 in 1830, reached 9,000 in 1840 and 21,000 in 1850.

By that time it had begun to appear that another lake port, younger than either Cleveland or Detroit, was likely to surpass both in every quantitative way. Although Chicago was a young city, not incorporated until 1833, interest in its site was very old indeed. Joliet and Marquette had noted as early as 1673 an easy passage between Lake Michigan and the Illinois River, running over the spot where the city would later appear. A few attempts to establish a Jesuit mission there seem to have failed, but a fur trading post did take root and later a United States fort was set up to protect it. The fort had to be surrendered during the War of 1812, however, and the entire white community—which numbered ninety-six at the time—was massacred by Indians.

But the location seemed an important one for Americans to try to hold; the fort was rebuilt after the war, and a government fur trading post was set up there. Meanwhile the idea of a canal connecting Lake Michigan with the Illinois River (and thus with the Gulf of Mexico), conceived first for its military value, had attracted the attention of highly placed people. They included John C. Calhoun who, as Secretary of War, began in 1819 to urge Congress to provide for such a canal. It did so in 1827 by granting to the State of Illinois alternate sections of land along the proposed route. Two years later, the state legislature established a Canal Commission; twenty more years were to pass before the canal was usable.

In the meantime, the commission laid out a town at each end of its canal line, Ottawa on the south, Chicago on the north, and proceeded to advertise its holdings in order to get enough money to begin digging the canal. Land sales were sluggish for a year or two; a couple of eighty-acre lots went for a hundred dollars each. Then came the brief flurry of Black Hawk's War, 1830–1832 —the Indians' last effort to reclaim their land east of the Mississippi River—which brought a good many soldiers into what had been the almost unknown lands of northern Illinois and southern Wisconsin Territory. This publicity, along with a gathering "boom" period in the nation's economy *and* the influence of the Erie Canal, suddenly created intense speculative interest in the Illinois canal and in the town at its northern end.

What this could mean to a town's growth is best shown by a few examples. In 1833, the county officials began to sell the school lands—the income, of course, to be used for educational purposes. Sale of 576 acres in that year brought in just under $40,000: about $75.00 per acre. But in 1837, just three and a half years later, three small lots in the school tract sold for $7,500. In 1830, 126

48

lots in the Canal Commission's town of Chicago sold for an average price of $35.00 each; four years later, lots on South Water Street were bringing $3,500 each. The next year, a local real estate firm sold a tract which had cost it $5,000 to some New York buyers for $80,000. One forty-acre plot was bought on January 2, 1835 for $4,000, and sold on April 10, for $10,000. As the real estate boom neared its climax, early in 1837, daily advances in land values of twenty and twenty-five per cent were not unusual.

All of this naturally attracted attention to Chicago, and its population swelled. There came the inevitable crash, in 1837, but by now enough people had sunk their fortunes (including their credit) in Chicago's prospects to give the place a nucleus of leaders who fought to sustain its growth. One of its first mayors, for example, was William Ogden, who had come in representing a group of wealthy New York investors. Thoroughout the depression which followed the speculative real estate inflation, Ogden and several associates busied themselves in pushing plank roads out from Chicago into its immediate farming hinterland. They agitated for harbor improvements as more and more lake ships sailed as far west as the southern end of Lake Michigan. By the mid-1840's, they were organizing railroad companies and seeking lines west into a lead-mining area around Galena, Illinois and east to Detroit and Buffalo, and ultimately New York City. They arranged for street-grading, for hotel building, and for social amenities including churches—Ogden a devout Presbyterian, contributed money to help build a Catholic church, no doubt on the grounds that by so doing he was helping the city to grow. Curiously, the canal project which had launched Chicago's career, went ahead only slowly and intermittently. Not opened until 1848, it had little direct effect upon the city's growth; its presence, as a project, may have done no more than help to sustain hope, during a dark period in 1837 and after, that the city would amount to something in the future.

Like Cleveland, Chicago quickly sought and found an industrial base for its economic growth. In the 1840's, meat-packing began to loom large among the businesses of Chicagoans; and in 1847 Cyrus McCormick moved his agricultural implement factory from

49

Virginia to the city at the tip of Lake Michigan. These beginnings, coupled with the complete success of Chicago's railroad planning, secured the city's place on the American metropolitan scene. By the outbreak of the Civil War its growth was a phenomenon discussed in the counting rooms of New York and in the drawing rooms of London and Paris.

Seventy miles or so to the north, along the western shore of the lake, a similar urban drama unfolded at almost the same time, on a somewhat smaller scale. Here, where the Milwaukee River enters the lake, there had been another small community of French, Indians, and halfbreeds, with the slow tempo of its life dictated by the fur trade. It did not have a fort, and there was apparently no attempt to establish any religious institution there before the appearance of the city of Milwaukee. During the early 1830's, as the Indians were driven out of the area and the Territory of Wisconsin advanced toward statehood, men began to arrive looking for promising land speculations.

One of these was named Morgan L. Martin, who was a member of the Territory's governing council, and he formed a partnership with the director of the shrinking fur trade business, Solomon Juneau. Martin went to Washington and lobbied for legislative favors, especially affecting land disposal, while Juneau and his brother remained on the spot and began filling out pre-emption claims to as much of the land around the river mouth as they could file for (it would cost them $1.25 per acre). Martin also called the attention of Easterners to his promising site, and the Juneaus began to lay out streets and prepare for newcomers.

About the same time another hopeful speculator arrived in the person of Byron Kilbourn, who was the federal government surveyor for the district. He too had a partner, one Micajah T. Williams, who happened to be Surveyor General for Michigan Territory before Wisconsin Territory was separated from it. Since Juneau had pre-empted most of the land east of the river, Kilbourn concentrated on the southwest side, and very quickly two competing speculative interests were both doing what they could do to attract settlement. A month before government land sales opened in the district, *all* the land within two miles of the mouth of the Milwaukee River had been pre-empted! Soon a real estate boom began, and the inflation of values proceeded much as it had in Chicago, with quarter-acre lots selling for $600. The depression broke up this activity, but again there had been enough solid investment along with it to create the basis for a flourishing lake port in the 1840's and 1850's. Much of the early history of Milwaukee revolved around fierce rivalry between the Martin-Juneau and Williams-Kilbourn groups; they got together in 1846 in order to secure a municipal charter that would enable them to provide basic urban services for the rapidly growing community.

Although there were important differences between these lake towns, and between them and the older river towns, certain comparable features appear in their growth. Speculation aroused interest and drew money to the towns; the towns then sought commercial empires and later industrial bases to sustain themselves. In doing this, these communities aligned their public interests, or general welfares, with the growth of their surrounding areas. A Milwaukee editor in 1846 remarked that it was "clearly to the interest of our . . . businessmen generally to unite upon some plan for extending and improving the roads leading to Milwaukee." In almost the same terms, one of his Cleveland counterparts was urging, three years later: "let us, like the wise Cincinnati merchants, spend liberally for these roads and . . . arouse our farmers and everybody to the importance of increasing our facility for trade and travel and thus make Cleveland the center of a large region." They also strove to provide amenities for domestic community life, though probably none of the cities in the interior did as well in this line as Lexington, Kentucky had done in its halcyon days. Their efforts meant that American expansion was largely a function of urban expansion, and that the civilization which pushed the edge of wilderness always toward the Pacific drew most of its impulses and took most of its direction from cities.

3

The City in American Thought
1790-1850

During the early years of the American nation, reaction to the country's rapidly growing cities was inconsistent and often contradictory. Most prominently perhaps the city seemed to threaten decay in the ideals of an agricultural republic; a formal doctrine of political anti-urbanism, to which successful candidates had to pay a greater or lesser measure of homage, persisted long after we had become an urbanized nation. The American literary tradition, even as it established its independence from Europe, inherited old prejudices against the city. Strains of Hebraic agrarianism in Christian thought, which pictured the city as the home of vanity, carnal lust, and conspiracy, often gave an anti-urban cast to American religious writing. Yet to assume from these manifestations of ideology that nineteenth century Americans were overwhelmingly hostile to the city and to urban values is grossly to oversimplify the complexities and ambivalences of popular thought.

53

The easy assertion, made frequently by students of contemporary American culture, of a basically anti-urban tradition does not stand the test of historical analysis.

A number of sentiments and interests that are sometimes overlooked influenced early nineteenth century attitudes toward cities and their meaning in American life. Sectional considerations, for example, often determined the character of any such inquiry. Spokesmen of the South and West might attack the cities of the eastern seaboard as the seats of national evil and corruption, yet defend their own cities as representing the highest ideals of a republican civilization. The ante-bellum South, for example, is often portrayed as a bastion of agrarianism, yet a number of southern writers during the period were arguing the need for great commercial capitals in the region to free the southern economy from financial control in northeastern cities. Those who reflected on the meaning of America might attack features of national development associated in a general way with the city, such as the factory or the machine, yet vigorously defend some other aspect of urban life, such as the cultural opportunities presented by the city environment. The metropolises of the eastern seaboard might represent all that was evil in Old Europe; those of smaller size, particularly the cities of the West, might, as part of the same statement, represent all that was virtuous in the American experiment. The question of when a city reached a stage of growth at which it was transmuted from splendor to decay was never subjected to analysis. Nor was there much effort to distinguish between types of cities, between the commercial and manufacturing, for example. Concepts of "city" and "urban" were, in short, sufficiently vague to serve a variety of sometimes contradictory purposes. Even those who saw great social dangers in the rise of cities, still regarded them as one of the best indicators of the country's material growth. And in nineteenth century America, only an occasional isolated figure—Thoreau, for example—questioned the view that material growth meant progress.

The formal expression of opposition to cities owed much to the influence of Thomas Jefferson and the political tradition he left to the nation. Although Jefferson's reflections that bear directly on the city are limited, a vague anti-urbanism pervades his entire defense

54

of agriculture and the farmer and occasionally his view becomes explicit. In his early *Notes on Virginia,* written in 1784, he asserted in one of his most famous dicta that those who labored in the earth were the chosen people of God. "The mobs of great cities," he continued, "add just so much to support of pure government as sores do to the strength of the human body." During his travels in Europe from 1784 to 1789, Jefferson was greatly interested in the architecture of European cities and systematically collected city plans as guides for building the new American capital. But he reacted unfavorably to the "empty bustle" of European cities, and unlike his countryman Benjamin Franklin, responded to the pleasures of Paris with the traditional distaste of the American Puritan.

Overall, Jefferson's experience abroad reinforced his belief that cities represented a threat to American values. "I think our governments will remain virtuous for many centuries," he wrote to James Madison in 1787, "as long as they are chiefly agricultural; and this will be as long as there shall be vacant lands in any part of America. When they get piled upon one another in large cities, as in Europe, they will become corrupt as in Europe." In a comment to Benjamin Rush in 1800 on yellow fever epidemics, Jefferson supplied his most bitter observation on the American city. "When great evils happen," he wrote, "I am in the habit of looking out for what good may arise from them as consolations to us, and Providence has in fact so established the order of things, as most evils are the means of producing some good. The yellow fever will discourage the growth of great cities in our nation, and I view great cities as pestilential to the morals, the health and the liberties of man. True, they nourish some of the elegant arts, but the useful ones can thrive elsewhere, and less perfection in the others, with more health, virtue and freedom, would be my choice."

But practical man that he was, Jefferson could never act on the proposition that plagues should not be fought, even though theoretically they might have a beneficial influence in destroying cities; in fact as president he formulated plans explicitly intended to check the spread of yellow fever. In similar fashion, Jefferson accommodated his ideology to the political and economic implications of urban life. Late in his career, he recognized that as a result of the

55

developments stimulated by the Embargo Act of his own administration and by the War of 1812 the United States had to
become a manufacturing nation. In one of his frequently cited
pronouncements he declared in 1816 that "we must now place the
manufacturer by the side of the agriculturist." Jefferson recognized
that manufacturing meant cities and the rise of a propertyless
working class, but the realities of international life permitted no
other course.

Despite this realization, Jefferson never abandoned his deeply-
rooted hostility to the city and the city dweller. At the age of
eighty, writing in a vein similar to that of *Notes on Virginia* thirty
years earlier, he found city life offering "more painful objects of
vice and wretchedness" as well as more opportunities for wasting
time. New York seemed a "Cloacina of all the depravities of human nature." Philadelphia was little different. In contrast, life in
rural Virginia was orderly, rational, moral, and affectionate.

After 1820, large American cities, which grew in part through
the manufacturing Jefferson had feared, became fixtures on the
American scene, and the "urban mobs" that constituted a threat to
republicanism were part of the political constituency. Accordingly,
political leaders influenced by the Jeffersonian tradition were forced
to confront his anti-urbanism. Some, such as John Taylor of
Caroline, author of that classical defense of rural values *Arator,*
simply continued to express and to refine a pure Jeffersonianism.
Others tried to adjust the old truths to the new realities of city and
industry.

Attempts at reconciling urbanization to the principles of agrarianism were perhaps most evident in New York, a state which by
the 1820's had acquired many of the features of a modern capitalist
economy. In the fight over suffrage extension during the 1821
constitutional convention, conservative Federalist spokesmen chided
Democratic delegates for their abandonment of their leader's principles. Would not suffrage extension spread the content of urban
sores through the whole body politic, Elisha Williams asked, and
expose the yeomen interest to the will of the "ring streaked and
speckled population of our large towns and cities, comprising people of every kindred and tongue?" "These cities," he warned, "are
filled with men too rich, or too poor to fraternize with the yeomen

of the country." By the 1830's many Democratic leaders were willing to adjust their principles and put the urban workman by the side of the Jeffersonian yeoman. Amasa Walker, a radical Jacksonian, argued in 1833 that "great cities are not *necessarily,* as the proverb says, 'great sores.' " A time would come, he predicted, when they would be "great fountains of healthful moral influence, sending forth streams that shall fertilize and bless the land." Another Jacksonian leader, the ex-New England Federalist Theodore Sedgwick II, argued that the reputation of cities did not involve a moral question at all but simply an economic one. Do something about people sleeping in cellars and garrets and living in holes and dens, clean up the filthy streets, provide the means of cleanliness and health: then the city, he asserted, would assume its place as the site of opportunity and no longer be a social problem.

That this kind of accommodation to the city involved difficulties was demonstrated in the editorials of the *Democratic Review,* founded in 1837 as an organ of Jeffersonianism. In its initial statement of principles the journal emphasized that the city often operated as an anti-democratic force in society. It was in the city that wealth accumulated, luxury unfolded its corrupting tendencies, and social divisions grew. It was here also that the mercantile classes, and their allies in the law and the ministry, worked against the democratic movement. Two years later, the *Review* noted that unfortunately the New York democracy did better in the metropolis than in outlying parts of the state and confessed that the suffrages of the country were to be preferred to those of the city. The atmosphere of competition and emulation in the city and the lack of leisure to reflect were not conducive to a proper independence of mind in a voter. "In the city," the editorial writer observed, "men move in masses. They catch the current opinion of the hour from their class, and from those public organs of the press on which they are accustomed to depend for their daily supply of superficial thought—for their morning dose of mental stimulus, in those flaming appeals to their passions, their interests, or their vanity, which it is the vocation of the latter daily to administer. . . . They are like men in a troubled crowd, swept hither and thither by the current of the huge mass, with a force which

57

the individual can rarely nerve himself to stem. Individuality in fact loses itself, almost of necessity, in the constant pressure of surrounding example, of the general habit and tone of society, and in the contagious excitements which rapidly chase each other in their successive sway over the multitudinous aggregate of minds."

Such views of urban life would be frequently expressed in another century—and would be up to date in a contemporary magazine. The writer's "troubled crowd" does not really differ much from the "lonely crowd" of our own time. But in the 1830's and 40's this kind of analysis seldom shaped the character of political dialogue. Although politics sometimes reflected divergent views of the American future, these were not expressed in terms of city and country as opposed social environments. And ordinarily the city, along with the machine and the factory, was accepted as a part of American progress. An 1852 orator commemorating Jefferson could, for example, praise all the Jeffersonian principles and yet still provide a vision of America's urban future: "May her villages which are fast becoming towns, her towns which are rapidly growing to cities, and her chief cities which are each one by itself, bidding hopefully yet to surpass in population a Pekin and a Canton; in enterprise and power, a London and a Paris; in art and intellectual and moral renown, an ancient Athens and Rome combined; finally exceed in every commendable respect, all the past achievements of men down to the discovery of the Western Continents."

It was only as the position of the farmer and of agriculture began perceptibly to decline, that Jeffersonian anti-urbanism reasserted itself as part of the rationale of an economic group losing its power in a changing society. Agricultural journals after 1850 began to fill their columns with proclamations against the city. A writer to the *Prairie Farmer* of Chicago typically asserted that the pursuits of agriculture "are so connected with everything around us which tends to enlighten and enoble the mind, improve the condition of society, and promote the common welfare—and its influences have so direct a bearing in all its ramifications, upon individual and national felicity, that it would seem as if a man must come from some other planet who could find anything to say in its disparagement." City life, he went on, "*crushes, enslaves,* and *ruins so many thou-*

sands of our young men, who are insensibly made the victims of *dissipation,* of *reckless* speculation, and of ultimate crime." In his reminiscences, a Michigan pioneer emphasized another aspect of the Jeffersonian view of the city which was frequently expressed as the century wore on. In his part of the country, he wrote, "a sturdy race of honest and patriotic men grow to counterbalance the effeminancy and wickedness of the old cities of the east. But for this, ruin and decay would have long since marked the gradual downfall of our great republic. There is today more leaven of salvation right here by the lonely shores of the mighty waters of Lake Michigan, than in all the borders of all the cities of the corrupt civilization of the older east. The wide extent of our country is the conservative influence that will save it from the fate of the ruined dynasties of the old world for ages yet to come."

These kinds of anti-urban sentiments helped to sustain the farmer movements of the late nineteenth century. "The great cities rest upon our broad and fertile prairies," said William Jennings Bryan in his famous Cross of Gold speech, which provided a prelude to the last important political effort seriously based on the Jeffersonian vision of America. "Burn down your cities and leave our farms, and your cities will spring up again as if by magic; but destroy our farms, and the grass will grow in the streets of every city in the country."

But Bryan lost. It is doubtful that the anti-urbanism which was part of the agricultural fundamentalism of the late nineteenth century ever in any precise way reflected community ideology toward the city. The formality and rigor of the agricultural attack on the city might alone indicate that the argument provided a defense of self-interest, not a collective response to perceived circumstances.

The often superficial city-country argument that influenced the character of political debate reflected deeper strains in American and Western thought. Thomas Jefferson's view of the city rested on assumptions about man and the world that at least went back to Virgil's *Georgics;* it owed much directly to Adam Smith, who had found "unnaturalness and dependence" to be the urban dweller's vices and had argued that "to cultivate the ground was the natural destination of man." Enlightenment rationalism and eighteenth century Romanticism, although the latter developed in part as a reaction to the former, both posited a natural man created in a fixed image, not a social being whose nature was modifiable and partly determined by the workings of institutions. In much early nineteenth century thought, European as well as American, the city was looked upon as an artificial institution that might be corruptive of the elemental man.

The Transcendentalist philosopher, Ralph Waldo Emerson, held to such a conception. Emerson's view of the universe differed radically from Jefferson's, but his view of the city was similar. The city, Emerson argued, was the source of Understanding, the essentially empty knowledge of empirical science; the country was the school of Reason, the higher truth of intuition and vision. Like Jefferson, Emerson recognized the value of cities in providing such educational agencies as the opera, the museum, the library, and the lecture. But the city was also artificial; it denied man's creative facilities. The true test of a civilization was the kind of man the country turned out. And a choice between city and country was necessary. "I wish to have rural strength and religion for my children, and I wish city facility and polish. I find with chagrin that I cannot have both." Although he was not altogether consistent, Emerson fundamentally chose the country. He wrote to Thomas Carlyle in 1840: "I always seem to suffer some loss of faith on entering cities. They are great conspiracies; the parties are all maskers, who have taken mutual oaths of silence not to betray each other's secret and each to keep the other's madness in contenance." In a late essay on farming and the farmer Emerson went further: "That uncorrupted behavior which we admire in animals and in young children belongs to him, to the hunter, the sailor—the man who lives in the presence of Nature. Cities force growth and make men talkative and entertaining, but they make them artificial."

In one of the most famous passages of his works, Emerson argues the need of man to return to the woods. There "man casts off his years, as the snake his slough, and at what period soever of life is always a child." It was in the woods that one could return to reason and faith. There one could become the celebrated "Transparent eyeball" seeing all, becoming a part and parcel of God, loving "uncontained and immortal beauty." There all the associations of the city became mere trifles. "In the wilderness,"

Emerson wrote, "I find something more dear and connate than in streets or villages. In the tranquil landscape, and especially in the distant line of horizon, man beholds somewhat as beautiful as his own nature."

In American literature of the early and mid-nineteenth century, Emerson's metaphysical view of the unnatural city became part of a more general indictment of the city and of urban life. As Morton and Lucia White have demonstrated in their pioneering study of the intellectual and the city, the American literary tradition has often been an anti-urban one. A dominant theme in the important fiction of the period is that of America as the lost Eden. The city becomes the symbol of the fall from grace of the land and its people. Particularly as manufacturing becomes important, the city serves to represent materialism, commercialism, corruption, and the evil influences of Old Europe.

This kind of symbolic use of the city extends back past Emerson at least to the first important American novel, Charles Brockden Brown's *Arthur Mervyn* published in 1799. Brown uses Philadelphia during the yellow fever epidemic of 1793 as a setting that represents the reality of evil in the world; the dark and ominous, plague-filled city is entered by the young country hero, Arthur Mervyn, fled from, and returned to with fascination. As R. W. B. Lewis has pointed out, Mervyn is the first of the American Adams —the innocent who matures through knowledge of evil but aches for the freedom of his past. In Brown's novel, the city is specifically the vehicle of the hero's maturation; Arthur Mervyn is continually aware, as he puts it, of the "contrariety that exists between the city and country."

Melville, Hawthorne, and Poe, as the Whites observe, all had "bad dreams of the city." Their characters are attracted to the city but fearful of its effects. Melville's *Pierre,* for example, is a hero with the "choice fate to have been born and nurtured in the country, surrounded by scenery whose uncommon loveliness was the perfect mould of a delicate and poetic mind," and who is defeated by the heartlessness and commercialism of New York. In general, the three authors' bad dreams are of the European city— of London, Liverpool, Paris, or Rome—but there is usually present an implied warning that the evil may reach America's shores.

61

Lewis, in his analysis, has examined Hawthorne's frequent symbolic use of the city, the "frantic shuffling" between city and country in novel after novel. The two environments to Hawthorne represent a moral choice between freedom and restraint. Thoreau found the choice simple—retreat to the woods. Hawthorne, Lewis notes, perceived the complexities in this decision: "He acknowledged the dependence of the individual, for nourishment, upon organized society (the city), and he believed that it was imperative 'to open up an intercourse with the world.' But he knew that the city could destroy as well as nourish and was apt to destroy the person most in need of nourishment. And while he was responsive to the attractions of the open air and to the appeal of the forest, he also understood the grounds for Puritan distrust of the forest. He retained that distrust as part of the symbol. In the forest, possibility was unbounded; but just because of that, evil inclination was unchecked, and witches could flourish there."

Hawthorne's tale of an Utopian colony, *The Blithedale Romance,* based to a degree on the author's experience at the famous Brook Farm, addresses itself directly to the problem of community. The book provides a good example of the way in which city and country were used as symbols in the mid-nineteenth century novel. The book's hero, Miles Coverdale, who has decided to join the Blithedale experiment, feels regret as he leaves his comfortable bachelor rooms, his cigars, and his claret. But as the party of colonists starts out in a snowstorm he becomes aware of the oppressive force of buildings on all sides and "the old conventionalism" of the city—the smoke in the air and the tramping feet of passers-by that destroy the freshness of nature. Coverdale feels a sense of release as they leave the city and find better air to breathe. "Air that had not been breathed once and again! Air that had not been spoken into words of falsehood, formality and error, like all the air of the dusky city!"

At Blithedale, Coverdale experiences a degree of regeneration, but at the end of an unhappy summer, he realizes that the communitarian experiment represents merely another form of conventionalism and feels compelled to return to the city. He is immediately aware again of its smoke, cruelty, and conventionalism. But he finds satisfaction in the city's sounds and impressions.

"Whatever had been my taste for solitude and natural scenery, yet the thick, foggy, stifled element of cities, the entangled life of many men together, sordid as it was, and empty of the beautiful, took quite as strenuous a hold upon my mind. I felt as if there could never be enough of it." In an extended passage, Coverdale describes the sounds of the city—the stir of the hotel, the noise of the pavements, a marching band going by, fire engines, church bells, applause from a nearby public hall. "All of this was just as valuable in its way," Coverdale concludes, "as the sighing of the breeze among the birch-trees" at Blithedale.

Throughout Hawthorne's work there is fascination with the city but always coupled with the realization that the features that make it fascinating are those that make it dangerous. As one of his latter thoughts on the matter, he suggests in *The Marble Faun* that "all towns should be made capable of purification by fire, or of decay within each half-century . . . we may build almost immortal habitations, it is true; but we cannot keep them from growing old, musty, unwholesome, dreary, full of deathscents, ghosts and murder stains."

Themes of the evil city, elevated to the level of literature in the work of Melville, Hawthorne, or Poe, also served more popular writers of fiction. Sensational works on the sinful metropolises of America began to find a wide market as early as the 1840's. Osgood Bradbury in his *The Belle of the Bowery* (1846) and *Female Depravity, or, the House of Death* (1852) developed, in near pornographic fashion, the story of the innocent country girl who is led into evil ways in the city. The latter book has as a main character the intriguing Henry Luroff, who had "seduced more girls from the country than any other young man in the city." Edward Z. C. Judson in *The B'Hoys of New York* (1849) presented the complementary topic—the "green countryman" corrupted by the city's evil women. Under his pseudonym, Ned Buntline, Judson was later to popularize another genre of sensational American writing, the dime-novel Western. Often vice was portrayed attractively in these works on the city, as in *The Gamblers' League or the Trials of a Country Maid* (1857). The book tells the story of two New York confidence men and their tool the beautiful Arabella, who was forced to live a life of sin with one of them. The depraved Arabella develops special talents for ensnaring innocent victims from the country and lives luxuriously as a result.

Written at a similar level and often centering on the same themes were alleged guidebooks that revealed the mysteries and sins of American cities. One of the earliest writers of these exposés of urban life, which became particularly popular in the years after the Civil War, was a *New York Tribune* journalist, George G. Foster. In two books collecting his columns—*New York in Slices by an Experienced Carver* (1849) and *New York by Gas-Light: With Here and There a Streak of Sunshine* (1850)—Foster presented most of the themes and topics that were later to become standard in the genre. Here the reader encounters the gullible country lad seduced and robbed by the painted streetwalkers; the symbolic area of complete degradation—in this case the notorious Five Points district, which ordinarily served the purpose in writings about New York; the invidious comments on the city's "races," the Jewish, Negro, and Irish; the prostitute's confession—"Princess Anna," once an innocent country girl seduced and abandoned by a city boy, exploited by the clergy, and now steadily drifting downward to the lower depths; contrasts between the luxurious sexual immorality of the upper classes and the sordid life of the poor; Wall Street as a collection of temples to Mammon.

Often works of this type have been dismissed as lurid anti-urban tracts, designed to appeal to the prejudices of rural and small-town America. There is much that is lurid and much that is anti-urban in Foster's accounts. Yet his reaction to the city is more complex than simple hostility. Running through both books is the theme that the American city as it stands may be evil but that potentially it is the site of the good community and the locale for the fruition of Christian society. In *New York in Slices,* he states the theme explicitly: "A great city is the highest result of human civilization. Here the Soul, that most perfect and godlike of all created things, the essence and spirit of the visible world has put forth all its most wonderful energies. . . . Yes—man in isolation, or thinly gathered in feeble neighborhoods and scattered villages, is powerless to accomplish great works or to fulfill the mission of his race. It is only in a large city, where some hundreds of thousands combine their various powers, that the human mind can efficiently stamp itself on every thing by which it is surrounded—can transmute the insensible earth to a fit temple and dwelling place for immortal spirits."

These pious sentiments, which were often a part of the better known later exposés, can perhaps be dismissed frequently as window dressing for prurient sensationalism. Still, they were common sentiments expressed in a variety of contexts. The notion of the city as an arena where American society could either move toward a higher good or descend toward evil informs much of the pre-Civil War writing about the meaning of the city in American life. It is to be found, for example, in the first important demographic analysis of the United States. George Tucker, a Jeffersonian politician who became Professor of Moral Philosophy at the University of Virginia when it opened in 1825, examined the census returns from 1790 to 1840 and speculated on their meaning in a significant but little known work entitled *Progress of the United States in Population and Wealth* published in 1843. His compilations demonstrated that towns and cities were clearly growing at a much faster rate than the country as a whole and that this trend would continue in the future. Tucker was uncertain, however, as to what would be the effect of this development on American society. "The growth of cities," he wrote in a passage widely quoted in contemporary sources, "commonly marks the progress of intelligence and the arts, measures the sum of social enjoyment, and always implies mental activity, which is sometimes healthy and useful, sometimes distempered and pernicious. If these congregations of men diminish some of the comforts of life, they augment others: if they are less favourable to health than the country, they also provide better defences against disease, and better means of cure. From causes both physical and moral, they are less favourable to the multiplication of the species. In the eyes of the moralist, cities afford a wider field both for virtue and vice: and they are more prone to innovation, whether for good or evil."

The early religious studies of the city in America offered a related view—that the city could serve as the testing ground for the faith of a Christian. Amory D. Mayo in *Symbols of the Capital; or Civilization in New York,* published in 1859, established a pattern for the clerical examinations of American life, another genre which later in the hands of such figures as Josiah Strong and William T. Stead was to find a wide popular market. Mayo attacked the city with all the conventional romantic and agrarian arguments. The struggle for success in the city scarred the bodies and twisted the minds of both successes and failures. "All dangers of the town," he wrote, "may be summed up in this: that here, withdrawn from the blessed influence of Nature, and set face to face against humanity, man loses his own nature and becomes a new and artificial creature—an unhuman cog in a social machinery that works like a fate, and cheats him of his true culture as a soul. The most unnatural fashions and habits, the strangest eccentricities of intellect, the wildest and most pernicious theories in social morals, and the most appalling and incurable barbarism, are the legitimate growth of city life."

Yet Mayo understood the appeal and the reality of the city. He saw young people flocking there and being challenged by the experience. If they survived the ordeal, he thought their faith and character would unquestionably be strengthened. Moreover, an ideal city, a monument to Christian principles, was conceivable if there were only a way of removing the poor and the exploiters of the poor. "But, we cannot build cities 'to order,'" he wrote in a more realistic vein, "they are and will be huge receptacles for all varieties of humanity, and represent the worst as surely as the best in our American character. All the teacher of Christianity can do is to take men and women in towns as he finds them, and, in spite of disheartening influences, keep on forever warning, instructing and inspiring to virtue."

Numerous nineteenth century clergymen who became aware of the problems of the eastern cities had realized that the American city was here to stay and was not necessarily a threat to the good community. One of the more optimistic spokesmen of this point of view was Joseph Tuckerman, a Unitarian minister in Boston who pioneered community programs of social welfare in the United States. Tuckerman consistently argued that cities were not inherently un-Christian. With effort, he asserted, they could be made the centers of the "purest and highest religious and moral influences of the highest intellectual culture, and of the greatest advancement of the arts and sciences, and that the most vigorous growth of all the Christian virtues may be made a characteristic of cities." The most famous national spokesman of Unitarianism, William E. Channing, a friend and Harvard classmate of Tuckerman's, argued that American cities could become the metropolises of world civilization if individuals in the cities would face up to their responsibilities for the health and welfare of the poor. In eulogizing Tuckerman, Channing reflected his own as well as Tuckerman's view of the city when he wrote that it "became his deliberate conviction and one which he often repeated, that great cities need not be haunts of vice and poverty; that . . . there were now intelligence, virtue and piety enough, could they be brought into united action, to give a new intellectual and moral life to the more neglected classes of society. In this faith he acted, toiled, suffered and died."

The religious argument that the city could represent Christian good but that the American city, with its extremes of wealth and poverty, its materialism and its exploitation contradicted Christian principles worked its way into a substantial body of pre-Civil War writing about urban life. It received typical statement, for example, in an 1857 governmental investigation of the slums of New York. The writers argued that man was a gregarious creature who yearned for neighborhood. Theorists of all ages had conceived of noble cities. Even the Bible had "coupled the forms of earthly splendor with the more spiritual excellences of a New Jerusalem." The city could be the site of "intellectual and moral beatitude." If desolate nature was "symbolical of savage or barbarous life," then its opposite ought to be found where art, luxury, and industry existed in profusion. "Yet here," the report continued, "in reality, where pleasure wreathes perennial flowers, and magnificence runs wild with varied forms; here, in sad refutation of Utopian speculation, the leper crouches in dumb despair, the beggar crawls in abject misery, the toiler starves, the robber prowls, and the tenant-house —home of all those outcast beings—rises in squalid deformity, to mock civilization with its foul malaria, its poison-breeding influences, its death-dealing associations."

A number of questions, then, were part of the early nineteenth century dialogue on the American city and its relationship to the American future. Did the city, with its extremes of wealth and poverty, its spiritual impoverishment, its greed and oppression, constitute an overwhelming threat to the Christian community or did the existence of these problems of urban life provide a way of strengthening Christian ideals? In a broader sense, was the city, in Christian eschatology, really Sodom and Gommorah or the New Jerusalem, the "city on a hill?" Were the growing cities part of a new economic pattern that would undermine the foundations of republican government? Could man, a creature of nature, comprehend his place in the universe while restricted by an essentially artificial environment?

Underlying these and related social and philosophical questions, however, was a scientific conception—the city was essentially unhealthy, a dangerous type of environment that threatened man's physical existence. Observation tended to lend support to this conception, for it was largely city dwellers who were struck down by the frequent, dreaded nineteenth-century plagues of cholera, yellow fever, and other epidemic disease. Ebenezer Hazard, who had survived the Philadelphia yellow fever epidemic of 1793 in spite of the massive bloodletting prescribed by his physician, expressed a view that was to be echoed many times in the next fifty or sixty years when he observed that the plague might teach the country a lesson and check the "prevailing taste for enlarging Philadelphia, and crowding so many human beings together on so small a part of earth."

These ecological views related closely to prevailing medical theories concerning the nature of disease. Not until the 1880's was the germ theory of disease generally accepted in the United States, and before that time many diseases, particularly those that were epidemic in nature, were regarded not as entities but as dynamic conditions whose manifestations varied in terms of a range of moral, climatic, and environmental factors. This type of etiology generally supported the view that the city provided an unwholesome, unnatural atmosphere in human life. Miasmas which induced both physical and moral disease (and the two were not rigorously demarcated) were frequently associated with an urban environment.

Nineteenth century novelists conceived of the city as representing a danger to the soul of man or to his society, but they also feared the city in a physical sense—as the source of dangerous contaminating exhalations. When Hawthorne's Miles Coverdale, for example, finds "better air to breath" upon leaving the smoke-filled city, he is in part employing metaphor—but only in part. The same point could be made of Jefferson's observations on cities as "pestilential" or as "sores," which have too commonly been construed simply as comments on political or economic matters. The city as "cancer," a metaphor still frequently employed, has its roots in this kind of nineteenth century biological theory. Jefferson's friend, the distinguished scientist and physician, Benjamin Rush, a firm believer in miasmatic theories of disease, made the point of the physical danger of cities explicit in a letter to Jefferson: "I consider them in the same light that I do abscesses on the human body, viz., as reservoirs of all the impurities of a community."

In a little noted aspect of his Presidential career, Jefferson devised a plan to remove disease-causing vapors from American cities. He outlined his proposal after the acquisition of New Orleans from the French. "Such a constitution of atmosphere being requisite to originate [yellow fever] as is generated in low, close, and ill-cleansed parts of town, I have supposed it practicable to prevent its generation by building our cities on a more open plan. Take, for instance, the chequer board for a plan. Let the black squares only be building ones, and the white ones be left open, in turf and trees. Every square of house will be surrounded by four open squares, and every house will front an open square. The atmosphere of such a town would be like that of the country, insusceptible of the miasmata which produce yellow fever. I have accordingly proposed that the enlargement of the city of New Orleans, which must immediately take place, shall be on this plan. But it is only in the case of enlargements to be made, or of cities to be built, that this means of prevention can be employed." There is no evidence that the scheme was ever applied to New Orleans. But the town of Jeffersonville, Indiana later to be eclipsed by Louisville across the river in Kentucky, was initially plotted in the fashion Jefferson suggested, and the original plan for Jackson, Mississippi also followed his design. In both cases, the open squares offered too great a temptation as building sites for the system to endure longer than very briefly.

69

Until the 1860's, when it was recognized that epidemics could be combatted through systematic community programs of sanitation, each year of plague brought warnings to abandon the unhealthy cities. In 1849, for example, a physician wrote that the siege of cholera that year could be considered one of the "greatest *reforms* the world has ever known," for it might teach Americans "to forsake large cities . . . to choose the country's wholesome air with its quietude and competence." The first investigations of housing and other problems of urban life in America emphasized that the city sapped the moral and physical vigor of its residents. The famous 1845 report of John H. Griscom, a New York physician and pioneer in the public health movement, argued that the foul air of New York caused an individual's blood to become burdened with impurities, preventing it from imparting to the "system the qualities demanded by nature for the due maintenance of health and strength." All that was necessary to demonstrate this, the report argued, was a stroll in the country. The contrast between an atmosphere filled with "animal and vegetable exhalations" and the air of grassy plains, rivers, and mountains needed "no epicurean lungs to detect." The "superior corporeal activity" and the mental stimulation imparted by these latter surroundings provided "prima facie proofs" of the country's superiority.

Although efforts to introduce trees and parks into the city— which became a well-organized movement in the 1840's and 1850's —rested in part on a formalized enthusiasm for nature aroused by the romantic writings of John Ruskin, William Cullen Bryant, Andrew Jackson Downing, and others, fundamental also to the movement was the view that the city was inherently unhealthy and that parks and trees would bring it closer to the state of the country. Parks would serve as "lungs" or "ventilators," and both terms were used often, absorbing or dispelling the impurities created by the urban environment. A physician writing about the 1849 cholera epidemic speculated that the principal cause was insufficient electricity in the air, a result of the unnatural congestion of cities. Accordingly, the answer to epidemics was clear: "If cities must exist let many and large spaces be devoted to parks, and let all the streets on each side of the way be lined with trees, with two or three trees to every building, so that the people may be supplied

70

with electricity and oxygen in abundance from Nature's own laboratory." Regardless of the particular environmental theory of disease
advanced, parks were viewed as an urban public health measure of
fundamental importance. In gaining support for New York's Central Park and the other large urban parks that followed, considerations of health often proved more important than did arguments
stressing the aesthetic or philosophical value of bringing the countryside to the city.

The notion of an individual city as an organic structure subject
to inevitable decay because of its production of pervasive disease-
producing vapors absorbed many writers about the American future
in the early and mid-nineteenth century. Reflecting on the past
urban history of the world, a commentator in *De Bow's Review*
noted that great cities had always declined. Babylon, Nineveh,
Memphis, Tyre, and Carthage had been succeeded by Pekin,
Canton, Constantinople, Naples, Vienna, Madrid, London, and
Paris. The fate of ancient cities was now being prepared for the
present world capitals. "Most of these great cities," he wrote, "are,
in their oldest portions, exhibiting signs of decay. Like ancient
trees, while at the heart they are wasting away, they add circle to
circle of outward growth; now gaining in progress of growth on
the measure of interior decay, and again failing to increase out-
wardly as the interior portions waste away." This decay was chiefly
the result of exhalations of a great city caused by the accumulation
of filth at its interior. Would American cities face the same fate?
The author thought not. The next great metropolises, he predicted,
would be located in the interior valley of America. Because of the
pattern of the magnificent Mississippi River system, the natural impurities that led to deterioration of a city could be safely carried
away. A long life could thus be predicted for the future great cities
of the United States.

If the city as a place to live was viewed as inherently unhealthy,
the desirability of the city as an institution for the promotion of
economic activity was seldom questioned. Along with the telegraph, the railroad, and the factory, the growing city by the 1830's
was looked upon as a certain token of American progress toward
a magnificent future. From Christopher Columbus on, the New
World had in part meant wealth; the city had always been an im-

portant symbol of America as the land of material opportunity. The nineteenth century immigrant's vision of New York with its streets paved with gold continued a traditional cultural attitude as old as the seven cities of Cibola sought by the Spanish explorers. Moreover, the rationale that developed in defense and explanation of American capitalistic expansion had the city as one of its principal elements. We read Thoreau today and are moved by his prophetic remonstration against American materialism, against the city, the machine, and the factory. Yet in his own time people were more likely to read the poetic tributes to the telegraph, the iron horse, or the country's magnificent thriving cities to be found in their commercial magazines or local newspapers. Although the anti-urban philosophers and novelists of the nineteenth century intrigue the contemporary mind, the defenders and prophets of the material city perhaps reflect more exactly the early popular view of the city.

Much of the favorable writing about early nineteenth century urban growth grew out of the city rivalries of the period and stressed geographical theories of city location and development. Generally present in these discussions was a formal viewpoint that could be termed the doctrine of natural advantages: great cities were located and grew because of the influence of a variety of deterministic geographic influences involving river connections, distances, raw materials, and climate. Human enterprise was not entirely ruled out of the calculation; potentially great cities with all the natural advantages in the world might presumably fail through lack of enlightened effort by local leaders. But until well into the railroad era it was accepted that the forces of geography fundamentally determined the success or failure of attempts to build great cities.

This meant that a proper study of geography would enable a student to predict the future of urban growth in America. Prophecy was a salient part of the doctrine of natural advantages, and DeWitt Clinton's exuberant vision of New York's destiny expressed in 1825 was unusual only in that it proved largely to be true. The city, he declared, "will, in course of time become the granary of the world, the emporium of commerce, the seat of manufactures, the focus of great moneyed operations, and the concentrating point

72

of vast, disposable, and accumulating capitals, which will stimulate, enliven, extend, and reward the exertions of human labour and ingenuity, in all their processes and exhibitions. And, before the revolution of a century, the whole island of Manhattan, covered with habitations and replenished with a dense population, will constitute one vast city." Statements like this accompanied American city building for another century.

In the early nineteenth century the American West, not the urbanizing northeast, sustained the hopes of those who wished the United States to remain an agrarian republic. Yet, ironically, it was the American West that also spawned the most elaborate visions of an urban future for the nation. Just as historians long failed to recognize town and city building as a force in the economic development of the west, interpreters of the character of our national culture in their concern with the myths arising from struggle with the wilderness have tended to overlook the impact of a western urban experience on American thought. Those who saw American progress in material growth often perceived the west as an eventual land of magnificent cities. From the first days of settlement across the Appalachian Mountains, every region of the West had its newspaper editor, hired promoter, or local intellectual predicting greatness for a primitive hamlet or perhaps a city that existed only on its promoter's map. Writing in 1815, Daniel Drake, the frontier physician and long time promoter of Cincinnati, admitted it might seem visionary and boastful to speak of cities in the West. Yet, Drake argued that if one became familiar with the natural advantages of the region, it would be apparent that the primitive villages on the banks of the Ohio and Mississippi would attain the position of "populous and magnificent cities." The magnificent river transportation system of the interior, the fertility of the soil, and the region's bountiful resources betokened enormous population growth. Of all the great cities destined to develop along the Ohio, Drake predicted that Cincinnati with its unparalleled natural advantages was destined to be the foremost.

At each successive stage of westward movement, similar claims were made for other western cities. With more obvious justification than in many communities, St. Louis writers worked out the doctrine of natural advantages in elaborate detail. Located near an

73

unrivalled confluence of rivers at a key point on the great central waterway, the Mississippi, St. Louis struck many observers as nature's favorite. The city, the British traveler Alexander Mackay wrote near mid-century, "occupies as it were the central point, from which the great natural highways of the Union diverge in different directions. The different radii which spring from it bring it into contact with a vast circumference. The Missouri connects it with the Rocky Mountains, the Ohio with the Alleghenies, the Upper Mississippi with the Great Lakes, the lower with the ocean. It is destined soon to become the great internal *entrepôt* of the country."

Farther to the west Albert Richardson, the journalist and western traveler, wrote a few years later of the "New Babylons" springing up along the Missouri and Kansas rivers on the fringe of settlement. Each of these, he said, had beautifully lithographed maps showing magnificent city development and railroads converging from all directions. In many cases, however, not a single habitation had actually been built at the site. Richardson warned immigrants and investors to turn "deaf ears to plausible theorists with elaborate maps, who prove geographically, climatically, and statistically that the great city *must* spring up in some new locality."

Although the doctrine of natural advantages, utilized to justify prophecies of urban greatness for aspiring villages and towns, often represented little more than a narrow boosterism, in the hands of many western writers it was developed into an involved theory of city location and growth. In 1851 an obscure Cincinnatian named S. H. Goodin seized on the theory of gravitation to try to prove that his city was destined to be a great metropolis. Describing a process by which circles of varying sized urban settlements formed according to the fundamental law of centralization, he concluded that ultimately the competition of cities in the third circle would create a great central city in mid-America, which would have all the others as "satellites or outposts."

A number of threads of nineteenth-century thought were woven into the presentation of these theories: a geopolitical emphasis on the importance of central land masses in a society's development, the old geographical-historical idea that great cities are inevitably located along the major rivers of the world, and the view that mankind moves ever westward. In addition, these reflections were always informed by a vision of an urban future for the nation.

Particularly influential in shaping the outlook of the western urban writers was the German geographer and explorer, Alexander von Humboldt, whose multi-volume study of the universe entitled *Cosmos* was widely circulated in the United States in an English translation. Humboldt argued that nature determined the patterns of development of all society. He emphasized the importance of the continual movement of the peoples of the world along an isothermal zone where yearly temperature conditions were most favorable for civilization. Cities, he argued, would form at intervals within this favored habitat. These views and several related concepts advanced by Humboldt provided the foundation for much of the mid-nineteenth century speculation about the urban future of the West.

The American popularizer of Humboldt and one of the more significant of the western urban prophets was the explorer, military adventurer, and land speculator, William Gilpin (1813–1894). Gilpin participated fully in the frontier experience. He first arrived in the West as a young army recruiting officer during the Second Seminole War, became active in politics in St. Louis, participated in the early efforts of Oregon settlers to organize the territory, and after a year in Washington spent noisily advocating America's manifest destiny participated in Stephen Kearny's expedition to New Mexico during the Mexican War. After the war he again became active in politics, early supported the Republican party in Missouri, became territorial governor of Colorado in 1861, and late in his life made a fortune from land speculation in Colorado. All the while, he was speaking and writing about the West; his articles of the 1850's, later collected in a book first called *The Central Gold Region* and later *The Mission of the North American People,* won him national recognition as a spokesman of the West.

Gilpin's erudite but tangled writings are made up in large part of detailed topographical description but running through them all is a version of Humboldt's geographical determinism. Gilpin adopted Humboldt's conception of the Isothermal Zodiac, an undulating belt of land around the globe where climate was most favorable for man. Within this zone, and there only, Gilpin asserted, the great civilizations of the world had flourished. Upon the Axis of Intensity, running through the heart of the Isothermal Zodiac, had pressed the migratory movements of the human masses. Near this line of favorable median temperature, men had constructed the world's primary cities, the "foci from which have radiated intellectual activity and power."

Gilpin further asserted that North America was a vast bowl that focussed all forces to the center and led to a harmonious pattern of social development. The continent was a "symmetrical and sublime" geographic unit, the Mississippi Valley its dominant center. "The Great Basin of the Mississippi is the amphitheatre of the world," he wrote; "here is supremely, indeed, the most magnificent dwelling marked out by God for man's abode."

These geographical conceptions emphasizing population movement westward and the concentration of wealth and power in the interior of the nation could easily be fitted to a rationale justifying the future of the cites of the West. They were continually used in this fashion, and Gilpin himself in several instances made the necessary applications. As a resident of Independence, Missouri during the 1840's, he had formulated a plan to make an area of land near the small frontier community into "Centropolis," the pre-eminent city of the mid-continent. Although Gilpin had a magnificent map prepared that showed the national capital and national observatory located in the heart of a great city embracing an area of over a hundred square miles, the speculative scheme proved a complete failure and left Gilpin in debt for a number of years.

As part of this promotional venture, Gilpin in 1853 had advanced an explicit theory of city location to justify Independence's claim to urban greatness. His article on the subject incorporated many of the geographical arguments that were a part of the doctrine of natural advantages prevalent in western urban writing as well as his own version of Humboldt. Independence, Gilpin asserted, occupied a key point on the zodiac of the westward movement. Throughout history man had erected the world's cities along great navigable rivers, the Ganges, Nile, or Danube, which ran through broad fertile basins. A physical law locating emporiums a hundred leagues apart had operated along the rivers of North America. Gilpin argued that if a reader were to make even a slight inspection of a map of the river system of the world, such as Humboldt had prepared, his eyes would immediately be drawn to the portion of the Missouri River running east from the mouth of the Kansas to St. Louis, and he would see that Independence, because of its location at the western end of this natural throughway, was destined to be the next great American metropolis. St. Louis and Independence, he wrote, "stand out upon the face of the continent like eyes in the human head." No mere works of man could alter the rise of Independence to metropolis. "The peculiar configuration of the continent," he declared, "and its rivers and plains make these *two* natural *focal* points. This will not be interfered with by any railroads or any other public works which may be constructed by arts, as these latter are successful and permanent only when they conform with the water grades of nature and the natural laws which condense society."

At the time Gilpin wrote, numerous railroads were being projected west of the Mississippi River, and this had to be taken into account in any prediction about the future location of great cities in mid-America. Although it was soon to be conclusively demonstrated that railroads could be built virtually anywhere, decisively altering natural patterns of city location, prophecy lagged far behind technology, and spokesmen for aspiring communities generally argued that railroads would always be bound by the logic of river course and natural physical channels of trade and communication. In advancing the claims of Independence, Gilpin projected a great north-south railroad to run from Independence to Galveston and the Gulf of Mexico, which, he asserted, would conform to the pattern of continental forces. Advancing a common point of view that persisted in western promotional writing until late in the century, he argued that such a line would prove to be the means by which the West escaped the exploitation of the East.

In the late 1850's after the failure of his project, Gilpin abandoned his interest in Independence and moved the "*site* for the central city of the 'Basin of the Mississippi'" a few miles west to Kansas City, which by that time had clearly eclipsed Independence as the regional city. "There must be a great city here," Gilpin concluded, "such as antiquity built at the head of the Mediterranean and named Jerusalem, Tyre, Alexandria, and Constantinople; such as our own people name New York, New Orleans, San Francisco, St. Louis." A few years later, he found that the pioneer population moving ever westward along the Axis of Intensity had again begun to condense itself in force. The settlers had chosen Denver, a "focal point of impregnable power in the topographical configuration of the continent." Ultimately, Gilpin argued, Denver would also become the gateway for eastward migration along the Axis of Intensity toward the world's vital center, the Mississippi Valley. In the 1850's and 60's, Gilpin was considered a leading authority on the West. His kind of vision of the great cities of the West, as fanciful as his notions seem, supported the hopes of hundreds of ambitious promoters in the towns and hamlets of the region.

Jesup W. Scott (1799–1873), who ranks with Gilpin as a student of early western cities, was influenced by a similar view of the significance of interior geography. In the late 1840's and 50's, at roughly the same time Gilpin was winning prominence, Scott wrote a series of widely circulated articles designed to show that the future urban population of the United States would be concentrated in the Mississippi Valley and Great Lakes regions. Gilpin had been influenced by town boosting on the Missouri-Kansas border; Scott was the product of an earlier urban frontier. He came west to the booming Maumee Valley of Ohio in the 1830's at a time when twelve villages and paper town sites along a fifteen mile stretch of river were competing to become the metropolis of the lake region. The Panic of 1837 ended this boom brought on by interior canal building and nearly wiped out Scott. But after several years of newspaper work and land speculation, he eventually made a fortune from a key holding of downtown Toledo real estate that he had purchased at an early date.

In his writings, published in the widely known *Hunt's Merchants' Magazine* and *De Bow's Review,* Scott consistently advanced an urban interpretation of the westward movement. The rise of the city, he argued, was the fundamental economic development occurring in the west. It had not attracted sufficient attention; the country's "best minds" had tended to ignore it; yet surely, he asserted, the rapidity of the growth of cities was "among the most remarkable phenomena of human progress." Finding the natural laws that impelled mankind toward an urban society should in fact be a primary aim of the student of the United States.

Like Gilpin, Scott stressed the geographic unity of the interior of North America in shaping the growth of cities. "The centre of power, numerical, political, economical, and social," he wrote, "is . . . indubitably, on its steady march from the Atlantic border toward the interior of the continent. That it will find a resting place somewhere, in its broad interior plain, seems as inevitable as the continued movement of the earth on its axis." Scott argued that Europeans and their descendants in the United States had too closely associated great cities with "salt, sea and commerce"; the interior of America for too long had been thought of as a land of gloomy forests and desert prairies. People perhaps acknowledged in the abstract the potentialities of a vast transportation system of rivers, lakes, and railroads, supplemented by canals and macadamized highways, but had only begun to recognize by the 1840's how the locomotive and the steamboat were actually creating easy interior commerce and stimulating the growth of interior cities.

Substantial portions of many of Scott's articles consisted of elaborate population projections, both for the region as a whole and for individual cities, designed to show the future growth of urban population in the West. Although his methods of handling statistics were crude, Scott ranks among the first important American students of demography. In 1843, he set the pattern for his later calculations when he predicted that by 1890 the great interior valley would have a total population of 48 million, with 35 million people in cities. By this date the Atlantic slope would have grown only to a 21 million total; Canada and the region west of the Rocky Mountains would have respective totals of five and two million. These figures clearly indicated the future dominance of the interior cities of America, Scott asserted, particularly since he felt that he had been unduly generous in assigning the number of people that would still be required in agriculture. Although Scott's statistics become more and more detailed over the years, his projections were always shaped to demonstrate the same trend—the inevitable rise to dominance of the cities of the West over those of the eastern seaboard. In an 1854 article, for example, he estimated the population of the great central plain—which he defined to in-

79

clude portions of Canada and the American Southwest—at 15
million, seven-eighths of this population on farms. He counted
600,000 people living in the cities and towns that bordered on the
Great Lakes and the St. Lawrence River; the Mississippi and Mobile
river basins added urban population of 800,000. Natural increase
for the region could be calculated at 800,000 a year. Owing to
technological advances in agriculture, most of this growth would be
absorbed in the interior cities, particularly in those located along
the Great Lakes.

By the late forties, the Great Lakes cities performed a key function in Scott's calculations. He argued that although the cost of
railroad transportation would steadily decline, commerce on the
waterways would always be less expensive than overland commerce. The future great cities, therefore, would be located at strategic positions along the Great Lakes, where the interior railroad
system would join lakes and rivers. Although over the years he
had picked a number of cities as the site of the future great metropolis of the interior, by the 1850's he had narrowed the rivals for
supremacy down to Chicago and Toledo—the holders of the "keys
of commerce, soon to become immense between the great rivers
and lakes of the continent." The "great manufacturing hives of the
North American plain" would also come as naturally to these two
sites as "teeth in the mouth of an infant child." In his later years,
he became increasingly interested in Humboldt's geography and
built his arguments more explicitly upon geographical determinism.
On the great interior plain of North America, he predicted in one
of his last pieces, "will grow up the greatest aggregation, the
greatest nation, the noblest empire of man, and the greatest city."

Scott was convinced that the growth of cities was the most vital
and most progressive aspect of American development. If one is to
sustain the thesis that American intellectual energies have been
directed against the city, it is necessary to rule out the influence of
a host of lesser popular writers like Scott who viewed the nineteenth-century city as the exemplar of American progress. "All
people take pride in their cities," he wrote in 1848. "In them
naturally concentrate the great minds and the great wealth of the
nation. There the arts that adorn life are cultivated, and from them

flows out the knowledge that gives its current of thought to the national mind." The western urban writers, and probably a goodly proportion of all Americans at mid-century, would have agreed with these sentiments.

4

The Urban Milieu
1800-1860

Foreign travelers who visited early nineteenth century American cities were impressed by their bright airy appearance and the absence of the decaying congested districts to be found in the cities of Europe. English visitors often compared American cities to the larger villages they knew at home. Even New York, in spite of its rapid growth during the early part of the century, shared in this evaluation. "No dark alleys, whose confined and noisome atmosphere marks the presence of a dense and suffering population," the Utopian reformer Frances Wright wrote of America's largest city in 1821, "no hovels, in whose ruined garrets, or dank and gloomy cellars crowd the wretched victims of vice and leisure, whose penury drives to despair, ere she opens them to the grave."

Yet by this date the view that American cities were different

83

was already illusory. As early as 1815 slums had begun to take root on a half dozen streets or so around Chatham Square on the lower east side of New York City. By this time also Boston had begun to develop districts inhabited by a class of urban poor; to local reformers like Joseph Tuckerman this circumstance seemed to represent a transfer of the abuses of Old Europe to the New World. In the years of great urban growth and industrialization after 1830, eastern seaboard cities rapidly acquired the characteristics associated with the manufacturing cities of Europe. Within a decade and a half after Frances Wright wrote, visitors to New York were noting the presence of precisely the things she had found absent—misery, filth, and overcrowding. Areas such as the notorious Five Points district had become standard symbols of the evil city.

As early as the 1830's, New York had also acquired its reputation as the city of frenetic hustle and bustle. Asa Greene, a New York physician, newspaperman, and literary figure, noted in his 1837 commentary on the city that to cross Broadway "you must button your coat tight about you, see that your shoes are secure at the heels, settle your hat firmly on your head, look up street and down street, at the self-same moment, to see what carts and carriages are upon you, and then run for your life. We daily see persons waiting at the crossing place for some minutes, before they can find an opening, and a chance to get over, between the omnibuses, coaches, and other vehicles, that are constantly dashing up and down the street; and after waiting thus long, deem themselves exceedingly fortunate if they can get over with sound bones and a whole skin."

No other nineteenth century city was quite like New York, nor for that matter were any two city environments entirely similar. In physical appearance, early nineteenth century cities had more personal character than they did later on. Baltimore and Philadelphia were distinguished by rowhouses and stoops; Savannah had its attractive park squares, Charleston its gracious verandas. Nationality influences—French in New Orleans, German in Philadelphia, Dutch in New York, or English in Baltimore—contributed to distinctive architectural patterns. But already building methods and the technology of municipal services were making cities more alike.

In 1819, Benjamin Latrobe, architect and designer of municipal water systems, made this point in his diary, noting that the standards of Baltimore and Philadelphia were diluting the French influence in New Orleans. "We shall introduce many grand and profitable improvements," he wrote, "but they shall take the place of much elegance, ease, and some convenience." The general acceptance of Georgian architecture and the use of balloon-frame construction broke down regional diversity in houses and other buildings. By the 1840's travelers found a monotonous similarity in the appearance of American cities, particularly those that had been newly built in the West.

Although cities were coming to look more alike, visitors still noted striking sectional differences in the kind of urban environment they represented. By the 1830's signs of decay were evident in the southern seaboard cities tied to a plantation economy; in contrast, the interior river towns of the South such as Louisville and Memphis had begun to boom and were viewed as seats of opportunity. Pittsburgh early in the century had already acquired its reputation as the "large workshop" of America. The towns and cities of the West consistently seemed to represent American progress and the conquest of a hostile wilderness. To virtually all travelers, such places as Chicago, Cincinnati, and St. Louis presented a picture, as Alexander Mackay wrote of the latter, of "bustle, enterprise, and activity." Because of their warmer climate, southern cities were often portrayed as especially unhealthy, and there was evidence to support this view. The cholera epidemic of 1833 nearly destroyed the small thriving city of Maysville, Kentucky and New Orleans had the highest death rate of any city in the union. In spite of this, New Orleans was frequently labelled the most cosmopolitan and urbane of American cities. The indefatigable English traveler, James Buckingham, for example, thought the city's St. Charles Hotel had no equal in beauty anywhere in the world. He commented that New Orleans' fine restaurants, its concerts, balls, operas, and masquerades, in fact its whole mode of life, merited comparison with Paris.

These sectional contrasts were often extended to cities in the same region, New Orleans and Charleston, for example, or even to neighbors as in the case of Chicago and Milwaukee. To Frederika

85

Bremer, the Swedish novelist who visited the West in 1850, Chicago was "one of the most miserable and ugly cities" which she had seen in America. People had apparently come there, she observed, "to trade, to make money, and not to live." Milwaukee, on the other hand, appeared to be "a splendid city" which "grows and extends herself every day" increasing "with all its might."

Although most American cities before 1850 escaped the congestion of the growing slums of New York and Boston, all of them shared a number of unpleasant features. Since streets were paved only in a few sections of larger cities, mud was always present in rainy weather. Joshua T. Smith in an 1837 journal provided a comment echoed in virtually every account of western cities but also customary in those of the eastern metropolises. "One characteristic of Detroit should have been noticed before—its *mud*. It is the common topic of conversation & exceeds credibility—After a little rain the cart wheels sink literally up to the axle-tree in the filth—*No single* street in the town is paved or lighted—This of course adds to the numerous advantages of which the city has to boast." In addition to mud, there was refuse and garbage clogging the streets; in all parts of the country, bands of hogs protected as scavengers roamed about town, a condition that usually aroused protest only when children were attacked. Frances Trollope in her famous account of America's domestic manners found it "decidedly unpleasant" to live in Cincinnati surrounded by herds of "unsavory animals" but admitted the necessity of their "Herculean service." Without them, she observed, streets would soon be choked with filth in every stage of decomposition.

In the 1830's and 40's, New York was often considered the showcase city of America—the exemplar of growth, change, and progress in the new society. Local residents were proud of its role, but not until past mid-century did the community do much to make the city presentable. Philip Hone, the ex-mayor of the city, had written in 1832 that New York was "one huge pigsty" but that a prudent farmer would avoid putting his pigs into it for fear they might catch the plague. In 1844 the editor of the *New World* made the same point: "That our streets have been horrible enough in times past no one denies, but they are now . . . more abominably filthy than ever; they are too foul to serve as the styes for the hogs which perambulate them. . . . The offal and filth, of which there are loads thrown from the houses in defiance of an ordinance which is never enforced, is scraped up with the usual deposits of mud and manure into big heaps and left *for weeks together* on the sides of the street." Not until after the establishment of the New York Metropolitan Board of Health in 1866 was there reasonably systematic and permanent clean-up of the city. As part of this program, hogs were finally eliminated from the city's streets.

The absence of adequate sewage facilities also contributed to the unpleasantness and unhealthiness of urban life in the nineteenth century. Before 1850 methods of removing waste were still largely those of the country, even in larger cities. Privies or water closets emptied into vaults or cesspools, and the waste material soaked into the soil or was hauled away as receptacles became filled. Kitchen waste was run into the street and left to evaporate or was led off by open drains to watercourses. Ditches provided for this purpose often carried urine and fecal matter as well as house slop, since privy facilities were often hopelessly inadequate in the congested districts of cities. A Cincinnati board of health report of 1865 told of a two-story tenement which housed 102 people for whom only one privy had been provided. When a municipal department of sewers was created in New York in 1849, only 70 miles of sewers had been built. Eight years later the mileage had grown to 158 for 500 miles of city streets, still leaving three-fourths of the city, including most of the slum areas, without facilities.

Inadequate sanitation, a laissez-faire governmental tradition which made measures of public control difficult, and erroneous beliefs about the causes of disease contributed to one of the most serious problems facing the nineteenth century urban dweller—epidemic. Diseases, particularly those spread through water contamination, flourished in the congested districts of cities; outbreaks of typhoid, dysentery, and typhus were continual. In addition, there was the most dreaded plague of all—cholera—which struck the United States with force in 1832, 1849, and 1866. Cholera becomes epidemic largely through water contamination, but neither its cause nor etiology was known at the time. The disease was particularly terrifying with symptoms comparable to those of arsenic poisoning. Its spectacular presence led city dwellers to question the fundamental character of American society. Initially, cholera was interpreted as a scourge of God, a punishment for national sins, which would strike those who were filthy, intemperate, and immoral. Accordingly, many spokesmen of the urban upper classes accepted as natural its depredations among immigrants in congested slums. John Pintard, the aristocratic founder of the New York Historical Society, reflected the views of his segment of society when he wrote to his daughter that the 1832 epidemic was "exclusively confined to the lower classes of intemperate dissolute & filthy people huddled together like swine in their polluted habitations." He argued that the epidemic could not be coped with; it would simply have to run its course. "Those sickened must be cured or die off, & being chiefly of the very scum of the city, the quicker the dispatch the sooner the malady will cease."

Not until 1883 was the microorganism that caused cholera isolated; until that time there was debate over the nature of the disease and how it was transmitted. But by the time of the 1866 epidemic, the social and moralistic explanations of the disease that had earlier been common were no longer generally accepted. It was recognized that the disease was specific and contagious, that it struck both rich and poor, both moral and immoral. New York's success in checking the epidemic through a vigorous program of sanitation reinforced the conviction that cholera could be prevented through public health measures and that communities had the duty to make this effort. The Metropolitan Board of Health organized in response to the epidemic had power to deal with problems of quarantine and urban sanitation. Its success led within a few years to the establishment of similar agencies in other large American cities and marked a beginning stage of the modern urban public health movement.

An equally serious plague that struck the early American city was yellow fever, a virus disease transmitted by a variety of mosquito. Although its cause was not directly related to the unsanitary conditions of cities as was the case with cholera, fetid pools of water to be found within most cities did provide excellent breeding places for the disease-carrying insect. Those who argued, as many did, that yellow fever was the result of locally created miasmas urged the necessity of cleaning up the cities. Although their explanation was wrong, their program when adopted helped to check the spread of the disease. Accordingly, yellow fever was controlled to some extent long before its etiology was established in the twentieth century.

Yellow fever appeared frequently in the eighteenth century American towns; it struck Philadelphia, then America's largest city, with unusual intensity in 1793. Over 4,000 deaths, a figure which represented almost ten per cent of the city's population, were attributed to the disease. Business and government in what was then the national capital came to a halt as over half the residents fled to the countryside. Other eastern cities faced the dreaded plague before the decade was over—Baltimore and New Haven in 1794, New York, Baltimore and Norfolk in 1795. The 1798 Philadelphia epidemic was nearly as serious as that of five years earlier; New York with 2,000 deaths was hit again as were Boston and seven smaller port cities. In 1799 yellow fever continued its ravages of the decade with visitations to Philadelphia, New York, and Boston.

For reasons not clearly known, yellow fever generally disappeared from northern cities after 1825. But it continued to be one of the serious problems of the south. A major epidemic struck New Orleans in 1847 leaving over 2,000 dead. This attack, though, hardly compared with the epidemic five years later when during one hot week in late August yellow fever claimed 1,365 victims in the city, and for the whole summer the death toll stood at 8,000.

During the early nineteenth century such endemic diseases as malaria and consumption killed many more city dwellers than yellow fever and cholera. But it was the presence of plague that produced speculation about the nature of the American urban environment and contributed to efforts to change it. Although spokesmen for contagion always remained vocal, the view that decaying filth and the resultant miasma in the atmosphere caused epidemics gained ground in medical thinking toward the middle of the century.

Mortality statistics, which for the first time had begun to be systematically compiled, lent support to the view that the rising death rate might be simply the result of urban congestion. In New York City, for example, the crude death rate rose from one death per 46.5 persons in 1810 to one in 27 in 1859; other large cities demonstrated a similar alarming tendency. Awareness of the un-healthiness of the city contributed to the view that community energies had to be directed toward alleviating the conditions that caused squalor, overcrowding, and decay. This conviction often rested on an unsound environmentalist theory of disease, but it still led to programs that improved the health of cities and the quality of the life to be lived in them. The New Orleans Board of Health, arguing unsuccessfully for enlarged power in 1849, expressed the sentiment that cities were here to stay and that their problems would have to be met through community action. "If large cities have been denominated the 'graves of mankind,'" its report de-clared, "it has been with too much reason, both reason and calcula-tion sanction it, but still they should not be unnecessarily so; it is perfectly apparent in this investigating age, what has made them so, and that they proceed from causes that are in a great measure removable. Were there not great social and intellectual advantages from them (as well as pecuniary) men would not willingly, with the knowledge of these facts, thus multiply the sources of their own mortality, by congregating together, and it is well known that the population of many cities is maintained by immigration alone; but it is a poor compliment to an intelligent, rich and free people, that the love of thrift is stronger than all the numberless enjoyments which health produces."

In the 1830's, George Templeton Strong, an aristocratic New York lawyer whose magnificent diary records the rise of a metrop-olis, accepted the views of his class that the poor became ill because of their moral derelictions. Yet, reflecting a general change in attitude among the urban elite, Strong by the time of the 1866 cholera epidemic was willing to argue that the whole community was responsible for the presence of the disease through allowing "poisonous rookeries" to exist in New York. "It is shameful," he wrote, "that men, women, and children should be permitted to live in such holes as thousands of them occupy this night in the city." The change of attitude among the urban upper classes not only contributed to the institution of public health programs but also led to more general efforts to make cities livable for all classes.

This change was reflected in new community sentiments toward the long standing urban problem of poverty. In the early years of the century poverty like disease was ordinarily considered the result of an individual's moral failure. A report of an 1809 investigation by the New York Humane Society into the "sources of vice and misery" in New York City nowhere mentioned economic causes. "By a just and inflexible law of Providence," the report declared, "misery is ordained to be the companion and the punishment of vice." The rise of a distinct class of poor in the eastern cities was often attributed to immigration; European nations were accused of exporting their problems to the New World and destroying the classless paradise. The *New England Magazine* in an 1834 article found the Irish who came in gangs responsible for the growing urban pauperism. "The consequence is, that they almost invariably continue gregarious, and will not assimilate with the rest of the inhabitants. They do not dispose themselves over our western savannahs, or fell the broad forests which stretch between us and the Pacific, but they nest together in thickly-settled places, and constitute, with some praiseworthy exceptions, the most corrupt, the most debased, and the most brutally ignorant portion of the population of large cities." The presence of large numbers of newly arrived immigrants in American cities was a principal cause of the growth of a strong, organized anti-foreign movement throughout the country in the depression period of 1837–1843. The nativist Know-Nothing Party, which became important in the 1850's, directed much of its energy against the European immigrant who remained in the eastern city.

Although poverty might be considered the result of individual failing particularly of the immigrant, the problem did exist and it was necessary for city leaders to try to deal with it in some fashion. The ideas and policies of Thomas Chalmers, a minister in Glasgow, Scotland who worked against the policy of providing outdoor relief to the able-bodied, influenced the character of American programs. The New York Society for the Prevention of Pauperism organized in 1817 was concerned with providing institutional relief as were similar agencies organized in Boston and Philadelphia.

The approach adopted by these early agencies is illustrated in the Baltimore experiment. In 1820, seventy-two city leaders, who had felt the pressure of heavy contributions to private charities during the hard times following the Panic of 1819, organized the Baltimore Society for the Prevention of Pauperism. The organization isolated the four "most obstrusive causes of pauperism"—excessive drinking, lotteries, houses of prostitution, and the types of charitable institutions that fostered the notion that something could be gotten for nothing. To counteract these forces, the Society emphasized the necessity for moral reform—to be achieved mainly by removing temptation from the citizenry. The Society's attempt to serve as a "moral police" for the city and to restrict the liquor traffic aroused opposition. Its opponents denounced a system designed to erect an "inquisitorial power" in Baltimore, terming the Society one for "foundation of a fanatic and gloomy despotism." Answering these charges, a leader of the Society reaffirmed the individualistic ethic that influenced so much of the nineteenth century program to deal with urban poverty. "In this country," he wrote, "the sober and able-bodied, if industriously disposed, cannot long want employment. They cannot, but by their own folly and vices, long remain indigent. Correct these vices, whether they are cherished by the bagnio or grog-shop, and you will prevent the consequent evils." Recovery from the depression that had altogether been ignored as a cause of distress ended the activities of the Baltimore society. But the point of view it had expressed continued to be influential; much of the justification for the temperance crusade that swept over the country in the years after 1825, for example, rested on its principles.

Yet many who worked day by day with the poor gradually changed their approaches to the problem of widespread urban pauperism. Joseph Tuckerman supplies the most striking example. His "ministry at large," a kind of city mission for the poor organized in the period of depression following the Panic of 1819, was based on the principle that the answer to urban pauperism lay in individual spiritual regeneration. But as a result of his investigations of the poor in their homes and his growing awareness of their everyday problems, Tuckerman became interested in a great many practical programs that involved wages, housing, education, and the delinquency of children. Although he never abandoned completely an individualistic explanation of poverty, he argued that the community had collective responsibilities to the poor and that to some extent at least these obligations could be met only through legislation. His experiments in defining categories of the poor and in coordinating charitable programs won him a reputation on both sides of the Atlantic as a pioneer of philanthropy.

Another leading charity worker of the early nineteenth century, Robert M. Hartley, who was responsible for the organization of the New York Association for Improving the Condition of the Poor in 1843, underwent a similar change of heart. Beginning as a deeply religious tract distributor and temperance worker, Hartley became convinced that concern with the material welfare of the poor would have to precede concern with their spiritual welfare. As secretary of the Association for over thirty years, he worked for the coordination of independent charities and pioneered housing reform. Louis M. Pease, a leader in New York's Five Points House of Industry, recognized early that before the poor could be expected to profit from reading tracts or listening to lectures on morality, it was necessary to provide them with regular jobs. Increasing community awareness of a collective responsibility to the poor led to a more efficient organization of private charities and the passage of legislation providing an institutional base for governmental relief. In addition, some measure of protection was provided to European immigrants who had begun to arrive at America's shores in great numbers in the 1830's.

The United States has traditionally been thought of as a refuge for Europe's downtrodden and oppressed who were welcomed and immediately launched out on a better life. To a considerable extent, this view represents a false social myth. The lot of the individual immigrant who came to American cities in the early nineteenth century was a particularly hard one. If he survived the voyage with its dangers of typhus, dysentery, and malnutrition, he faced exploitation on his arrival at an eastern port from a host of sharp operators—bond brokers, runners for forwarding companies, and boarding-house owners and agents. New York, where a high proportion of immigrants entered the United States, was a rapidly growing city in the 1830's. Immigrants could find employment in the burgeoning factories of lower Manhattan Island, and many of them remained in the city. Long and narrow Manhattan Island was not geographically suitable for the kind of rapid growth it experienced. Land values jumped, and considerable overcrowding took place early at the island's lower end. Those who could afford to moved northward. Houses were converted to tenements, and the profits made in this fashion stimulated the building of new tenements. Front and rear buildings on the same lot created an intricate array of dark foul courts and alleys in several sections of the city. The intense housing shortage caused basements, attics, and lofts to be rented. As a measure of the resulting congestion, the density of the seven lower wards of Manhattan increased from 94.5 to 163.5 persons per acre in the period from 1820 to 1850. In 1843, a survey found 7,196 people living underground in New York. Within seven years, as immigration expanded during the decade, the cellar-dwelling population of the city had increased to 29,000. By the time of the Civil War the urban slum had decisively destroyed the open character of New York and other eastern cities. Long before Jacob Riis at the turn of the century dramatized to the nation how the other half lives, housing reform had become a preoccupation of the urban reformer.

The problem of housing congestion was perhaps felt most acutely in New York, but immigrants who arrived in Boston, particularly the Irish fleeing starvation during the potato famine of the 1840's, faced the same general problems of overcrowding and disease. And in some ways, the Boston immigrant was worse off than his New York counterpart. There were fewer opportunities for work in manufacturing in Boston, and the city was more culturally self-contained than New York. The Boston immigrant became aware on every side of a hostile environment; in the period before the Civil War acute ethnic and class tensions developed in the city.

One of the more serious results of expanding immigration in the early nineteenth century was the continuing poverty of immigrants who remained in the cities. From the beginning a highly disproportionate share of paupers was to be found among the foreign born. In 1835, for example, there were 4,786 native-born paupers and 5,303 foreign-born in the almshouses of New York, Philadelphia, Boston, and Baltimore. New York City in 1837 was spending $279,999 annually for the support of its poor, three-fifths of whom were foreign-born. The rising cost of living after mid-century intensified the problem of the newcomer. In 1852 more than half those requiring public assistance in eastern cities were Irish and German.

By 1860 fully 86 per cent of the paupers in New York were of foreign birth. A class of pauperized immigrants crowded together in slums in huge cities seemed to many to present a fundamental challenge to traditional American values. In the period after the Civil War, this was the feature of urban life that most concerned those who attacked the evil city as the principal threat to the American nation.

Closely associated with the growth of poverty in eastern cities was an increase in crime. From the early colonial period, American cities had experienced the ordinary amount of lawlessness and immorality associated with organized communities anywhere. But until the nineteenth century, they had largely been spared the criminal districts and criminal gangs characteristic of European cities. By the 1840's, however, leaders in New York and elsewhere were concerned about the appearance of both phenomena. Particularly noted were the gangs of youthful criminals, who made war on each other and terrorized neighborhoods. Philadelphia had its Buffaloes, Blood Tubs, Rugs, and Copper Heads; Baltimore its Stringers; New York its Bowery Boys, Plug-Uglies, Highbinders, Swipers, and Dead Rabbits. The Crawfish Boys of Cincinnati indicated that western cities could not claim exemption from the problem. By 1849 juvenile crime had become so serious that New York's chief of police devoted his entire report for that year to the subject. In preaching a sermon on this report, Thomas L. Harris reflected the general point of view. "Of the young children in the denser part of our city," he lamented, "one in ten is doomed to a life of inevitable vice, misery and degradation, doomed to be ground to powder in the vortex of infamy and shame." Saving the children of the city became a major aim of such urban reformers as Charles Loring Brace, who organized the Children's Aid Society in 1853 and devoted the better part of his life to an essentially futile effort to move the less fortunate children of the city to foster homes in the west.

As to be expected, many people blamed the immigrant for the rising crime rate in the cities. John Pintard in 1828 wrote to his daughter that "as long as we are overwhelmed with Irish emigrants, so long will the evil abound." Although the immigrant in poorer areas of cities was often arrested for inconsequential crimes that

95

might be ignored elsewhere, there is little doubt that a life of desperation and the ready availability of alcohol contributed to a high rate of serious crime among immigrants, particularly among the Irish. In New York in 1859, for example, only 23 per cent of the people arrested were native Americans and 55 per cent were born in Ireland. Most of the persons committed to the city prison in New York City during the nine year period from 1850 to 1858 were immigrants, and seven-eighths of the total were recorded as "intemperate." In 1860 when just over half of the population of the city was foreign born, about 80 per cent of the 58,067 convicted of crime during the year ending July 1 were born in Europe.

The rising crime rate forced eastern cities to adopt more formal systems of police. Until mid-century, even larger cities used the type of law enforcement that had existed since colonial days—a combination of day policemen and night watchmen, hired part-time, often from the ranks of the unemployed, with little provided in the way of central organization, training, or discipline in service. The wearing of uniforms was successfully resisted for years by policemen, who argued that the uniform was a badge of European servitude. Since they were not identifiable, policemen often fled serious disturbances.

Change in this informal system came first in New York City. A law enacted in May of 1844 abolished the night watchman and other duplicating law enforcement officials. Substituted for this was a single body of police of 800 men. The politically controlled new force provided little significant reform until it was modified in 1853 by the establishment of a board of police commissioners. Over bitter opposition the commissioners required the wearing of a uniform consisting of a blue swallow-tailed coat with large buttons, gray pantaloons, and a blue cap labeled with the officer's number. Philadelphia established a central system of police in 1850 although uniforms were not required until 1860. Boston abolished its dual system of watch and police in 1854 and organized a department of 250 full-time officers. A Baltimore force was organized in 1857 with 350 uniformed policemen. With the creation of the metropolitan police district of New York in 1857, state influence began to be extended over large city police forces through state police boards.

Similarly in the provision of such other municipal services as water, fire protection, and streets, cities moved from casual, semi-private systems inherited from an era when municipalities were villages to formal programs that were entirely a part of government. In fire protection, for example, the resistance of volunteer Cincinnati firemen to the introduction of steam fire-engines led to the organization in 1853 of one of the first paid municipal fire-fighting forces in the United States. Chicago and other western cities followed the example almost immediately, and within a few years Boston, New York, and Philadelphia had adopted the method.

Philadelphia was the pioneer in the establishment of a municipal water system. The publicly owned Centre Square Water Works, designed by the brilliant architect and engineer Benjamin Latrobe and completed in 1801, was long a source of civic pride. But the supply of water it provided was often undependable until the completion of the Fairmount Water Works in 1822. The shoddy private system of the Manhattan Company furnished water to New York from 1799 until 1835, when an ambitious public system was begun which brought water by a closed aqueduct from the Croton Reservoir forty miles to the north. Completed in 1842 at a cost of twelve million dollars, the system had to be radically enlarged in 1858 owing to the great growth in the population of the city. Most cities underwent a similar pattern of development: wells and springs to privately owned systems to public ones. By 1861 there were eighty private and sixty-eight public systems in operation throughout the country.

Although the nineteenth century urban environment was often conceived as a series of problems and of efforts to resolve them, at the same time it could be viewed as the locale in which American culture was taking root and maturing. The city was the home of the theater, the museum, and the art gallery, a fact recognized by early nineteenth century city leaders. In all sections of the country, including the "agrarian" South and the "frontier" West, urbanism was partly defined as a process of furnishing cultural amenities. When spokesmen of western and southern cities attempted to describe the good city, they did not declare cultural independence from Europe or the East. On the contrary, they considered their

cities progressing to the extent that they could furnish the kind of
theater, art, and high society to be found elsewhere in the world.
Henry McMurtrie, who wrote one of the first important books on
a western city, described frontier Louisville in 1819 as a city
proud of its cultural refinement. "There is a circle, small 'tis true,"
he wrote, "but within whose magic abounds every pleasure that
wealth, regulated by taste, can produce, or urbanity bestow. There,
the 'red-heel' of Versailles may imagine himself in the emporium
of fashion, and whilst leading beauty through the mazes of the
dance, forget that he is in the wilds of America." A generation
later on another frontier, Robert T. Van Horn argued that the
booming "young metropolis" of Kansas City could not become a
real city until it had a permanent theater and other cultural institutions.

In all parts of the country, patronage of the arts was looked
upon as a responsibility of the urban upper classes. During the
latter part of the eighteenth century, for example, it was the support of the rich and fashionable that overcame the opposition of
intellectuals and clergy to the theater as an immoral institution.
The presentation of musical performances, particularly opera which
by the 1850's had become a regular feature of the social season in
New York, Boston, Philadelphia, New Orleans, and Chicago, was
also supported as part of an effort to consolidate the position of
the upper classes in the cities. As early as 1807, John Lambert in
writing of New York noted the association between rapid economic
expansion, the accumulation of wealth, and an interest in art,
music, and learning. This enthusiasm had tended to remedy the
"deficiency of the polite and liberal accomplishments among both
sexes in the United States." "The riches that have flowed into the
city, for the last twenty years," he continued, "have brought with
them a taste for the refinements of a polished society; and though
the inhabitants cannot yet boast of having reached the standard
of European perfection, they are not wanting in the solid and rational parts of education; nor in many of those accomplishments
which ornament and embellish private life."

Although such "refinements" were an important dimension of
the urban environment, the number of urban dwellers who were
able to take advantage of them was always limited. Theater, for

example, was initially expensive and frankly maintained for the rich. Alexis de Tocqueville, the most notable foreign visitor to Jacksonian America, observed that playhouses and plays had increased prodigiously but that very few Americans actually attended the theater. "People who spend every day in the week in making money," he wrote, "and Sunday in going to church, have nothing to invite the Muse of Comedy." There was, however, particularly in eastern cities a variety of popular entertainments patronized by all classes. In the early nineteenth century, for example, New Yorkers went to see Niblo's Columbian Gardens, which contained exotic plants, large transplanted trees, and colorful fountains; heard concerts or watched fireworks displays at Vauxhall Gardens; or visited several waxwork museums that featured biblical, historical, and patriotic exhibits. In a later period, curiosities of one kind and another—animal exhibits, experiments in mesmerism and lectures on phrenology, mechanical toys such as the automaton chess player and automaton Turk—drew substantial audiences in the cities.

More serious performers in the arts were also considered to some extent as curiosities, and as the "star" system developed, theater and music tended to become more popular among the middle and lower classes. Celebrities from Europe, some of them brought to America by the famous showman and promoter, P. T. Barnum, enjoyed financial success on their tours of the cities. The most famous of these, Jenny Lind—"the Swedish nightingale," "the angel of the stage"—earned $1,000 a performance at each of 150 highly successful appearances throughout the country in 1849–50. Earlier, the dancer Fanny Elssler, "the divine Fanny," who came to the United States in 1840, received $6,390 for eleven nights in Philadelphia and by the time she reached New Orleans on her tour, was asking $1,000 a night. William Macready and Charles Kean, who played at New York's New Park Street Theater in 1830, Fanny Kemble the most popular actress of her day, and the Swedish violinist Ole Bull were other European performers who won the favor of American urban audiences. American actors like Edwin Booth and Edwin Forrest also established star reputations.

Conflict among supporters of rival actors was common, and one

99

such conflict led to a significant challenge—perhaps the first of any consequence—to municipal authority in the United States. In 1849 a New York mob which championed Edwin Forrest stormed the theater on Astor Place where William Macready was playing. The quarrel had been building for some time; sides were taken along social lines with lower class groups making a hero of Forrest. Twenty-two people were killed and a large number wounded in the riot before troops could restore order. The episode aroused the reflection that the American city was not only creating a European-style class structure with extremes of wealth and poverty, but might also create the kind of revolutionary turmoil characteristic of Europe. Upper class observers in particular saw a close relationship between the Astor Place rioters and the Paris mob.

In the early part of the century, interest in the theater was a dimension of urban experience not confined to any one section of the country. The popular Irish actor, Tyrone Power, who recorded his travel impressions in the years from 1833 to 1835, wrote of his enthusiastic audiences in Baltimore, Savannah, and New Orleans. Macready during his last American tour in 1849 played a successful four weeks of Shakespeare in New Orleans shortly before the Astor Place riots. Ellen Tree, Fanny Kemble, Jenny Lind, Fanny Elssler, and other European performers included the cities of the South and West on their American tours. In addition to these well-known performers, traveling companies and amateur theatrical groups enjoyed greater or lesser successes in larger communities in all parts of the country.

As part of a growing interest in theater in the early nineteenth century, playhouses became established urban landmarks. Since a theater cost $30,000 or more to build, it was only in the larger cities that adequate facilities could be supplied. A boom in building in the 1820's saw the erection of the Bowery, the Chatham, the Lafayette, and the New Park Street in New York; the Tremont in Boston, probably not the only American theater with a connecting brothel; and the New Chestnut Street and Arch Street in Philadelphia. New York's Park Theater, located opposite City Hall, had seats for 2,500; after its remodeling in 1834 it became a favorite of the social elite. In the 1830's the Broadway, with seats for 4,000, also opened, marking the beginning of the most famous theater

100

district in the country. In this same period, civic leaders in such hinterland cities as St. Louis, Buffalo, and Mobile expressed considerable pride in the local playhouses. Because of the relatively high upkeep and taxes, as well as the large fees paid to star performers, theaters closed frequently or their ownership changed hands, but from this time on they were to be an established feature of the urban scene.

By the 1850's civic pride demanded that cities not only support theaters but also art galleries, opera houses, and museums. Boston acquired a new music hall early in the decade. Philadelphia citizens subscribed to a new $220,000 opera house; Chicago obtained a structure that combined an opera house, art gallery, and studio building. Increasingly, as part of the fruition of an urban outlook, city leaders argued that the worth of a city could be measured by how well it provided such cultural institutions. Discussing the future of New Orleans, a local writer in 1846 reflected a typical viewpoint of the era when he argued that there could be no significant "moral advance" in New Orleans unless the city supported the necessary educational and cultural agencies. Without a university, a historical society, public libraries, public lectures, and a lyceum, he argued, New Orleans could never become a truly great city.

The flourishing movement for tax-supported city libraries in the 1850's supplied a good example of this rising urban spirit. Private literary clubs and learned societies had maintained semi-public reading rooms and atheneums since the colonial period, but not until the 1820's was there organized effort to use taxes to establish free libraries open to all city inhabitants. It was several years before these efforts bore fruit. The Boston Public Library, which had been authorized in 1845, opened in 1854, and within a decade and a half had 100,000 volumes. The Astor Library in New York, made possible by a large bequest from John Jacob Astor, opened the same year, and the Peabody Library in Baltimore was established in 1857. Western cities, as remote as Leavenworth, Kansas also shared in the enthusiasm. During the decade of the fifties, the number of public libraries in the country increased eight-fold to over 1,000 and their volumes multiplied five-fold, reaching a total of nearly eight million. Reflective of another aspect of the transfer

of eastern cultural institutions to the West, the Chicago Historical
Society was organized in 1856. It soon had a collection of 11,000
books and began accumulating maps and manuscripts. Its holdings
were proudly displayed to foreign travelers as an indication of an
advancing American scholarship. The growth of a reading public
established the bookstore as an urban institution. The Old Corner
Bookstore of James T. Field and William D. Ticknor in Boston
was a famous gathering place for writers and intellectuals during
the period of the New England literary renaissance. By the 1850's,
Chicago had three prospering bookstores, one of which advertised
itself as the largest in the Midwest.

In spite of the view expressed by many writers that American
culture ought to reflect democratic ideals, the cultural agencies of
the city—the bookstore, the theater, the music hall, the fine restau-
rant—could for the most part be enjoyed only by the few. But
to the urban leader and spokesman, who shaped the character of
the American urban environment, it was the presence of these
cultural amenities that made life worthwhile. The career of George
Templeton Strong supplies a case in point. Strong won a measure
of national attention for his work on the Sanitary Commission,
the relief agency of the Civil War, but in general he preferred to
avoid public life, and is by all odds most notable for his massive
diary covering the years from 1835 to 1875, one of the great
diaries in the history of western letters. Although Strong was concerned with many other matters than the city in which he lived, his
diary supplies a vivid picture of life in New York and an intelligent, cultivated man's reaction to it in a period during which
New York grew into one of the foremost cities of the world.

Strong was representative of an early nineteenth century group
of New York merchants, bankers, lawyers, and men of affairs, who
could make their way in the world of business but still had time
for the leisure of systematic reading, literary discussion, and occasional writing. Many of this group, for example, gathered together
in the select circle of Lewis Gaylord Clark, publisher of the
Knickerbocker magazine; Clark's "Table," in existence through
the 1840's and 1850's, constituted one of the notable elites in the
history of American cities.

Like most members of the upper classes who wrote about nineteenth century cities, Strong had little sympathy for the democratic forces in American life. He found the social structure of New York natural and proper; he disliked the horde of immigrants pouring into the city and often held them responsible for the congestion and disease that had taken root in the districts they inhabited. He preferred to stay away from the poorer sections of the city. "Such a ride uptown!" he wrote on June 19, 1852. "Such scalding dashes of sunshine coming in on both sides of the choky, hot railroad car, and drawing stale, sickly odors from sweaty Irishmen in their shirt sleeves; German Jew shop-boys in white coats, pink faces, and waistcoats that looked like virulent prickly heat; fat old women, with dirty-nosed babies; one sporting man with black whiskers, miraculously crisp and curly, and a shirt collar insultingly stiff, who contributed a reminiscence of tobacco smoke—the spiritual body of ten thousand bad cigars. Then the feast of fat things that came reeking under one's nose at each special puddle of festering filth that Center Street provided in its reeking, fermenting, putrefying, pestilential gutter! I thought I should have died of the stink, rage, and headache before I got to Twenty-first Street." Yet for all his revulsion from the immigrant and the slum, Strong did have compassion for the city's poor. One of the more moving passages in his diary consists of an extended reflection in 1851 on how the abuses of the English industrial city, "the thousands and tens of thousands that are perishing hopelessly in profligacy, drunkeness, and starvation in the cellars and workshops . . . ," the men, women, and children who lay "rotting and alive, body and soul at once, in those awful catacombs of disease and crime . . . ," were being replicated in New York. Immigrant women in the city were leading lives "barren of hope and enjoyment;" children were brutalized "almost beyond redemption by premature vice." And while all this was happening, scholars were "laboriously writing dissertations for the Historical Society on the First Settlement of the Township of Squankum" and clergymen were "compiling treatises on Ancient Egypt." Strong implied that their labors might better be devoted to the problems at hand. To help "one dirty vagabond child" out of the "pestilential sink," he concluded, "would be rather more of an achievement than the writing of another *Iliad*."

In spite of such occasional sentiments, Strong never became

directly involved in the various organizations that sprang up near mid-century to do something about the lot of the poor. Yet he did spend much of his life trying to improve the quality of urban experience. As a trustee of Columbia College, he dedicated time and energy to making an inadequate college into a great university. He worked assiduously in a number of programs for cultural improvement, expanding the work of the New York Historical Society, or heading the city's Philharmonic Commission, for example. Strong's father had acquired a horse and rode regularly through the city with the avowed ambition of becoming better acquainted with it than any other man. The younger Strong had the same kind of commitment to an urban way of life. He found many things to complain about in New York: he was continually exercised by the city's atmosphere filled with malarial and "morphic influences;" by the "tadpoles and animalculae" in the local water; by the heat, dirt, and noise of Wall Street; by mud the consistency of molasses; and by the "tepid mucilage of fog," which represented the "gaseous form of mud and civic filthiness." On occasion, Strong, like many urban intellectuals of the period including those of the *Knickerbocker* circle, might even denounce cities in general, as "sinks of vice, corruption and misery—enlightened on the surface by the false glare of unhealthy exhalations." Yet, he was never happy for long away from the metropolis. "Got back to town this morning 'for good,' " he wrote typically in 1840, after a sojourn on Long Island, "and right glad am I to see this city of abominations again for the last three weeks or so have been as heavy and dull as the *Statutes at Large* or Rollin's *Ancient History*." A book collector, a student of music, a patron of the arts, Strong obviously loved the cultivated life of an urbane, intellectual aristocrat in America's largest city. Although he lived in the era of rural America, Strong was as much the New Yorker as the most sophisticated mid-twentieth century representative of that cultural type.

Strong's outlook was shaped by the cultural advantages of the urban milieu; the cultural institutions of the city absorbed much of his energies. But his was not the only kind of commitment to a nineteenth century pattern of urban life. Representative leaders of western cities of the nineteenth century often cared little about the culture of the city; instead they became fascinated with the process

104

of growth itself—with technology and demography, with the material city as a symbol of American progress. Jesup W. Scott of Toledo was the best known spokesman of this outlook, but there were many lesser western urban leaders who reflected this view. A good example is provided by Robert Thompson Van Horn, journalist, politician, and a local hero of the western railroad center of Kansas City, Missouri. Like Scott, Van Horn believed that the multiplication of western cities and their rapid growth was one of the most dynamic aspects of the American experience. His life calling was in reality that of a professional urban promoter, a not uncommon craft in the nineteenth century American West.

Born in Pennsylvania in 1824, Van Horn as a young man taught school, studied law, learned printing, and drifted west to Pomeroy, Ohio where he acquired a newspaper. Here he began arguing the typical view of the region that the nation's wealth and population and its future great cities were to be concentrated in the Mississippi Valley. After several unsuccessful ventures, in 1855 he took over the operation of a struggling newspaper in the town of Kansas, then a small frontier trading entrepot on the western edge of settlement. Van Horn devoted his efforts to making the village a magnificent western city. He became an expert on railroads and turned his newspaper into a textbook on how to promote them. He took the lead in getting charters for railroad corporations, organizing a chamber of commerce to promote them, defeating the efforts of rival towns with their own railroad plans, and mobilizing his community behind bond issues and other inducements to corporate leaders. Unlike many promoters in the aspiring hamlets of the West, Van Horn saw his hopes realized as Kansas City in the years immediately after the Civil War quickly developed into an important railroad, livestock, and meat-packing center. He lived to be ninety-one, served for years as spokesman of the city's origins, and saw his chosen community mature into the interior metropolis he had early predicted it would become.

To an urban spokesman like Van Horn, cutting streets through imposing hills, spanning a river with a magnificent bridge, installing the machinery for a meat-packing plant, or turning prairie land into a thriving city addition were the vital aspects of the nineteenth century. But he was also able to savor the good life of a man of

105

power in a growing city. He clearly loved the lavish meals, the meetings over bourbon, the holiday parties that were a part of community leadership. Strong's diary records the diversions of an urban intellectual in a center of culture; Van Horn's editorials supply an enthusiastic account of the recreations of a frontier outpost being transformed into a bustling metropolis—of summer circuses, touring Shakespearean companies, visits with travelers to the West, lyceum speakers, Swedish bell-ringers, and winter ice-skating parties. Robert T. Van Horn's Kansas City was not George Templeton Strong's New York, but both men identified with an urban milieu. Early and mid-nineteenth century cities—large and small; in the East, the West, or the South—provided arenas where the able and energetic could realize their talents and enlarge their experience. The urban leader of the period responded to the opportunities and challenges of the urban environment with little reflection on the serious social problems already being created in America by the rapid growth of cities.

5

The Completion
of the Urban
Network,
1860-1910

Between 1860 and 1910 the modern American city emerged. From 1820 on, technological and economic transformations had contributed to a high rate of urbanization in the United States. The continuance of this urban trend in the years after 1860 led to an ever increasing concentration of Americans in cities of all sizes and engendered the view on the part of many social critics that the "rise of the city" was a fundamental problem facing American society. During this fifty year period in which the total population of the United States increased from 31,443,321 to 91,972,266, the number of people living in incorporated munici-palities of 2,500 or more increased from 6,216,518 to 44,639,989 —a percentage change in urban population from 19.8 to 45.7 of the total. Urbanization did not proceed at an even pace during the fifty years. Movement to the city naturally accelerated in times of prosperity and fell off in times of depression when economic opportunities in the city diminished, as was illustrated in the percentage changes in urban population during each census decade:

1860–70	59.3
1870–80	42.7
1880–90	56.7
1890–1900	36.4
1900–10	39.3

But throughout the period the urban trend was unmistakable; the United States was clearly becoming a nation of cities and city dwellers.

Most public attention during the period focused on the growth of the very large cities. The burgeoning metropolises of the East seemed, in particular, to represent to many a fundamental threat to American civilization. Here were the sites of the ghetto and the slum; here the abuses of Old Europe seemed to be growing in the New World. When Josiah Strong in his best-selling book, *Our Country* (1885), argued that the city had become a "serious menace to our civilization," he was referring primarily to the large cities of the East where he found the flourishing of inequality, socialism, political corruption, and Roman Catholicism. Other commentators on American society considered the cities of the East emblematic of the country's dynamic material progress. Scores of foreign travelers, for example, repeated the observation that in New York could be observed the essence of all the vital forces sustaining the rapidly expanding nation; it was as one of them put it, "the magnum opus of modern material civilization."

Despite the contemporary preoccupation with the large city of the eastern seaboard, it should be emphasized that cities of all sizes, in all sections of the country, were growing rapidly. Again, the details of the federal census revealed the pattern. During the period from 1860 to 1910, while the number of cities of over 100,000 increased from nine to fifty, the number of urban places of ten to twenty-five thousand increased from fifty-eight to 369. The period traditionally marks the rise of the great American city; it also marks the emergence of a national urban network—a complex, interrelated system of national and regional metropolises, specialized manufacturing cities, and hundreds of smaller subordinate cities of varying size and function. The rapid development of new regions of the country after 1860 created great opportunities in building new cities, but by 1890 this possibility was no longer open as the urban network had been substantially completed. With the exception of an occasional city such as Miami, Florida which sprang up after a railroad was built along the east coast of Florida in 1896, or Tulsa, Oklahoma located at the site of an oil discovery, most of the American cities destined to achieve even moderate size had been founded by 1890. Less than a fifth of the municipalities incorporated after 1890 had obtained even the minimum urban size requirement of 2,500 by 1910. Opportunities in the exploitation of urban growth, a fundamental force in nineteenth century American economic development, now lay in taking advantage of possibilities in established urban centers, not in creating new cities in new regions. New urban communities that became important in the twentieth century developed largely as satellites or suburbs of older nineteenth century cities.

During the period from 1860 to 1910, the important pre-Civil War cities for the most part maintained their position. New York, of course, became one of the great cities of the world. With its five separate boroughs brought under one government in 1898, its population by 1910 approached five million. Still the leading commercial center of the nation, it had also developed important manufactures and was the center of many of the complex financial functions that were part of a national metropolitan economy. "New York," wrote Williard Glazier in his adulatory but perceptive 1884 survey of American cities, "is one of the most wonderful products of our wonderful western civilization. It is itself a world in epitome. Thoroughly cosmopolitan in its character, almost every nationality is represented within its boundaries, and almost every tongue spoken. It is the great monetary, scientific, artistic and intellectual centre of the western world." Philadelphia, though it dropped from second to third in the rank of American cities, trebled its population during the fifty years, reaching a total of over one and a half million in 1910. Baltimore, Philadelphia's great ante-bellum trade rival, grew more slowly, falling from third place in 1860 to seventh in 1910. Boston dropped one notch from fourth to fifth. Of the major pre-Civil War cities only New Orleans showed a drastic decline in rank. Reflecting the deterioration of interior river commerce, the coming of the railroads, and the east-west pattern of trade and population movement, the city fell from fifth rank in 1860 to 15th in 1910.

Large midwestern cities recorded important gains. St. Louis, Cleveland, and Detroit all grew rapidly to rank fourth, sixth, and ninth respectively in 1910. And the Midwest supplied the most dramatic example of individual city growth in the period—the rise of Chicago. In 1860 Chicago ranked eighth among American cities, with a population of 109,620. It had boomed during the fifties, and local leaders in the next decade took advantage of the city's ten trunk railroads that had earlier been won to build thriving meat-packing, milling, and iron industries. They also continued their struggle with St. Louis for control of the trade of the West. During the Civil War the blockade of the lower Mississippi River and the diversion of trade northward damaged the interests of St. Louis, but its quick recovery renewed the hopes of its leaders. Chicago, however, through its magnificent railroad system continued to advance even more rapidly. Despite the disastrous fire of October 1871, which leveled two-thirds of the city and left 100,000 people homeless, Chicago had eclipsed its rival in population by 1880. By that date, 15,000 miles of railroads connected Chicago with regions of the Northwest and upper Mississippi—an area that grew more rapidly than territories naturally tributary to St. Louis. In addition, St. Louis leaders for too long assumed that the city's magnificent river connections would assure its continued supremacy and consistently demonstrated less willingness to take risks and to pursue bold policies to expand the city than did their counterparts in Chicago. As a result of its victory over its mid-continental rival and its continued development, Chicago passed the million mark in population in 1890 to become the country's second largest city. In 1910 its population stood at 2,185,283.

As Manchester, England had done fifty years earlier and Los Angeles was to do later, Chicago during the late nineteenth century served as the world's "shock city." Constantly visited by foreign travelers, constantly written about, Chicago with its dynamic but often brutal environment seemed to provide a portent of a new and

110

frightening kind of urban future. To Rudyard Kipling in the nineties, Chicago, unlike San Francisco or Salt Lake, was "a real city," the first American city he had encountered. But it was a place of barbarism, boasting, and violence. "Having seen it," Kipling wrote, "I urgently desire never to see it again." But the British reformer and editor, William T. Stead, author of *If Christ Came to Chicago,* and the leader of a crusade for civic betterment in the city, argued in the same period that Chicago had the "opportunity at her feet" to become the ideal city of the world. "She is not laden down by any *damnosa hereditas* of the blunders and crimes of her past; her citizens are full of a boundless elan, and full of faith in the destiny of their city. . . . It seems to me nowhere on the whole of the earth's surface, for one of my ideas and aspirations, could I have been more profitably employed than I was in Chicago in the winter of 1893–94."

Although Chicago supplied the most noted example of the effects of American urbanization in the late nineteenth century, numerous smaller cities demonstrated spectacular growth rates. During the decade of the 1880's, a period of prosperity following the long depression after 1873, 101 cities of 8,000 population and above doubled their size. Among the cities of the Midwest, where urbanization centered during the decade, Omaha grew from 30,500 to 140,000; Kansas City, Missouri from 60,000 to over 132,000; Wichita from 5,000 to 23,000; Duluth from 3,300 to 33,100; and Minneapolis from 47,000 to 164,000. Elsewhere, Birmingham, the new industrial city of the South, jumped from 3,000 in 1880 to over 26,000 ten years later; a southwestern city, El Paso, increased its population thirteen fold. Among the cities of the Far West, Spokane, Washington grew from a settlement of 350 to a city of 20,000; Tacoma jumped in population from 1,100 to 36,000; and Denver, already a good-sized city of 35,000 in 1880, more than tripled its population by 1890.

Numerous specialized technological and economic developments contributed to the possibilities of individual cities. Some grew through invention—Dayton, Ohio provided the site of the operations of the National Cash Register Company; Schenectady, New York in 1886 became the home of General Electric. Others grew through specialized manufactures: Holyoke, Massachusetts in paper, Corning, New York in glass, or Hershey, Pennsylvania in candy. Minneapolis in milling, Milwaukee in beer, and Memphis in cotton-seed oil were examples of cities that profited from the processing of regional agricultural products. Although manufacturing was fundamental to the rapid urbanization of the period, industries often grew in places, such as Pittsburgh, Philadelphia, or New York, which were well established older cities with a diversified economic base. Manufacturing alone was seldom responsible for the creation of the large cities that became part of the urban network.

Similarly, the colorful mining booms of the late nineteenth century in gold, silver, copper, coal, and oil created a number of small urban communities, but many of these, in the west particularly, failed even to survive once the local mineral resources ran out. Only an occasional mining city—Butte, Montana near copper deposits, and Wilkes-Barre and Scranton in the anthracite region of Pennsylvania—achieved major-city status. More often than not in the long run, an older city benefitted from new mineral sources, as Pittsburgh did from coal and Cleveland from petroleum.

In large measure, the location and initial growth of important cities that sprang up in this era of the completion of the American urban network was tied to the building of a national system of transportation. In the early part of the nineteenth century, the outcome of struggles for transportation had drastically affected the rank and importance of the cities of the East. After 1850 this conflict was transferred to the West. The rivalry among city promoters and real estate speculators to win railroads for their communities in newly developed regions supplied one of the most dramatic chapters in the history of American urbanization. Earlier rivalries had been limited by nature—by the location of rivers and lakes. But railroads were not bound by topography, by the paths of river commerce, or by natural trade patterns. Railroads could be built anywhere, creating cities where they chose. Since the building of railroads was dependent to a considerable extent on subsidies from local communities, railroad leaders were willing to bargain with competing towns to obtain the best possible deal in stock subscriptions, bond issues, and right-of-ways. It was sometimes possible, therefore, for towns with few natural advantages to triumph over better situated rivals for the prize of regional dominance. The "boosterism" associated with the Midwest and areas farther west is largely a legacy of the late nineteenth century era of urban rivalry. Numerous cities in the West owe their importance to the fact that groups of energetic local promoters with substantial investments in local real estate were able through superior organization of their communities, superior advertising, or often simply through good luck, to persuade railroads to build to their particular locations.

From early in the railroad era, railroad officials were well aware of the possibilities of profit in urban growth in the West. The platting of town sites and the sale of town lots became an established aspect of the process of building railroads into new regions. The techniques of town development and the system of bargaining with competing communities were perfected by the Illinois Central Railroad, chartered in 1851 to build southward from Chicago through the heart of the state. The company used the threat of building new towns or running its tracks through neighboring places in order to force local officials in established communities to offer concessions of right-of-ways, railroad station site donations, or stock purchases. Centralia, Kankakee, Champaign, and La Salle were established as competing towns by the Illinois Central when agreements could not be effected with Central City, Bourbonnais, Urbana, and Peru. Creation of new towns was often advantageous, for it permitted a larger share of the profits from increased land values to go directly to railroad owners. The company's charter prohibited the railroad from laying out towns on its lines, but Illinois Central leaders circumvented this restriction by creating a land company called "The Associates" for the specific purpose of managing town-site speculations. The company's concern with town promoting contributed to considerable urbanization along the line of the Illinois Central. In 1850, there were only ten towns in the immediate vicinity of the railroad's route; ten years later there were forty-seven; in 1870, eighty-one. The combined population of these urban places, excluding Chicago, rose from 12,000 in 1850, to 70,000 in 1860, and to 172,000 by 1870. Profits from the Illinois Central's town promotions were large. The development at Kankakee, for example, cost "The Associates" some $18,000 to May 1855. By the end of that year the group had collected nearly $50,000 through lot sales and the value of the property remaining was estimated at more than $100,000. After ten years of large dividends, the Kankakee business was sold for $50,000.

In advancing their town projects, the Illinois Central leaders frequently had to head off the plans of rival town promoters. The contest for the location of the University of Illinois provides a case in point. After the passage of the Morrill Act of 1862, which provided federal lands for the support of higher education, several communities competed for the prize of the state university. The Illinois Central supported Champaign, where a number of town lots remained unsold, and offered $50,000 in freight transportation as part of the city's bid of $285,000 to the state. The bids of the three other leading contenders were higher: Lincoln offered $385,000; Bloomington, $470,000, which included $50,000 from the competing Chicago and Alton Railroad; and Jacksonville, $491,000. But, owing to the bribery of legislators and political bosses, Champaign's bid was finally accepted in 1867. The Illinois Central's investment again reaped large dividends. Real estate boomed, and by 1870 Champaign had become the most populous community south of Chicago on the branch line of the railroad.

As railroads built westward, other lines engaged successfully in town development, though their gains were not as spectacular as those of the Illinois Central. The Chicago, Burlington, and Quincy also used the device of the independent association to lay out numerous town sites in Iowa. These were widely advertised as places with magnificent futures. Charles Perkins, the land agent of the Burlington, commented more frankly to his wife in referring to the towns of Batavia, Whitfield, and Agency City in 1864: "*Towns* they are on paper, meadows or timber land with here and there a house, in reality." Two years later, near Ottumwa, Perkins supplied insight into the methods of town development by railroads. "I shall have two or three more towns to name very soon. . . . They should be short and easily pronounced. Frederic, I think is a very good name. It is now literally a cornfield, so I cannot have it surveyed, but yesterday a man came to arrange to put a hotel here. This is a great country for hotels."

The rise of Kansas City, Missouri as a western railroad center

114

and regional metropolis supplies one of the best examples of the relationship of real estate, local promotion, and railroad planning to the growth of individual cities in this era of booming development of new regions.

The community began its existence as an insignificant frontier trading depot. During the 1830's and 40's, as trade moved up the Missouri River from St. Louis, a complex of small trading communities sprang up along the western edge of Missouri to serve a vast western empire. For its first fifteen years, the town of Kansas, founded in 1838, was little more than a collection of warehouses and general stores near the juncture of the Kansas and Missouri Rivers. The settlement functioned as an entrepot of the river-caravan trade—a convenient location where goods could be easily transferred from steamboat to wagon for shipment to far-flung points of a distant hinterland. With the expansion of the Santa Fe trade in the 1850's and particularly with the migration of settlers into Kansas after the opening of the territory in 1854, the town began to grow, and a group of local property holders, who were joined by investors from the East with an interest in promising western town sites, set out to build a regional city through obtaining railroads. Despite a well-organized local program, by the time of the Civil War, Kansas City, as it was now called to distinguish it from the territory, was not yet connected to the railroads being built across Missouri, nor had a frantic effort to build a local railroad succeeded. The town had grown to four and a half thousand, and it had eclipsed the cluster of communities in the immediate vicinity—Parkville, Weston, Westport, and Independence. But St. Joseph, some forty miles to the north, already had railroad connections through the Hannibal and St. Joseph line, completed in 1859. Another river town, Leavenworth, Kansas a few miles north had begun to boom and was nearly twice as large as Kansas City.

The outbreak of the Civil War nearly destroyed Kansas City. Guerrilla fighting broke out in the region. The town's population declined by a half; it acquired a reputation as a center of secessionist sentiment, and many of its pro-southern business leaders were driven from the community; the overland wagon trade, which had earlier centered there, went to Leavenworth, near a military fort and the center of Union military operations in the region.

115

Most observers who toured the region at the end of the war predicted that Leavenworth would be the next great city of the West. Albert Richardson, the well known western traveler, found Leavenworth in 1866 to be more like a "great city than any point between St. Louis and San Francisco." Five newspapers, gaslights, well-built brick buildings, all gave it the "air of a metropolis."

But Leavenworth's promising hopes were never to be realized. As railroad building revived in the western regions during the closing period of the war, a few property holders in Kansas City, who had held on during the days of adversity, revived their local railroad program. Using stocks in their paper railroad companies, a congressional land grant to one of their companies, local bond issues, and blocks of potentially valuable real estate, the Kansas City leaders were able to persuade officials of the Hannibal and St. Joseph to connect with a transcontinental branch being built in Kansas—the Union Pacific, Eastern Division (later the Kansas Pacific)—by way of Kansas City rather than by way of Leavenworth. The Hannibal and St. Joseph's construction of a railroad bridge at Kansas City—the first across the Missouri River—assured the city's rapid development. By 1870 the federal census gave its population as 32,260. Within another decade, Kansas City had developed its important meat-packing facilities, and its population in 1880 stood at 55,785. Leavenworth, to a lesser extent St. Joseph, Wyandotte, (which Horace Greeley in 1859 had thought the likely site for the next great western city), and numerous other Kansas and Missouri towns, whose claims to future urban greatness had once seemed plausible, had been eclipsed by the rise of Kansas City.

The growth of Kansas City owed much to the location of a federally supported transcontinental branch in Kansas. It was through the Kansas Pacific Railroad that Kansas City became established as a cattle market and meat packing center. Many important western cities owe their existence directly to the western railways provided by the Pacific Railway Acts of 1862 and 1864. Cheyenne, Wyoming, for example, began as a railroad construction camp casually chosen in the summer of 1867. By fall there was a hastily constructed town of 4,000 people who had got there ahead of the rails. When the trains arrived in November, another 4,000 people came in. Railroad construction moved on the next

116

spring, but Cheyenne was already large enough to be named as territorial capital. The development of the Wyoming cattle industry and gold discoveries in the Black Hills provided a base for its continued growth. Reno, Nevada, founded as a mining provision center, became a station on the Central Pacific Railroad in 1868. M. C. Lake, a rancher, offered the company eighty acres of land as a town site provided he could retain the alternate lots. The offer was accepted, the town was laid out, 200 lots were sold on the first day of public auction, and the community was a fact. Other small isolated western trading or mining sites—El Paso, Albuquerque, Santa Fe—boomed with the coming of the railroads.

Cities of the West frequently grew almost accidentally as the result of the location of railroads. However, the early history of Denver, like that of Kansas City, indicates that community enterprise was also important in the establishment of the principal cities in the western segment of the American urban network. Well before the coming of the railroads, the gold discoveries in Colorado in 1858 had led to the creation of numerous mining communities, particularly along Cherry Creek. The possibilities in city development attracted an ambitious promoter, General William Larimer, who had lost a fortune in Pittsburgh in the early fifties and had sought to recoup through speculative town-building activities in La Platte and Omaha, Nebraska and in Leavenworth, Kansas. Arriving at Cherry Creek to found a town, Larimer learned that a rival group had already staked a claim. Undeterred, he merely set up his own town called Denver City on the opposite bank of the stream. Promoters of the original town of Auraria and those of Denver engaged in vigorous rivalry, but in 1860, after an exchange of real estate among Larimer and other leaders, the two towns merged as Denver. Larimer, who had asserted in 1859, "I am Denver," became the "Donating Agent" for the community. He was responsible for providing lots for those who would build there and took charge of setting up the necessary urban institutions for an aspiring city—hotels, newspapers, general stores, sawmills, and a cemetery. Nourished by the mining boom, Denver began to establish itself as a regional metropolis.

Local leaders of course recognized that railroads were essential to the city's continued growth, and with the construction of the

Union Pacific westward after the Civil War they campaigned for a route to cut through the mountains west of the city. When Union Pacific engineers decided to build through passes to the north in Wyoming, Denver promoters recognized a vital threat to their interests. The city had not grown much since 1860 and without a place on the line it was likely to languish. Accordingly, in 1869 local leaders organized a local company which successfully built a 106 mile line north to Cheyenne. In June 1870 the first train pulled into Denver, and in August the Kansas Pacific reached Denver providing an alternative eastern connection. But Denver leaders did not rest on these successes. Despite the ridicule of many eastern investors, in 1871 they began the construction of a narrow gauge trunk line to the south, the Denver and Rio Grande. The railroad tapped new mineral areas and proved enormously profitable to its owners and to the city. Denver leaders consistently demonstrated promotional zeal and skill. For example, the location of a United States mint at Denver, which provided official recognition of the city's regional status, owed much to local organizational activity. Partly as a result of this kind of effort, by 1890, though its population was still under 107,000, Denver had established its economic influence over a vast area of the West.

In addition to contributing to the location and growth of western cities, the transcontinental railroads fed grandiose schemes of countless visionaries of an urban West. Wildly speculative urban land booms were a vital aspect of the history of the growth of the region. During the early years of debate over the route for a railroad to the Pacific, spokesmen for a federally supported project, Thomas Hart Benton and William Gilpin, had continually advanced a dream of a great chain of magnificent cities that would spring up along the line, and as railroad building actually got underway in the 1860's, promoters attempted to realize the design. One of the more ambitious efforts was that of George Francis Train, an investor in the Union Pacific, who had been one of the organizers of the scandal-ridden Credit Mobilier established to construct the railroad. Train owned 600 acres of land in Omaha, and decided to apply the separate company device employed so successfully in the Credit Mobilier to urban promotion. His Credit Foncier was set up specifically to build and develop cities along the line of the

118

Union Pacific. "One of my plans," he recorded in his autobiography, "was the creation of a chain of great towns across the continent, connecting Boston with San Francisco by a magnificent highway of cities." His proposals were advanced with the usual extravagant appeals to the optimism stimulated by the country's rapid development. "Would you make money easy?" asked a Credit Foncier prospectus about Columbus, Nebraska. "Find then the site of a city and buy the farm it is to be built on! How many regret the non-purchase of that lot in New York; that block in Buffalo; that acre in Chicago; that quarter section in Omaha. Once these city properties could be bought for a song. Astor and Girard made their fortunes that way. The Credit Foncier by owning the principal towns along the Pacific line to California, enriches its shareholders while distributing its profits by selling alternate lots at a nominal price to the public."

Train realized only limited gains from his exuberant promotions. Omaha did not grow as fast as he had anticipated, nor did the towns that the company founded along the railroad automatically sprout into great cities. Train shifted his operations to Denver, and later to Tacoma, which he proclaimed the future great city of the world. To advertise its claim he made a sixty-seven-day trip around the world from the city, breaking the record of the celebrated Nellie Bly set the year before in 1890. But this effort was also largely a failure. Train broke down and was legally adjudged insane. He died penniless in 1903—one of the last of a succession of nineteenth century prophets of a west of magnificent cities whose visions were but partly realized.

The recurrent town booms in southern California in the late nineteenth century provide one of the best examples of the general influence of the urban enthusiasm that motivated promoters like Train. As elsewhere in the West, these booms were closely tied to railroad building. In the late 1860's, local promoters in Los Angeles, then a city of less than 6,000, were encouraged by rumors of a possible transcontinental railroad connection. In order to advance this possibility, they organized a local railroad called the Los Angeles and San Pedro to build a twenty-one mile line to a harbor site on the ocean. When the Southern Pacific planned a connection southward from San Francisco, local officials passed over control of their company, paid a cash subsidy of over $600,000, and offered numerous other concessions to ensure that the line would build by way of the city rather than choosing a route behind the mountains to the east. The Southern Pacific completed its line to the city in 1876. By 1881 it had connected with the Texas and Pacific east of El Paso, which gave Los Angeles access to New Orleans as well as San Francisco.

Owing to the effects of the depression of the seventies, Los Angeles did not boom as local promoters had hoped until a rival line, the Atchison, Topeka, and Santa Fe, obtained its own tracks into the city in 1887. A rate war between the Southern Pacific and the Santa Fe lowered passenger fares to the Mississippi River to five dollars, and for a day or two one could go from Kansas City to Los Angeles for a dollar. In order to build up passenger traffic, both railroads sponsored excursion tours and engaged in lavish advertising of the virtues of southern California. The crowds of tourists and settlers who came to the region were joined by professional town promoters—the veterans of booms in Minneapolis, Kansas City, and Chicago—who came west to lay out new towns and new subdivisions in older sites. In an atmosphere of brass bands and circus exhibitions, new cities were platted throughout Los Angeles County. Within three months, thirteen town sites were laid out along thirteen miles of the Santa Fe and nearly as many along the Southern Pacific. On one day in 1887 real estate sales in Los Angeles reached nearly three times the amount of the subsidy paid to the Southern Pacific in 1872; total real estate sales for the year ranked the city third behind Chicago and New York. From January 1, 1887 to July 1, 1889, speculators laid out sixty new towns in southern California with estimated space enough for two million people, but at the end of the boom the sites had an aggregate population of less than 3,000.

Many of these promotions were the work of outrageously unscrupulous speculators. Sidney Homberg sold about 4,000 lots in Border City and Manchester to easterners unfamiliar with Homberg's site on the edge of the Mojave Desert. Border City, a historian noted, "was most easily accessible by means of a balloon, and was as secure from hostile invasion as the homes of the cliff-dwellers. Its principal resource was a view of the Mojave Desert." The collapse of the boom in 1888 destroyed the paper cities; abandoned, uncompleted buildings were the principal souvenirs of the boom. At least sixty-two of the more than a hundred towns platted in Los Angeles County between 1884 and 1888 passed out of existence. At the end of the boom, the town of Carlton had 4,060 lots, Nadeau 4,470, Manchester 2,304, but none of the places had a single resident. Chicago Park had 2,289 lots and one resident while Sunset had 2,014 lots and a watchman.

Despite the destruction of an estimated $14,000,000 in property values in a single year, Los Angeles still had its advantages of climate, space, and energetic promoters. Led by Harrison Gray Otis, the publisher of the *Los Angeles Times,* city leaders organized the Los Angeles Chamber of Commerce, launched a program of encouraging manufactures, established an inter-urban railway system, and advertised the natural advantages of southern California throughout the country. Moreover, a number of the boom towns in the area—Glendale, Monrovia, Burbank, and Azuza, among others—became permanent communities. Although the population of Los Angeles fell a third in the two years after the collapse of the boom, it resumed its steady growth thereafter. During the 1890's Los Angeles was second in size only to San Francisco among the cities west of the Rockies, and its rate of growth during the decade was exceeded only by Seattle.

As new cities were founded and grew in the West, the region's first metropolis, San Francisco, maintained its leadership until well into the twentieth century. In the wake of the gold rushes of the late forties and early fifties, the city had become the focal point of economic development throughout the Far West. Recognizing the commercial possibilities of a city located at one of the few west coast sites with a suitable natural port, speculators from the early 1850's had invested in San Francisco real estate, and the city experienced one of the early real estate booms. Lots that had sold for $1,500 each in 1850 had risen to from $8,000 to $27,000 three years later. Until the coming of the railroads, virtually all trade to the interior went through San Francisco or Portland, also located at a natural port. Railroads limited but did not destroy San Francisco's influence over a vast hinterland. The power of local capital assured that habitual commercial patterns would persist even after rival cities sprang up along the routes of railroads. "San Francisco dwarfs the other cities," Lord Bryce wrote in the late eighties, "and is a commercial and intellectual centre, and source of influence for the surrounding regions, more powerful over them than is any Eastern city over its neighborhood. It is a New York which has got no Boston on one side of it, and no shrewd and orderly rural population on the other to keep it in order." By 1880 it had become the country's ninth ranked city and was by far the largest city west of Chicago.

Limited in its growth by its location on a narrow peninsula, San Francisco early developed a group of suburban communities closely tied to the city. Oakland across the Bay, for example, became the center of railroad and industrial development in the area, and in 1880 was actually the second largest city of the Far West. This complex of communities in the Bay region was largely the work of real estate speculators, and for each successful town promotion, such as Oakland and Alameda, a failure could probably be cited. As the center of this urbanized region, San Francisco early established its reputation as an American showpiece, where the visitor could experience a varied urban environment that ranged from the dives of the Barbary Coast to the exotic castles of Nob Hill, and where local citizens prided themselves on their diligent practice of the graces of a sophisticated, cosmopolitan society. San Francisco was "the city" of the west, recognized as such in this period even by residents of rival Los Angeles.

The coming of railroads to the Pacific Northwest limited San Francisco's influence in that distant part of its vast hinterland by creating new regional cities. The development of the Pacific Northwest also contributed another important chapter to the history of nineteenth century urban rivalry—the struggle between Tacoma and Seattle for regional supremacy. Seattle, located on Puget Sound at the best natural port north of San Francisco, had gotten its start in the 1850's as a sawmill town in a magnificent timber region. Although the community had only 182 inhabitants in 1860, early in the next decade local residents through a donation of a site and buildings persuaded the territorial legislature to make Seattle the site of the university. Despite the continually stated faith of local residents in the community's magnificent resources and its

122

future, by 1870 the town had grown to only 11,000. Again, as in other western cities, local leaders recognized that railroads were necessary to end Seattle's isolation. They hoped and assumed that the Northern Pacific would choose the town as its western terminus, and in order to further this possibility offered the railroad the usual concessions—land, choice waterfront wharfage, and a quarter million dollars in cash and bonds.

However, their hopes were not immediately realized. In 1873 the Northern Pacific announced that Tacoma, a tiny settlement at Commencement Bay twenty-four miles south of Seattle, had been chosen as the railroad's terminus. The decision was largely the result of an effort to realize speculative real estate profits from development of a virtually new rather than an established town site. At the other end of the line, Jay Cooke, the financial backer of the Northern Pacific, had followed a similar policy in choosing Duluth as a terminus rather than the older neighboring town of Superior, where a group of outside investors had already obtained the choicest urban sites. The Northern Pacific leaders organized a subsidiary company, the Tacoma Land Company, which acquired 3,000 acres of land in the town and 13,000 acres nearby. Frederick Law Olmsted, the distinguished landscape architect and the father of American city planning, prepared a detailed curvilinear street plan for the city that took advantage of the site's topography. But the plan was derisively rejected as totally impractical for quick real estate profits. A contemporary observed that it was "the most fantastic plan of a town that was ever seen. There wasn't a straight line, a right angle or a corner lot. The blocks were shaped like melons, pears, and sweet potatoes. One block, shaped like a banana, was 3,000 feet in length and had 250 plots. It was a pretty fair park plan but condemned itself for a town."

Officers of the company quickly adopted a more conventional gridiron plan. Pamphleteers began advertising Tacoma as the future great city of the world; like so many western cities it was portrayed as the successor of Babylon, Tyre, Rome, and London. "No one can doubt," stated one brochure, "that the sum total of Tacoma's resources, domestic and foreign, together with the entire aspect of her own and the world's present environments, are vastly superior to those of Chicago in 1852, and that it is only a question of TIME

123

when a greater city than Chicago or New York will flourish on the more salubrious shores of Puget Sound." The Tacoma Land Company offered its lots for sale and built a magnificent hotel. The boom was on. Rudyard Kipling, who visited Tacoma in 1889, described the effects of a decade of mushrooming development. "Tacoma was literally staggering under a boom of the boomiest. . . . The rude boarded pavements of the main streets rumbled under the heels of furious men all actively engaged in hunting drinks and eligible corner lots. They sought the drinks first. The street itself alternated five-story business blocks of the later and more abominable forms of architecture with broad shanties. Overhead the drunken telegraph, telephone, and electric-light wires tangled on the tottering posts whose butts were half-whittled through by the knife of the loafer. . . . We passed down ungraded streets that ended abruptly in a fifteen-foot drop and a nest of brambles; along pavements that beginning in pine-plank ended in the living tree; by hotels with Turkish mosque trinketry on their shameless tops, and the pine stumps at their very doors; by a female seminary, tall, gaunt and red, which a native of the town bade us marvel at, and we marvelled; by houses built in imitation of the ones on Nob Hill, San Francisco—after the Dutch fashion; by other houses plenteously befouled with jigsaw work, and others flaring with the castlemented, battlemented bosh of the wooden Gothic school."

Despite a series of booms in the eighties which produced a population increase from 1,100 to over 36,000 for the decade, Tacoma's magnificent aspirations were never realized. Again, as elsewhere, the community organization of a rival and the ability of that rival substantially to affect the pattern of railroad connections altered urban ambitions and calculations. After the failure to obtain the Northern Pacific terminus, Seattle residents in the typical fashion of western urban promoters organized a local railroad company to build a line southeastward across the Cascade Mountains to tap the productive agricultural region around Walla Walla. After the line reached Newcastle, a site of coal fields twelve miles inland, Henry Villard, who had become president of the Northern Pacific following the collapse of Jay Cooke's financial empire, purchased the coal fields and the railroad. Villard promised to extend the

Northern Pacific from Tacoma to Seattle, but the company's financial difficulties forced cancellation of the plan. Seattle interests next launched a local project, the Seattle, Lake Shore, and Eastern Railroad, to connect with the Canadian Pacific. When the project received the support of eastern financial interests, the threat of competition forced the Northern Pacific to buy the local company and to connect Seattle to the Northern Pacific system. After a twenty year struggle, Seattle had its tie to a transcontinental railroad. Two years later, in 1893, the Great Northern Railway of James G. Hill located its main terminal at Seattle providing the city with alternative connections to the east.

During the nineties, Tacoma languished while Seattle nearly doubled its population and established a stable, three to one ratio in size over its rival. The victory of the community over the Northern Pacific and Tacoma became symbolic in local legend of the "Seattle Spirit," just as Kansas City's victory over Leavenworth thirty years earlier provided the central episode in the growth of the "Kansas City Spirit." In subsequent years, Seattle became noted for its support of community enterprises including extensive public works projects, sponsorship of an international exposition, and vigorous promotion of itself as the jumping off point for Alaskan gold. Tacoma, on the other hand, though it continued to grow, followed the course of most losers in the great nineteenth century urban rivalries and emphasized its fine homes, genteel living, and preservation of historical traditions.

Portland, Oregon the third of the major cities of the Pacific Northwest to emerge with the completion of the urban network, got its start during a period of town promotion along the Willamette and Columbia rivers in the 1840's. In many ways, this boom resembled those that took place along the rivers of the Midwest, the Maumee in Ohio, for example, in the period before the Panic of 1837. "Nearly every man in Oregon has a city of his own," an observer reported in 1850, "and it is impossible to tell what point on the Columbia will take the preference." Missionaries founded Oregon City; a group of Missourians, settled at Linnton; Wisconsin settlers established Milwaukie. Spokesmen for these and other communities supplied free lots, advertised their sites, and predicted that their hamlet would become a great western metropolis. But

125

the New Englanders who founded Portland had the advantage of good port facilities and considerable capital. They successfully established the city as the commercial center of the region though the entire area was in a sense still tributary to San Francisco. Portland's conservative railroad policy, based on the assumption that any lines built into the region would have to reach her, permitted Tacoma and Seattle to rise to positions of regional urban prominence. Although Portland eventually obtained transcontinental connections and steadily grew as an important western city, it acquired the reputation of a city fundamentally conservative in outlook. "The Columbia River has made the spirit of Portland," wrote a member of an old Portland family. "Portland people were toll takers at the gate. In time, they became conservative, took fewer chances and relied upon the geographic position of their tollgate. . . . Maybe too much sitting at the tollgate."

The growth of the Pacific Northwest cities illustrates the importance of urbanization in the development of new regions and points up the continuance into the latter part of the nineteenth century of the urban frontier fundamental to the growth of the Trans-Appalachian regions of the country. During the decade of the eighties, as Portland grew from 17,500 to 46, 385, Oregon's urban population rose from 14.8 to 26.8 per cent of the total; statistically Portland gained one in five of Oregon's new population, and two in five went to the two most urbanized counties. Similarly, during the decade three urban counties in Washington received half of the new population, and Seattle, Tacoma, and Spokane got one of every three new arrivals.

The cities of the West were founded as commercial enterprises; railroads and real estate were fundamental in their development. The Mormon settlement of Salt Lake, which became an important regional city, was untypical in its founding, since initially its leaders were driven by a goal of achieving isolated self-sufficiency for a community of saints. But Salt Lake was soon subject to the same forces that influenced other western cities. From the beginning, the settlement had performed urban functions, including complex religious activities, for a hinterland of nearby farmers. In spite of Brigham Young's resolution to avoid commerce with the Gentile world, Salt Lake early developed trade ties to St. Louis and became a stopping point for overland travelers to the West. "Salt Lake is the city of the future," Albert Richardson recorded of his visit there in 1865, "the natural metropolis of all Utah and portions of Nevada, Idaho, Montana, and Colorado. It contains nearly twenty thousand people, and bids fair to continue the largest city between St. Louis and San Francisco. The overland telegraph connects it with the Atlantic and the Pacific, mail coaches ply daily to Nebraska and Kansas on the east, California on the west, Montana on the north, Idaho and Columbia river on the northwest, and the Pak Ranager silver region four hundred miles to the southwest. . . . Some of the trading-houses do an immense business. A single merchant has sold more than a million dollars worth of goods per annum." At this time, Mormon community leaders were actively involved in an effort to influence both the Central Pacific and the Union Pacific to choose a route that ran through Salt Lake City. When both railroads decided to build by a more northern route, church leaders, through a series of land transactions and inducements offered to U.P. and C.P. officials, insured that the Mormon settlement of Ogden rather than the "Hell on Wheels" railroad camp at Corinne—twenty-five miles northwest of Ogden —would be the terminal point of the two transcontinental lines. Outside professional speculators had chosen Corinne as the most logical place for the regional city, and at one time the town supported nineteen saloons and an Opera House. Within ten years, Corinne had become a ghost town.

After this victory, Mormon leaders next sponsored the building of a thirty-seven mile railroad between Salt Lake and Ogden. The completion of this line made certain that Salt Lake rather than Ogden would continue to be the regional city. As the flow of traffic stimulated the economic development of the region, the isolation of the Mormon religious community broke down further, and by the eighties Salt Lake City increasingly resembled other western cities. The president of the Salt Lake Chamber of Commerce argued in 1888 that an increase in the price of real estate was enabling the city to become more like its western neighbors. In so doing, he sounded a dominant theme in nineteenth century urban ideology: "The present extraordinary prosperity and development of Denver, Los Angeles, Omaha, and Kansas City had their origin in real estate speculation. The one almost necessarily succeeds the other, as prices of land can be sustained in times of speculative excitement only by the building up of manufacturing and mercantile industries, to which the speculator himself is often driven for self-protection."

The importance of urban entrepreneurship—of organized civic enterprise that enabled one community to triumph over another and win railroads, manufactures, or the other necessities of urban growth—is clearly evident in the histories of the major cities in the American urban network. Its importance is sometimes more evident, and more precisely delineated, in the histories of lesser places that did not achieve metropolitan status but which proved successful urban enterprises. The example of Wichita, Kansas supplies a case in point. Wichita was a late founded Kansas town; in 1868 urban speculators chose a town site at a convenient spot on the Chisholm Trail, the route of cattle drives from Texas to railheads in Kansas. The promoters advertised that the new center would shorten the cattlemen's trip to market, but this contention was meaningless since the nearest railroad was still some eighty miles to the north. Wichita had no unusual geographical advantages, and the older Kansas towns on the route of the Kansas Pacific seemed much more promising as potential urban centers. But, as elsewhere, community enterprise altered these considerations. Wichita leaders, through a bond issue of $200,000, persuaded the Atchison, Topeka, and Santa Fe Railroad being constructed southwestward to build a branch toward the town. Even more important, they encouraged Joseph G. McCoy, the leader in the Kansas cattle marketing industry, to transfer his operations to Wichita from Abilene, where local opposition to the sometimes violent cattlemen had developed. The first train reached Wichita in May 1872; by the end of the year a total of 3,530 carloads of cattle had been shipped from the city. Wichita had become a booming cow town, while Abilene began its slide toward relative insignificance.

With the decline of the open range drives and the end of the colorful era of the cattle kingdom, Wichita leaders faced a period of adversity, but they energetically converted the economy of the city into activities suitable to its location in a rapidly developing wheat-raising area—flour milling, lumber yards, brick making, stove and farm machinery manufactures. They also launched a vigorous advertising campaign lauding the virtues of the "Peerless Princess of the Plains." A pamphlet of 1888 announced an inflated claim of 40,000 population and labelled Wichita, "the largest city in Kansas, a city of fine Educational Institutions, Magnificent Business Blocks, Elegant Residences and Extensive Manufactures, with more Railroads, more Wholesale Trade, More Manufacturing, More Enterprise than any city in the Southwest."

The success of this promotional campaign set off a real estate boom in Wichita, and during the decade of the eighties the city recorded a population growth from 5,000 to 24,000. Again demonstrating an exceptional degree of community spirit, Wichita leaders initiated a program that provided the city with adequate municipal services and a range of cultural and educational institutions. Local boosters could now proclaim the city "the new Athens" of the West. After the region recovered from the depression of the nineties, the expansion of wheat raising stimulated banking and the manufacture of farm machinery in Wichita. During the 1900–10 decade the city doubled its population to 52,000. The success of local leaders in building Wichita into a large regional marketing and manufacturing center permitted the city to take advantage of new opportunities that presented themselves in the twentieth century. Oil and airplanes enabled the city to become an important industrial center and the largest city in Kansas. Wichita lacked substantial natural advantages; yet at each stage of its development local leaders had been willing to support the community projects necessary to growth. In the completion of the urban network, the quality of urban entrepreneurship often dictated whether the enterprise of city building succeeded or failed.

The history of American cities largely emphasizes the successful urban enterprises and fails to examine the failures and partial failures of community organization that doomed a number of promising places to oblivion or to second rank. Superior, Wisconsin once attracted national attention as the potential site for a great metropolis of the interior, but the failure of outside investors to agree on necessary promotional policies led to its becoming the lesser community of a middle sized urban complex. Galena,

Illinois once seemed one of the more promising cities of Illinois, but lead supplies in the region began to run out, and local leaders were unable to obtain a railroad connection. Galveston, Texas, an important pre-war port on the Gulf of Mexico and a magic name in the writings of early western urban promoters, also failed as a community to take advantage of the possibilities of railroads and lost its position to Houston. Scores of small lumber, mining, transportation and manufacturing cities throughout the Middle and Far West did not diversify their economies at the proper time or were unable to profit from opportunities exploited by more unified or more energetic rival communities.

During this period of the completion of the urban network, urban growth in the South in important respects resembles that of the undeveloped regions of the West. In both cases, Eastern and European capital financed ventures in town-building, the pattern of railroads determined the location of important new cities, and frenzied real estate booms were typical.

In the period before the Civil War, the South had its important cities and a pattern of urban life similar to that in cities elsewhere, yet the region had clearly lagged behind the Northeast in the extent of urbanization. In 1860 only fourteen of the country's ninety-three cities above 10,000 (15.1 per cent) were located in the South, and the percentage of urban population in the region (in places above 2,500) was only 7.2 compared to 19.8 for the country as a whole. Probably the twenty-year period of war and reconstruction did not significantly retard urbanization, but neither did it, of course, stimulate it. Opportunities of profit from urban enterprise arose primarily with the rapid economic development of the New South after 1880. Older communities, the river towns for example, developed a more diversified economic base. Recalling his days as a pilot on the Mississippi in 1883, Mark Twain observed: "I was not expecting to live to see Natchez and these other river towns become manufacturing strongholds and railway centres." Newer interior cities—Atlanta and Nashville, and later Louisville, Memphis, and Dallas—boomed as a network of railroads was built in the region. Atlanta, in particular, was the site chosen by Northeastern investors in urban enterprise.

As part of this growth, the South experienced the customary real estate booms so common in the West. Birmingham, a new industrial city in Alabama founded in 1871, had a particularly spectacular boom in the late eighties. "Why, men would come in at four o'clock in the morning and begin making trades before breakfast," an early resident recalled. "Property changed hands four and five times a day. . . . Men went crazy two hours after getting here. A brand-new sensation was born every day." During this period, a dozen paper towns were launched within a seventy-five mile radius of Chattanooga. "The great bulk of both capital for the project and people who buy the lots, come from the East and North, some of the money from England," commented a Chattanooga newspaper. The projected town of Cardiff, Tennessee announced an auction of town lots for April 22, 1890, for which "Ten Solid Vestibuled Special Trains Will be Run from New England Alone, beside Specials from All Over the South and West." The fate of this project was indicated by the fact that Cardiff never achieved sufficient size to rate a census listing. General Fitzhugh Lee, nephew of the more famous general, led the Rockbridge Company organized to boom Glasgow, Virginia. Lee announced the sales of "Lots number 35 and 37 in Block 153 on Rockridge Road to Her Grace Lilly the Duchess of Marlborough" and two others "to George Spencer Churchill, Duke of Marlborough." The company sold large amounts of stock and began the construction of a magnificent hotel. But with the collapse of the boom the company failed, and the hotel which was never opened stood for years as a decayed ruin.

Despite the urban booming and the sometimes spectacular growth of individual cities, the South, in sharp contrast to regions of the West, remained in this period primarily a rural region with a rather consistent level of urbanization at any census period corresponding to that for the nation as a whole about fifty years earlier. In 1900, for example, urban population in the South was 15.2 per cent of the total while the national figure in 1850 had been 15.3. In 1920 the percentage for the South was 25.4; the national figure in 1870 had been 25.7. This supports the general conclusion that urbanization in the South paralleled closely the national process, with a fifty year time lag. However, it should be noted that a disproportionate share of the increased urban population was located in the border regions of Maryland, Delaware, and the District of Columbia. After 1920 the rate of urbanization (that is the percentage change in urban population from one census to the next) became greater for the South than for the nation as a whole, and the time lag by 1950 was down to forty years. In the period from 1850 to 1910, the South occupied a distinctive position in the national culture and economy, and this was influenced by its lower level of urbanization. Yet, despite its much emphasized agrarian tradition, the region was fully affected by the transforming forces that led to the growth of cities throughout the nation.

The importance of city promotion and city building in the growth of the American economy in the nineteenth century has been insufficiently appreciated and little assessed. In a very significant respect, as Richard C. Wade has clearly demonstrated for the period before 1830, the town promoter was the true "frontiersman" in the development of new regions of the country. The speculative city he founded in the wilderness was often the cause not the result of growth and settlement. Moreover, historians have tended to ignore the cultural drama that was a part of the violent competition for success in the enterprise of city building; town rivalry was one of the great games of nineteenth century America. "Tell them we are building a great city," a promoter of the small frontier settlement of Kansas City had typically proclaimed in the fifties. By 1910, however, this kind of urban rallying cry, once heard through the land at every promising spot on road and river, could no longer reflect the creating of magnificent cities in the wilderness through hope, enthusiasm, and energy. The urban network had been substantially completed, and something vital had passed from American life.

6

Transformation and Complexity
The Changing City
1860-1910

Creation of new cities in undeveloped regions, rivalries among communities competing for urban supremacy, prophetic visions of America's urban future, and frenzied booms in town sites and urban land contributed fundamentally to the cultural drama of nineteenth-century America. But the rapid urbanization of the United States after 1860 involved much more than the establishment of individual cities and their organization in a complex inter-urban network. It also involved profound changes in the nature of the city itself and in the pattern of life in organized communities both urban and rural. By 1910 American culture can be said, in a number of senses, to have become urbanized, and this marked a significant change in the character of American society. During the fifty years from 1860 to 1910, American cities absorbed nearly a seven-fold increase in population, much of it in the larger cities; this striking demographic development was a concomitant

133

of radical institutional and technological changes that altered the social and physical environment and the way people were conditioned by that environment.

The accretion of urban population alone does not necessarily cause changes in the fundamental patterns of society. In fact, the growth of population and its spatial regrouping may in some circumstances be considered an element in social change independent of—but of course influenced by—levels of technology and industrialization. Tokyo, for example, grew to a city of a million in the middle of the nineteenth century but remained in organization a kind of extended town which functioned much as it had for centuries past; a similar point could be made about many of the large cities of Africa. But urbanization in a narrow demographic sense, when coupled as it was in America with an advanced level of technology and dynamic capitalistic institutions, provided a vital force in the transformation of society. In the nineteenth-century cities of the western world, specialization, variety, complexity, and regularity were substituted for the simplicities and lack of differentiation in earlier communities. Such fundamental human institutions as the household, the family, and the church underwent significant modification in the new environment. Observers, conditioned by the outlooks of the past, often found the city the site of social disorganization. But this disorganization was sometimes in reality only a complicated pattern of accommodation to the conditions of a new environment. As Oscar Handlin has observed, no earlier human experience had imposed the demands of the late nineteenth-century western city. Even the concept of time had to be altered. "The complex interrelationships of life in the modern city," Handlin writes, "called for unprecedented precision. The arrival of all those integers who worked together, from whatever part of the city they inhabited, had to be coordinated to the movement. There was no natural span for such labor; arbitrary beginnings and ends had to be set, made uniform and adhered to. The dictatorship of the clock and the schedule became absolute." By 1910 in urbanizing America, this new social order of the city was already being imposed on the country, and in large measure defined the character of a national culture.

The great increase in the population of American cities, which underlay these fundamental changes, was the result of population movement—of migration into cities from abroad and from the American countryside. Although the relationship between migration, birth and death rates, and urban growth cannot be examined historically with any precision, it seems reasonably certain that not until well into the twentieth century did city dwellers in America reproduce at replacement levels. Examination of this circumstance, however, is complicated by the fact that *migrants* to a city during a given period (the decennial federal census period constituting the ordinarily available span of measurement) did reproduce at a rate above replacement levels; therefore for a chosen period urban population would show a statistical natural increase. Special data available for the census period 1900–1910 suggests the characteristic demographic pattern in this era of rapid urbanization. Of 11,826,000 *new* city dwellers in 1910 some forty-one per cent were immigrants from abroad, 29.8 per cent were native rural-to-urban migrants, 21.6 per cent represented natural increase, and the remaining 7.6 per cent were the result of incorporation of new territories into existing cities. Virtually all demographic evidence indicates that the growth of cities in the period 1860 to 1910 was sustained by high birth rates on the farm, including the rural areas of Europe, and among people newly arrived in the city.

Although the mass migration of the polyglot peoples of Europe to America has rightly been viewed as one of the notable themes of the national experience, in examining urbanization demographically it is convenient to consider foreign migration as one aspect of a general movement of people from the farm to the city. Most European immigrants who came to the United States were rural dwellers, and when they arrived, they settled in the cities. The use of machinery in farming, the introduction of techniques of scientific agriculture, and the opening of new fertile areas of production in Argentina, Australia, and the American West improved the efficiency of agriculture and drove surplus workers from the soil. In the United States, the productivity of farm labor increased strikingly so that by the 1890's a much smaller work force than that of the 1830's could bring in even larger crops of many of the main agricultural products. For example, through the use of modern machines, the work of one man in a wheat field in 1896 could be more than eighteen times as effective as it had been in 1830. To the economic forces pushing people from the farms were added the pulls exerted by commercial and industrial demands for ever larger labor forces in the cities. As a result of the population movement encouraged by these developments, about eleven million of the forty-two million city dwellers of 1910 had come from American farm homes after 1880; it also seems fairly certain that at least one third of the total urban population of 1910 were American natives of rural origin. Migration to and from the United States, and the internal movement of immigrants, left a net total of over nine and a half million foreign born in American cities in 1910. The large numbers of people pouring into cities after 1860 forced striking changes in their function and organization. Both the European peasant and the American migrant from the farm faced the problem of adjusting to a new and rapidly changing environment, in which they were themselves a vital element in the process of change.

As early as the 1850's, spokesmen of the values of the country, such as Amory D. Mayo, had lamented the increasing movement of young people from the farm to the city and had noted the fundamental social change this movement was producing. By the 1860's the rural exodus was the subject of increasing attention. The *New York Times,* for example, complained in 1863 that the Civil War had accelerated rather than retarded urbanization: throughout the nation "the tide of population" was pouring toward the city "with undiminished impetuosity." Later in the decade, Horace Greeley emphasized the same theme: "We cannot all live in cities," he wrote, "yet nearly all seem determined to do so. . . . 'Hot and cold water,' baker's bread, gas, the theatre, and the streetcars . . . indicate the tendency of modern taste. Away behind these is the country. 'God made it.' The 'town' may have its allurements. Long valleys with independence and health whispering among the oaks and pines speak of a more vigorous race." Arthur M. Schlesinger, in his seminal study of the growth of urban America, has vividly described the "lure of the city" during the 1880's, a decade of prosperity and rapid urbanization. Although in this decade—as in every decade until the 1950's—non-urban population for the country as a whole increased absolutely, certain states and areas did show marked reductions. This selective depopulation intensified the alarm of the defenders of rural America against the wicked city. As a result of internal migration during the decade, forty per cent of the nation's 25,746 townships showed a decline in population. Portions of rural New England were particularly hard hit as nearly sixty per cent of the townships (932 of 1502) registered a drop. State studies recorded a wide-scale abandonment of farms— 3,300 in Maine, 1,500 in Massachusetts, 1,300 in New Hampshire, and, 1,000 in Vermont. In the rapidly urbanizing Midwest, there were similar pockets of rural decay. Portions of central Missouri, eastern Iowa, northern and western Illinois, and central and south-eastern Indiana were drastically depopulated, largely as a result of the movement of farmers to towns and cities. There were 7,500 fewer farmers in Michigan in 1890 than there had been ten years before, although the total population of the state grew by half a million. In Ohio 755 of 1,316 townships and in Illinois 800 of 1,424 decreased in population during the decade, though both states, like all midwestern states during the period, grew in total population.

The predominant urban trend of the period was not the result of individuals migrating directly from the isolated farm to the huge metropolis. More frequently, people moved from rural areas to a local hamlet, then to a town or regional city, and then perhaps to Chicago, New York, or another metropolis. Young men and women often moved from the small towns in which they had been born to the larger city. "The reasons that impelled a person to leave the farm to go to a crossroads village," Schlesinger writes, "were likely to cause the ambitious or maladjusted villager to re-move to a larger place, or might in time spur the transplanted farmer lad himself to try his fortunes in a broader sphere. The results were seen in the records of city growth. The pyramid of urban population enlarged at every point from base to peak, and the countryside found itself encroached upon by hamlet, town and city."

Hamlin Garland has vividly recorded the effects of this move-ment on individuals in describing the migrations of members of his family back and forth from farm to village to city. His work captures the feeling of rootlessness that resulted from the constant mobility so characteristic of American society in this era of migration. Late in his life, for example, Garland could sum up numerous advantages of big city life in New York, where he had settled with his family after a futile attempt to recapture the stability of the village environment in West Salem, Wisconsin. Yet, at the same time, he reflected disillusionment over something fundamental that had been lost: "No! I am not *entirely* content. Deep down in my consciousness is a feeling of guilt, a sense of disloyalty to my ancestors, which renders me uneasy. It may be that this is only a survival of the mental habit of my boyhood, a tribute to my father and his self-reliant generation." Although Garland and other writers expressed nostalgia about the land and a simpler past that probably mirrored a general cultural anxiety toward the complex new urban environment, Americans in the years 1860 to 1910 moved toward the place of opportunity and challenge—the city.

More dramatic in its effects than the "urban drift" of native population was the large scale settlement of European migrants in the cities of America. For this, in general, was a movement of people directly to the city—and predominately to the larger city. The report of the famous Dillingham Commission, which reflected a bias in favor of immigration restriction and hence drew too sharp a line between the effects of the "old" and the "new" immigration, found that in 1910 78.6 per cent of the more recent "new" immigrants from southern and eastern Europe lived in urban communities compared to 68.3 per cent of the old immigrants from northern and central Europe. Overall, about seventy-two per cent of the foreign born were classified as urban residents, compared to about forty-six per cent for the nation as a whole. Certain immigrant groups had a particularly high proportion of urban dwellers. Over five-sixths of the natives of Ireland and Russia lived in cities. The proportion was above seven-tenths for those born in England, Scotland, Austria, Greece and China; two-thirds for Germans; and three-fifths for Swedes. Only two nationalities—Montenegrins and Norwegians—had a lower percentage of city dwellers than did the population as a whole. In addition to their concentration in cities in general, immigrants also tended to live in larger cities, so that the percentage of foreign born increased directly with categories of city size in the 1910 census. The influx of immigrants to the cities, particularly during the decade of the 1880's when over five million arrived in the United States, produced some striking statistics for individual cities. In 1890, New York (including the still legally separate municipality of Brooklyn) contained more foreign born residents than any city in the world. The city had half as many Italians as Naples, as many Germans as Hamburg, twice as many Irish as Dublin, and two and a half times the number of Jews in Warsaw. In 1893, Chicago contained the third largest Bohemian community in the world; by the time of the First World War, Chicago ranked only behind Warsaw and Lodz as a city of Poles. Notable also was the fact that four out of five people living in greater New York in 1890 had either been born abroad or were of foreign parentage.

As a result of this influx, the residential areas of many larger cities began after 1860 to form a mosaic of immigrant neighborhoods and ethnic ghettos. Nationality groups tended to live in distinct areas of the city; when newcomers from another country or region began to arrive in a neighborhood, the older ethnic group moved elsewhere. New York's Lower East Side, for example, underwent an ethnic transformation in the years after the Civil War. The Irish and Germans, who had earlier lived in the district, went northward up Manhattan Island or to Brooklyn; Italians moved into the old Irish neighborhoods while Jews from Russia and Poland occupied the German districts. In Chicago during this era, Poles and Bohemians migrated into areas that had earlier been German, Scandinavian, and Irish in character. Contemporaries, particularly in commenting on New York, frequently used the metaphor of the multi-colored quilt to describe the complexity of population patterns in the late nineteenth century city. Jacob Riis, for example, in his famous *How the Other Half Lives* employed the technique: "A map of the city, colored to designate nationalities, would show more stripes than on the skin of a zebra, and more colors than any rainbow. The city on such a map would fall into great halves, green for the Irish prevailing in the West Side tenement districts, and blue for the Germans on the East Side. But intermingled with these ground colors would be an odd variety of tints that would give the whole the appearance of an extraordinary crazy-quilt. From down in the Sixth Ward, upon the site of

139

the old Collect Pond . . . the red of the Italian would be seen forcing its way northward along the line of Mulberry Street to the quarter of the French purple on Bleecker Street and South Fifth Avenue, to lose itself and reappear, after a lapse of miles, in the 'Little Italy' of Harlem, east of Second Avenue. Dashes of red, sharply defined, would be seen strung through the Annexed District, northward to the city line. On the West Side the red would be seen overrunning the old Africa of Thompson Street, pushing the black of the negro rapidly uptown, against querulous but unavailing protests, occupying his home, his church, his trade and all, with merciless impartiality."

Behind this kind of contemporary description and analysis was an assumption of ethnic "clannishness;" in general the new immigrant was regarded as more clannish than the old. Loyalty to the old country was associated with a reluctance of the immigrant to give allegiance to his adopted land—an unwillingness to become "Americanized." But in reality, the intense immigrant group loyalties that gave cohesiveness to the ethnic communities were often provincial rather than national. New York, for example, did not contain a "Little Italy" but rather a number of distinct groups of Italians—Neapolitans and Calabrians in the Mulberry Bend district; a group of Genoese on Baxter Street; north Italians in the Eighth and Fifteenth wards west of Broadway; and a small colony of Tyrolese Italians on Sixty-Ninth Street, near the Hudson River.

Still, for the most part, with the exception of the trade union, immigrant life was organized along lines of nationality, giving support to the argument that the "new immigration" represented a threat to established American culture. In the late nineteenth century, it was the presence of the urban colonies of immigrants from eastern and southern Europe in the larger metropolises, made up of people predominately Roman Catholic and Jewish in religion and differing in manner and appearance from older Americans, that stimulated renewed attack on the evil city. In this critique, "urbanism" was equated with ethnicity, only one characteristic— and in some respects a minor characteristic—of emerging urban life in America. Many interior cities, Kansas City and Indianapolis, for example, and most of the rapidly growing cities of the South, did not experience the influence of the immigrant colonies, and certainly urbanization involved a much broader process of social change than the mere acculturation of immigrants. Yet the immigrant did become a stock figure in statements of urban ideology. Those who attempted to formulate a cultural defense of the city and to advance a kind of counter-myth of the good city became imprisoned in the old view and tried too narrowly to define "urbanism" as a function of cultural and ethnic diversity. In short, much of the argument about the city in American life down to the present day has had only limited application to the whole of the American urban experience. "New York is not America," asserted Ford Maddox Ford; by the same token, the city where ethnic diversity flourished does not necessarily represent historical urban America.

Rather than to consider the color or the contributions of the urban immigrant, as has so frequently been done, it is perhaps more relevant to examine the influence of his arrival on patterns of urban life. The presence of ethnic groups in large numbers in many American cities did force institutional change and institutional adaptation. Immigrants were overwhelmingly peasants, but the village of Europe, which provided the primary means of organizing life in the homeland, could not be transplanted to the city, nor could it really be transplanted anywhere in America. Hence, as in so many areas of urban life, there was a series of makeshift responses: the boss-machine system provides the best known example, and the special parts played by the immigrant church and the immigrant press in the cities have been similarly well noted. But there are numerous other examples of special institutional forms. The immigrant bank, for example, frequently appeared in the urban colonies to serve the needs of newly arrived settlers. The bank received money for safekeeping and took care of sending funds abroad to relatives, but it also served as a kind of information bureau and clearinghouse where the immigrant could obtain information and business services. The mutual aid or fraternal benefit society, which had its origins in the traditional death and burial associations common in European countries, was found among most immigrant groups. Uncertainty of employment in American cities accentuated the need for mutual insurance, but many of the organizations performed other functions, often sup-

141

porting schools and cultural events. At first organized on a local basis, the mutual aid societies eventually were federated along nationality lines, in such organizations as the Order of Sons of Italy (1905), the Polish National Alliance (1880), and the Pan Hellenic Union (1907). A variety of philanthropic associations took root in the immigrant communities, many of them designed directly to help those who had just arrived in the United States. To cite just one example, the New York Hebrew Free Loan Society, organized in 1892, made interest free loans of from $10 to $200 to immigrants eager to set up independent businesses. The society's funds had grown to over $100,000 within little more than a decade, as grateful borrowers who had succeeded contributed to its capital. Cooperative societies, clubs, and stores (common among a number of Slavic groups); physical culture organizations; patriotic societies; the Greek and Turkish coffee houses, which served the function of the neighborhood tavern for those opposed to the use of alcohol, were all part of a complex institutional network providing means by which the immigrant could order his life in the American city.

Expanded population, and the character of this population, produced significant institutional change within American cities and provided a fundamental force altering the character of urban life. But migration to the city took place within a framework of technological change, which encouraged the movement of population at the same time it provided the means that made possible the accommodation of vast numbers of new urban dwellers. As Edward C. Kirkland has indicated, the building of American cities supplied a fundamental generative factor in the growth of the economy of the late nineteenth century. City building, in this period, substituted for the construction of a transportation network which had stimulated the creation of capital goods in an earlier era. To build cities on a new scale, and to order the movement within cities of vast numbers of new residents required a variety of new techniques and inventions. Fundamentally, of course, buildings in which people could live and work had to be provided. In fact, private expenditure for construction was the single most important contribution cities made to the economy in the late nineteenth century, as the dollar value of building permits (in terms of 1913 dollars) reached a peak in 1880 that was not again approached until 1925.

In cities where it was possible to spread outward conveniently, the wide-scale adoption of an innovation in building of the 1830's —the balloon frame—made possible the construction of individual houses and smaller buildings with the speed and economy necessary for the quick and orderly development of new cities and of new neighborhoods in established cities. This style of construction, developed by a Chicago carpenter-architect named Augustine Deodat Taylor, utilized 2″ by 4″ or 2″ by 6″ "studs" of sawed lumber nailed together as a frame for a building instead of relying on heavy timbers with mortised and tenoned joints for support as had earlier been the case. The balloon frame eliminated the need for a highly skilled carpenter and an army of assistants to lift the supporting timbers into place when a building was erected. "If it had not been for the knowledge of balloon frames," Solon Robinson, an Indiana agricultural spokesman, told a New York audience in 1855, "Chicago and San Francisco could never have arisen, as they did, from little villages to great cities in a single year. It is not only city buildings, which are supported by one another, that may be thus erected, but those upon the open prairie where the wind has a sweep from Mackinaw to the Mississippi, for there they are built, and stand as firm as any of the old frames of New England, with posts and beams sixteen inches square." The balloon frame, coupled with abundant timber resources and the development of efficient woodworking machinery, greatly enlarged the possibility of rapid city growth in America.

Opportunities for concentrated commercial and industrial activity in cities with growing and mobile populations also spurred innovations in non-residential building. As early as the 1840's, large cast-iron warehouses, some of which reached the height of eight stories, had been constructed in eastern cities to accommodate the demands of large-scale merchandising. A pioneer in the development of a functional type of commercial and industrial building suitable for the modern city was James Bogardus (1800–74), an ingenious inventor who began his career as a watchmaker and devised such items as an engraving machine which produced the first English postage stamps, a pencil with lead always sharp, and a deep-sea sounding machine. Turning his talents to architecture and engineering, Bogardus, in building a five-story factory in New

143

York in 1848, put into practice a system of construction that substituted cast-iron columns for load-bearing masonry walls as supports for floors. This lessened the need for thick, space-consuming masonry in erecting large buildings. Bogardus' system made practical the construction of just the kind of building demanded for business and industry in the large city—one that was externally compact with space secured through additional height and with its floors virtually unobstructed to house huge machines or large stores of merchandise. Bogardus and others carried his method of using cast-iron columns a step further to construct entire buildings of cast-iron. In the years 1850 to 1880 cast-iron business buildings became common in larger American cities; Bogardus built numerous warehouses, department stores, and office buildings in every section of the country and using prefabricated techniques that he had developed, even exported a building to Santiago, Cuba.

Bogardus argued in the early 1850's that cast-iron buildings could be erected to great heights and submitted a design for an exhibition building at the New York World's Fair of 1853 that envisaged construction of a circular amphitheater with sixty-foot high walls and a 300-foot tower rising from the center. Although such buildings might be built, in order for them to be practical for business purposes it was necessary to devise ways of transporting people efficiently to their higher stories. The idea of the elevator was an old one, and for some years various systems, often using horse power, had been utilized for hoisting merchandise to the tops of warehouses. Bogardus suggested a steam-powered hoist to carry passengers to an observation platform atop the tower of his proposed exhibition building, which was never constructed.

The "invention" of the elevator in reality consisted of a series of refinements on a well established principle. In the year Bogardus submitted his design—1853—Elisha G. Otis perfected a safety device to protect passengers from injury should the cable controlling a hoisting platform break while in operation; the first Otis elevator was installed in a New York store in 1857. Another system—designed by a Boston inventor and called a "Vertical Screw Railway"—was used in a New York hotel in 1859. With the introduction of hydraulic power and gearing techniques, the elevator became more efficient by the 1870's and with its adaptation to

144

electric power in the 1880's came into general use in cities. Through considerable evolution, a device had been developed to take advantage of the economies in intensive use of urban space. And a new urban experience was possible for visitors to the big city. "In the tall buildings are the most modern and rapid elevators," wrote Julian Ralph in his account of a tour of Chicago in the early 1890's, "machines that fly through the towers like glass balls from a trap at a shooting contest. The slow-going stranger, who is conscious of having been 'kneaded' among the streets, like a lump of dough among a million bakers, feels himself loaded into one of those frail-looking baskets of steel netting, and the next instant the elevator-boy touches the trigger, and up goes the whole load as a feather is caught up by a gale. The descent is more simple. Something lets go, and you fall from ten to twenty stories as it happens. There is sometimes a jolt, which makes the passenger seem to feel his stomach pass into his shoes, but, as a rule, the mechanism and management both work marvellously towards ease and gentleness. These elevators are too slow for Chicago, and the managers of certain tall buildings now arrange them so that some run 'express' to the seventh story without stopping, while what may be called accommodation cars halt at the lower floors, pursuing a course that may be likened to the emptying of the chambers of a revolver in the hands of a person who is 'quick on the trigger.' "

As Ralph's comment indicates, late nineteenth-century Chicago employed the elevator with great efficiency, for it was in the Windy City that the techniques for pushing buildings ever higher were first perfected. Here, in the 1880's, the modern skyscraper succeeded the cast-iron "cloud scraper." The need to rebuild Chicago after the 1871 fire, rapid growth, and rising land values encouraged experimentation in construction. The city moved toward tall buildings. In 1884 William Le Baron Jenney, in erecting the ten-story Mutual Savings Bank Building, used a steel skeleton as a frame without supporting walls for the upper portion of the building. Whether Jenney was forced to employ the technique as a result of a bricklayers' strike or whether, as legend has it, he was inspired to the experiment as a result of laying a book on Mrs. Jenney's wire birdcage is a question for architectural history. Nor is the

145

claim of the Minneapolis architect, Leroy S. Buffington, to having invented the steel frame before Jenney worthy of extended examination. As with any fundamental change in building methods, the steel frame was the result of an evolution of technological means, not of a sudden dramatic discovery. (Even a method as innovative as Taylor's balloon frame was dependent for its success on the mass production of nails.) Cast-iron columns and the iron skeleton developed by a French builder, Jules Saulnier, in 1871 were precursors of the American engineering triumph.

The new system of construction, fully utilized in Jenney's Leiter Building constructed in Chicago in 1889, has been vividly characterized by Lewis Mumford as "the iron cage and the curtain wall." "This," Mumford writes, "translated into colossal paleotechnic forms the vernacular frame and clapboard construction of the old American farmhouse. The outer wall became a mere boundary of the interior space . . .; instead of the building's being a shell, it became essentially a skeleton—a skeleton with internal organs for equalizing the temperature and for circulation, with a tough external skin." The steel frame greatly simplified difficult construction problems and proved an enormously efficient form for taking advantage of valuable urban land sites. Huge supporting walls that absorbed lower level space were no longer necessary in tall buildings. Innovations such as hollow tile for fire proofing and methods of speeding up construction such as the use of salt in brick mortar during freezing weather meant that skyscrapers could be quickly and efficiently erected. In the hands of Louis Sullivan and other members of the famous Chicago school of architecture, the new form could produce an architectural triumph such as the Guaranty Building (later the Prudential Building) constructed by Sullivan in 1895 in Buffalo, New York. But the skyscraper from the beginning contributed to greatly intensified land speculation and increasing traffic congestion, and, since human needs were subordinated to pecuniary considerations, to a frequent lack of daylight and adequate working space within buildings.

The skyscrapers were part of a new pattern of urban life based on specialization and the concentration of economic activity that necessitated great mobility on the part of city dwellers. The possibility of this mobility and the opportunities it created in the heart of

146

cities resulted from another series of technological developments involved in the evolution of an urban system of transportation. In this sector of urban activity, there has been a consistent technological lag—or what might be more properly termed a socio-technological lag—in that certain theoretical possibilities in urban transportation required changes in customary living patterns too drastic to be accepted and the movement of large numbers of people back and forth through the space of the city has never been efficient. Moreover, improvements in transportation—including even the ingenious system of railway electrification adopted by cities at the turn of the century—were in some ways self-defeating, since they stimulated further differentiation and specialization and, accordingly, further congestion. It is historically true, as well as true of our own time, that all new means of urban transportation were almost immediately utilized beyond their maximum effective capacity. As early as the 1850's travellers to New York were noting the frequency with which the "whole traffic of the city" came to a "dead-lock;" the "diurnal stampede" from office buildings to streetcars "loaded and incrusted with double burdens in which men clung to one another like caterpillars" was a standard part of the day in late nineteenth-century Chicago. In spite of the long-standing existence of the urban traffic problem, changes in urban transportation were fundamental in creating the spatial expansion and the specialization characteristic of the modern city.

Although American cities grew rapidly in population in the early nineteenth century, they were still, until about 1850, reasonably compact; a man might walk through all the neighborhoods of even the larger places in a day. Expanded population was absorbed through a more concentrated use of residential space near the sites of work; this caused a considerable increase in population density and a high degree of congestion in eastern seaboard cities. In the late 1820's, the introduction of the horse-drawn omnibus, carrying twelve to twenty passengers back and forth to areas outside of cities, had led to some differentiation in urban land use and the creation of distinct "downtown" districts to which people came from some distance to work or to shop. The steam railroad—almost from the beginning of its use in the United States—played a part in this development. In the 1840's eastern lines began hauling regular commuters from the large cities to neighboring towns. The Boston and West Newton Railroad, for example, reported in 1857 that during the year it had carried one-half million passengers between Boston and stations no farther than ten miles away. But large trains could not conveniently be utilized within the limits of cities themselves, and charters of railroads, though generous in extending right-of-way privileges through cities, generally forbade the use of steam locomotives on city thoroughfares. The horse-drawn railway provided the first real answer to the problem of large-scale movement of people within cities. The "horse-car" was invented in 1832 by James Stephenson, a New York carriage maker, but it was not until a rail that could be laid flush with a city street was devised in the late forties and early fifties that this system could be practically applied. In building horse-cars, Stephenson also perfected a number of necessary improvements in brakes and springs which were later used on motorized street-cars. The horse railway came into general use by the 1850's. By 1858, for example, the five principal street railways of New York City were carrying nearly 35,000,000 passengers a year. The Metropolitan Railroad Corporation of Boston, operator of the longest horse-drawn railroad in that city, transported nearly 6,500,000 people in 1860. Although Philadelphia had been slow to adopt the system, by 1860 the city had 148 miles of street railway—the greatest of any city. The street railways existed in combination with a variety of other forms of horse-drawn transportation; the resulting congestion was sometimes fantastic. In 1866 in New York there were seven omnibus lines with 300 cars on regular routes; sixteen horse-railway lines using 800 cars and nearly 8,000 horses; 1,400 hackney coaches; and a few odd hansom cabs. Traffic was frequently so dense that it was often easier to proceed on foot. "You cannot ride," wrote Mark Twain in 1867, "unless you are willing to go in a packed omnibus that labors, and plunges, and struggles along at the rate of three miles in four hours and a half, always getting left behind by fast walkers, and always apparently hopelessly tangled up with vehicles that are trying to get to some place or other and can't. Or if you can stomach it, you can ride in a horse-car and stand up for three-quarters of an hour, in the midst of a file of men that extends from front to rear (seats all crammed, of course,)—or you can take one of the platforms, if you please, but they are so crowded you will have to hang on by your eye-lashes and your toenails." The horse-car railway was dirty, slow, and not suitable for long distances. But the rail system was more efficient than any other form of urban transportation that used animal power. Accordingly, the horse-cars continued to spread. By 1880 they had appeared in most cities of over 50,000; in that year there were about 19,000 street cars in operation over 3,000 miles of track.

In the larger cities by the 1860's, inventors and engineers were seeking ways to take advantage for urban transport of the only other source of power available—steam. In 1864, Hugh B. Willson, who had studied the London underground opened the year before, organized a company with capital of $5,000,000 to build a New York City subway in which a railroad could be operated, but the bill for the franchise was defeated in the state legislature through the efforts of street-transit interests. The other obvious possibility was to elevate railroads above the street. No great technological problems were involved in laying tracks on pillars, but there was the danger, particularly acute in view of the frequency of train accidents, of trains jumping the tracks and hurtling to the pavement below. Despite this fear and despite the opposition of horse-car interests and property owners along the railroads, an elevated line was begun in New York in 1867 and finally completed in 1870. An elevated railroad was expensive to build, and hence suitable only for larger cities. It was also noisy and dirty; passing trains caused vibration for some distance and locomotives often scattered oil and hot ashes on pedestrians below. But, owing to the intense traffic problem of New York, the elevated proved successful. In 1878, a second line—the Sixth Avenue Elevated— was added to the original, which initially ran from the foot of the island up Ninth Avenue to Thirtieth Street and had later been extended as far as Fifty-ninth Street. Three years later, the New York "L's" were hauling 175,000 passengers a day. New lines were built and extended across the Harlem River into the northern suburbs. The system spread to other cities. Kansas City and Brooklyn built elevated lines in the 1880's, and Chicago constructed its system early in the next decade. But by this time, it

149

had become clear that in larger cities such as New York and Chicago the capacity of elevated railroads was too limited. Trains were being run as close together as safety permitted. To employ faster or longer trains would require larger locomotives and expensive reconstruction of the elevated structures. It was virtually impossible to build new lines, since by the 1890's municipal leaders were unwilling to extend additional franchises owing to popular opposition to further extension of a noisy and dirty system of transportation.

In the meantime, another innovation in urban transportation, the cable car, came into use in American cities. Developed by a Scotch immigrant named Andrew Smith Hallidie, the cable car utilized an endless cable attached to a stationary steam engine as motive power. A grappling device suspended below the car passed through a slot running down the center of the railway where it was attached to the cable. The cable car system, which essentially involved a kind of towing operation, was particularly suitable for cities with sharp street grades such as San Francisco, where it was first employed. It also offered the advantage of speed—a ten-mile-per-hour average speed was easily attainable compared to a maximum average speed of about six miles per hour for horse railways. Under ordinary circumstances, the cable car was about twice as fast as the horse railway. Primarily because of this advantage, it was adopted in a number of cities including Chicago, New York, and Philadelphia. By the middle of the 1890's eastern cities had 157 miles of cable lines in operation, the Middle West 252, and the Far West 217. But the cable car system soon proved to have a number of serious disadvantages—its installation costs were high; there was no possibility of making up time or of varying service at busy hours on a line since all cars had to travel at the same rate of speed; and dangerous mechanical breakdowns were frequent. As a consequence, cable cars were never in use in more than fifteen of the larger cities, and in these only in the downtown areas.

The major technological breakthrough in urban transportation was provided by the application of electric power. The development of the trolley and the electrified railroad constitutes one of the important chapters in the history of American technology and indicates how profoundly the requirements of the city affected the patterns of American science and invention. The challenge of the problem of urban transportation and the profits to be realized from successful innovations stimulated extraordinary effort on the part of individual inventors and manufacturing firms. As early as the late 1830's inventors had started experimenting with vehicles run by electric motors. But it was not until the development of the dynamo in the 1870's that the possibility could be practically considered; until that time the only source of current available was the battery, and power from this source was over twenty times as expensive as that furnished by a steam engine. Nearly a decade of effort went into the solution of the major problems of electric traction; the problems defeated even the inventive mind of Thomas A. Edison.

A satisfactory system, which utilized the results of the experimentation of the preceeding years, was finally devised by Frank Julian Sprague, an Annapolis graduate and a practical engineer, who had worked for Edison and then had gone into business for himself organizing the Sprague Electric Railway and Motor Company in 1884. In 1887 Sprague accepted a contract to build an electrified street railway in Richmond, Virginia and the twelve-mile line over which forty cars were operated was completed the next year. Sprague's system, which used current from a central power source passed to the trains through an overhead wire, embodied a score or more of highly technical features that became standard in street railway operation. But to construct the system had required almost superhuman effort; it eventually cost twice as much as Sprague was paid on his contract. Ten years later, he calmly reflected on the difficulties: "When the Richmond contract was signed, we had only a blueprint of a machine and some rough experimental apparatus. The hundred and one details that were essential to success were as yet undetermined. Fortunately for the future of electric railways, the difficulties ahead could not be foreseen or the contract would not have been signed." But his system was an immediate success, and he made up his financial losses many times over through the sale of equipment. By 1890 fifty-one cities had installed trolley systems; five years later 850 were in operation with lines totalling 10,000 miles. The suitability of the new system of urban transportation was demonstrated most clearly by the rapidity with which it replaced horse-car lines. In 1890, 69.7 per cent of the total trackage in cities was operated by horses; by 1902 this figure had declined to 1.1 per cent, while electric power was used on 97 per cent of the mileage.

Sprague made a second major technological contribution to urban transportation when he designed a complex multiple-unit system of control that provided the means by which elevated steam railroads could be efficiently electrified. This innovation encouraged the building of another means of urban transportation, the subway, since one of the principal objections to underground railroads had been the accumulation of gas, smoke, and dirt resulting from the operation of steam locomotives in confined tunnels. But with electrification this problem could be eliminated. Between 1895 and 1897 Boston constructed an underground line a mile and a half long at a cost of four and a quarter million dollars. New York followed with an even more ambitious tunnel system opened in 1904, which ran from City Hall on the south to 145th Street on the north.

During the years in which systems of transportation were being established within cities, engineers also worked out the principles and techniques to build the bridges that would link parts of the expanding cities separated by rivers and harbors. Much of the necessary technology was developed during the construction of railroad bridges across the major interior rivers: Octave Chanute, who bridged the Missouri at Kansas City in 1869, and James B. Eads, whose famous bridge across the Mississippi at St. Louis was completed in 1874, produced the significant innovations through which piers could be put down in deep, swift flowing water. These two railroad bridges, and those across the Missouri linking Council Bluffs to Omaha and at Cincinnati across the Ohio, were utilized for ordinary traffic in expanding urban areas. The first large bridge financed by municipal funds was constructed across the Schuylkill at Philadelphia in 1863; for many years this cast-iron structure remained the most distinctive of the American bridges. But it was eclipsed by the famous Brooklyn Bridge, which realized an old dream of American inventors and engineers and which became a cultural symbol of national growth, progress, and power. "You see great ships passing beneath it," wrote the French traveller, Paul Bourget, "and this indisputable evidence of its height confuses the mind. But walk over it, feel the quivering of the monstrous trellis of iron and steel interwoven for a length of sixteen hundred feet at a height of one hundred and thirty-five feet above the water; see the trains that pass over it in both directions, and the steamboats passing beneath your very body, while carriages come and go, and foot passengers hasten along, an eager crowd, and you will feel that the engineer is the great artist of our epoch, and you will own that these people have a right to plume themselves on their audacity, on the *go-ahead* which has never flinched."

Brooklyn Bridge was a magnificent engineering achievement that required thirteen years to complete. Its designer, John A. Roebling, died from a tetanus infection after an injury suffered while returning by ferry from the bridge site before construction had even begun. His son, Washington A. Roebling, carried on the project despite a serious attack of the bends that left him crippled. He was forced to direct construction from his sick bed while his wife using field-glasses helped oversee operations. But despite difficulties and accidents that took twenty lives, the project was completed, and the bridge was formally opened on May 24, 1883 with a great celebration attended by President Chester Arthur, his cabinet, and a number of governors. It was the longest suspension bridge in the world —over a mile long with a passageway wide enough for two railroad lines, two double carriage lanes, and a footpath. Other cities also built major bridges during the period. Pittsburgh bridged the Allegheny River, Rochester the Genessee Gorge, Boston the Charles River, and St. Paul and Minneapolis the Mississippi. By the later part of the century, the suspension principle of the Brooklyn Bridge was frequently employed—in the Williamsburg Bridge over the East River in New York; in the Grand Avenue bridge in St. Louis over railroad yards; and in the bridge across the bay at Galveston, Texas. By 1909, this era of bridge building had produced 365 bridges over 500 feet in length, greatly facilitating the possibilities of movement in the growing urban regions.

The system of urban transportation developed in this period permitted American cities to spread out and maintain their functional identities rather than to fragment into a number of distinct urban units. For example, had the electrified railway not succeeded the horse-car when it did, it is possible that an independent metropolis would have developed to the north of New York, because by the 1880's travel time for those who poured into lower Manhattan each day had about reached its limit. Population densities had also reached a near maximum point in some sections of the larger cities, but the innovations in transportation permitted enough movement to outlying residential areas to relieve the most intense pressure. At the close of the century—a time when the suburbanization movement was viewed with a great deal of enthusiasm—an observer accurately described past and future patterns: "When a pair of legs was the only vehicle of locomotion which the ordinary man could afford, large cities were unavoidably compressed into very small quarters. The horse-car and the bus added a mile or two to this area, but did not dispense with the necessity of severely economizing space. The trolley has stretched it out several miles further, while future improvements in the machinery of transit may well make any spot within fifty miles of the center of an important city available as a place of residence for its wage earners. The extent to which the urban population may be distributed will be restricted only be the means of transit."

From the beginning of the growth of towns and cities in the United States, the possibility of combining the benefits of the country with the advantages of the city—the "happy union of urbanity and rusticity"—had been a part of the American conception of community. The village of Brooklyn early in the nineteenth century provided a place where New Yorkers could escape the city; a Brooklyn real estate man in 1823 advertising lots on Brooklyn Heights encouraged this possibility in very modern terms: "Situated directly opposite the s-w part of the city, and being the nearest country retreat, and easiest of access from the centre of business that now remains unoccupied; the distance not exceeding an average fifteen to twenty-five minutes walk, including the passage of the river; the ground elevated and perfectly healthy at all seasons; views of water and landscape both extensive and beautiful; as a place of residence all the advantages of the country with most of the conveniences of the city. . . . Gentlemen whose business or profession require their daily attendance in the city, cannot better,

154

or with less expense, secure the health and comfort of their families, than by uniting in such an association." A Cincinnati handbook in 1851 utilized considerable space in describing the advantages of suburban life in areas "unsurpassed for healthfulness, removed from the smoke and dust of the city, enjoying pure air and wholesome water." By the 1870's, Chicago promoters could claim the existence of nearly one hundred suburbs, with an aggregate population of 50,000, located along the railroads running from the city and offering the charms of "pure air, peacefulness, quietude, and natural scenery."

Although the rural ideal was always influential in American life, only the very wealthy were able to maintain homes away from the heart of cities until the coming of the horse-car lines in the late 1850's, and even then only a few people lived any substantial distance from the sites of work. In a meticulous and unique case study of three towns near Boston—Roxbury, West Roxbury, and Dorchester—that became late nineteenth century "streetcar suburbs," Sam B. Warner, Jr. has described the pattern of the outward movement of people in relation to changing systems of transportation. Boston, he points out, was still a walking city in 1850 with dense settlement extending outward only within a two-mile radius of city hall; a small minority of the rich maintained country cottages and estates some distance away. Horse railroads pushed settlement outward only about another half-mile by 1873 and about another mile and a half by 1887, extending the edge of dense settlement to about four miles from city hall. In the late 1880's and early 1890's, electrification pushed the area of convenient transportation six miles outward. It was in this latter period, that the three communities became genuine suburbs; virtually all the new buildings constructed were individual residences. As a result of the suburban growth of the three towns and in other directions as well, by 1900 the character of Greater Boston had been transformed. Great expanses of land had become urban. The three communities composed only the southern segment of metropolitan Boston, but their combined area of twenty-five and a quarter square miles was more than double that of the original city in 1850.

Moreover, the population growth had been striking. In 1870, after about fifteen years of the horse-car lines, the population of the three towns combined was 60,000. In 1900, the figure was 227,000 —a growth rate comparable in order of magnitude to that of San Francisco. If the three communities had been counted together as a single city, it would have ranked above Minneapolis, Louisville, and Jersey City in population and just below Newark and Washington. During the thirty years after 1870, more than 22,500 new houses were constructed in the three towns, providing living space for 167,000 suburbanites.

By examining 28,000 building permits and a variety of other records, Warner has been able to determine just what groups actually moved to these new suburban areas, and the Boston experience was probably reasonably typical of other large American cities during the period. Predominately, the suburbanites were from the upper half—perhaps the upper forty per cent—of Boston society in wealth. The suburbs were rather rigidly segregated into three economic classes—the wealthy five per cent, the central middle class of fifteen per cent, and the lower middle class of twenty to thirty per cent. The varying incomes and the different transportation needs of the three groups were reflected in large areas of similarly priced residences. In a number of respects the Boston suburbs were drab and monotonous. Architecture was undistinguished; each house looked much like the one next to it—not through municipal zoning measures or building codes, which were virtually nonexistent at the time, but through the natural tendency of an individual to build about what his neighbor had. There was little civic vitality, little diversity of life. But in spite of this, the Boston suburbs were a source of great contemporary pride. Buildings were new, and the area was bright, clean, and healthy. In commenting on the character of the Boston suburbs, Warner has perceptively indicated the often neglected, and in our day frequently maligned, positive side of the suburban experience in American life: "To be sure, the costs of new construction were such as to exclude at least half the families of Boston; but the suburban half, the middle class, was the dominant class in the society. To middle class families the suburbs gave a safe, sanitary environment, new houses in styles somewhat in keeping with their conception of family life, and temporary neighborhoods of people with similar outlook. In an atmosphere of rapid change, the income-graded neighborhoods rendered two important services to their residents. Evenness of wealth meant neighbors who would reinforce an individual family's effort to pass on its values to its children. The surrounding evenness of wealth also gave adults a sense of a community of shared experience, and thereby gave some measure of relief from the uncertainties inherent in a world of competitive capitalism.

"In addition to benefitting their own residents, in one important way the suburbs served the half of Boston's population which could not afford them. The apparent openness of the new residential quarters, their ethnic variety, their extensive growth, and their wide range of prices from fairly inexpensive rental suites to expensive single-family houses—these visible characteristics of the new suburbs gave aspiring low-income families the certainty that should they earn enough money they too could possess the comforts and symbols of success. Even for those excluded from them, the suburbs offered a physical demonstration that the rewards of competitive capitalism might be within the reach of all."

During the latter part of the nineteenth century, particularly after the advent of the street car, most larger American cities reflected Boston's experience and began to develop extensive residential suburbs. In Milwaukee, to use an interior city as an example, considerable outward spread began to occur by the middle 1880's. Older communities, such as the village of Humboldt, were swept into the expanding city. Other communities were able to maintain their identity as part of the metropolis. The hamlet at Oak Creek, founded in 1835, was subjected to development by the South Milwaukee Company; the Milwaukee Street Railway Company reached the community in 1896, and in the same year South Milwaukee was incorporated as a city. To the west, by the middle 1880's, the village of Hart's Mill had become the thriving suburb of Wauwatosa, "the city of homes," with "no factories to speak of," "no smoke to contend with in any form," "an ideal place in which to rear a family having the best possible schools." To the north, exclusive residential communities were being developed in the 1890's at Shorewood and Whitefish Bay. Industrial suburbs such as West Allis and Cudahy were also growing rapidly. As a result of the suburban trend, the population of the city itself was spread out

157

over a much wider area by 1900. In 1880 around thirty-four per cent of the city's population lived within one mile of the business center at the corner of Third Street and Wisconsin Avenue; by 1900 the percentage had dropped to less than seventeen. In 1880 only 17.4 per cent of the population of Milwaukee lived more than three miles from the business district; by 1900 the figure had risen to nearly thirty-one per cent.

A southern city, Norfolk, was also transformed by the street car in this period. Inspired by the example of neighboring Richmond, where Sprague had introduced his system, local horse-car companies began under public pressure to electrify their roads. The first trolley line went into operation on October 17, 1894 and within a decade the system reached a ring of suburbs—Sewells Point, Ocean View, Willoughby Spit, South Norfolk, Berkley, Portsmouth, and Pinner's Point. A real estate company purchased a tract of farm land and within a short time converted it into the suburb of Ghent, one of the city's most exclusive residential areas. By 1893 only about twenty houses had been erected or were in the process of being erected in the area; within a decade the former piece of farm land had been completely built up. Other outlying areas around the city experienced similar development; as a consequence the area of Norfolk was soon three times as large as it had been before the coming of the street car.

The effect of this movement of people to the suburbs on the growth of cities themselves is difficult to evaluate, since it introduces the problematic consideration of what might have happened had efficient devices of urban transportation not been developed when they were. Late nineteenth century observers had high hopes that suburbanization would provide the means of relieving congestion in cities. Adna F. Weber, the most systematic and the most able nineteenth century student of demography, concluded his monumental 1899 study of city growth with an optimistic forecast: "The 'rise of the suburbs' it is, which furnishes the solid basis of hope that the evils of city life, so far as they result from over-crowding, may be in large part removed. If concentration of population seems destined to continue, it will be a modified concentration, which offers the advantages of both city and country life." Carroll D. Wright, United States Commissioner of Labor in

158

the early nineties, found some evidence on the basis of governmental examination of the slums that congestion was lessening, and Weber, after careful study of New York population statistics for the early nineties, concluded that, with the exception of the wards of the city occupied by the most recently arrived immigrants, the congested districts of New York were losing population. It is clear that suburbanization enabled rapidly growing cities to mitigate the worst aspects of high concentration of population. Moreover, the development may have prevented eastern cities from reaching a kind of "saturation point" in growth. On the other hand, as Warner's careful study of Boston indicates, movement to the suburbs was possible only for a limited part of the urban population. The suburban pattern of life was not in accord with the notions of community brought over by many immigrant groups, but whatever their sentiments might be, well over half the people in cities, and the great bulk of the immigrants, were unable to move to the suburbs for economic reasons. The poorer districts of many cities continued to show an increase in density of population even after the general introduction of street cars. The notorious Tenth Ward of New York, which increased in population density from 432 an acre in 1880 to 747 an acre in 1898, was quite possibly the most crowded district in the world by the turn of the century. One block, not the most crowded, had a population of 2,781, and in a large section of the ward the concentration was at the rate of over 1,700 to the acre. Overall, the population density of New York in the early nineties was at the reasonable figure of 58.7, but this was misleading since the density below the Harlem River, the urbanized part of the city where the vast majority of New Yorkers lived, was up to 143.2 per acre in 1894—a figure substantially above that for such compactly built European cities as Paris (126.9 residents per acre) and Berlin (100.8 residents per acre). Other American cities did not experience this problem to anywhere near the degree of New York, but nonetheless congestion elsewhere was considerable. In 1890, for example, one-fourth of the wards in seven of the ten largest cities had high densities of more than one hundred people per acre.

The accommodation of larger numbers of people within cities required new methods of housing and stimulated innovations in building. Annual returns of from ten to twelve per cent were common on rental property, and an annual return as high as forty per cent possible. Most city dwellers rented their living quarters in the nineteenth century—in 1890 the percentage in cities above 100,000 was over seventy-seven. A number of cities exceeded this percentage: New York 93.67 (with Greater New York about 85), Brooklyn 81.44, Jersey City 81.20, Boston 81.57 were the highest. Rochester (56.02) and Milwaukee (57.87) had the lowest percentage of renters of the larger American cities. The importance of urban land rents—which Henry George among others found the key to the economic problems of American society—encouraged property owners to make the maximum use of valuable urban land sites. Since the few building regulations in effect before 1900 were seldom stringent, experimentation in housing consisted largely of finding methods of using available space up to its limits.

Urban building styles throughout the country varied according to the topography of the individual city, the kind of urban transportation system and the timing of its building, and local custom. In Philadelphia and Baltimore, where the tradition of home ownership was relatively strong, row houses were common, and mile after mile of these extended toward the suburbs. Boston and Newark utilized the four-story "three-decker," which acquired its name from the three wooden galleries or "decks," built one above the other initially at the front and in later years at the rear of the building. Three-deckers were particularly appropriate along horse-car lines, where the lower floor of a building was often converted to business use. Chicago and St. Louis constructed two- and three-deckers in almost solid rows greatly increasing the population density of the two cities toward the close of the century.

New York builders and landowners, facing the enormous demand for housing caused by the arrival of immigrants in great numbers and operating under the circumstances of the city's unusual topography, evolved the most ingenious—and by the standards of our day the most inhumane—methods of crowding people together on a limited amount of space. In the 1850's and 60's the older converted structures, which had first accommodated the new arrivals, were torn down and rebuilt as tenements. (Initially, the word "tenement" was used to apply to any multiple family rental

160

building, and New York law defined the tenement house as a unit occupied by more than three families. Later the word was generally applied to any residential building in a slum.) One of the first large tenements, built in 1850, was hailed by civil leaders as a "praiseworthy enterprise and well worthy of imitation." The *Evening Post* commented favorably on the project: "It is built with the design of supplying the laboring people with cheap lodgings, and will have many advantages over the cellars and other miserable abodes, which too many are forced to inhabit. The depth of the building is two hundred and forty feet, with a front of thirty-five feet. Each tenement consisting of two rooms and a hall, is nearly eighteen feet in width, and about twenty feet in length giving twenty-four residences to each floor." Within a few years, flimsily constructed, three- and four-story "railroad" tenements, with closet-like rooms and dark interior bedrooms, had sprung up throughout the lower part of the city. One of the larger of the new barracks-like structures was located at Number 36 Cherry Street and was called Gotham Court. The building was five stories high, thirty-four feet wide, and ran back from the street 234 feet between two alleys. Twelve doors opened onto the wider of the two alleys, and each door provided entry for the ten families living in each section of the building—two families to a floor in identical two-room apartments, with a main room about 15 by 9½ and a bedroom about 15 by 8½. The structure housed around 500 people without provision for plumbing or heat. Ten years later a row of privies had been placed in the basement, but by then more than 800 people had crowded into the structure. An 1865 report of the Council of Hygiene, one of the early New York housing reform groups, argued that Gotham Court represented "about an average specimen of tenant-houses in the lower part of the city in respect to salubrity" and asserted that there were many more "in far worse condition." The Council counted 15,511 tenements in 1864, housing approximately 500,000 of New York's 800,000 people. The Council also found 15,000 people still residing in basements and cellars.

In these circumstances, it is not surprising that the infamous dumb-bell tenement, which came into use in the late 1870's, was greeted by housing reformers as a major improvement. The dumb-bell, an American contribution to world building styles, was encouraged by the Tenement House Law of 1879 enacted by the New York legislature which required a window in the bedrooms of newly built tenements. The structure acquired its name from the indentation at its middle which, combined with indentation of the tenement built up against it on the adjoining lot, formed an air-shaft usually about five feet wide. The air-shaft provided a small measure of light and ventilation for interior rooms, and gave the plan of an individual tenement the appearance of a dumb-bell. The dumb-bell tenement was a very efficient structure designed specifically to take advantage of the standard sized 25 by 100 New York lot. It was usually built to five or six stories, and contained fourteen rooms to a floor—seven on each side running from the front to the rear of the lot. One family occupied the four rooms to the front, another the three to the rear, thus providing space for four families to a floor. With ten tenements on a block, quite ordinary blocks of dumb-bells contained as many as 4,000 people. By the time significant legislation regulating housing was passed in 1901, the dumb-bell had spread over New York "like a scab." This kind of housing, occupied chiefly by immigrants, lay at the heart of one of the chief concerns of late nineteenth century urban reformers—the slum problem. By 1900 the number of tenements in Manhattan had increased to 42,700, and they housed 1,585,000 people, an average of 33.58 people per building. Although no American city was comparable to New York in regard to congestion, slum areas had spread in numerous cities—Cleveland, Boston, Cincinnati, and Chicago, for example. In spite of the establishment of fairly stringent building codes in the early part of the twentieth century, slums would continue to grow until at least the time of the New Deal when a number of housing reforms including slum clearance may have checked their further enlargement.

New ways of building within cities, no matter how unsatisfactory the social results might be, and improved transportation, which enabled some people to move outward, permitted cities to keep expanding their population and enlarging their land area. But in order for these late nineteenth century agglomerations to continue to function as cities, something else was vital—improved communication. The telegraph had earlier provided the kind of information system that enabled cities to become tied together in national and international networks. But it could not be the means for relaying large amounts of complex information back and forth within cities. Free urban mail delivery was established in New York in 1863 and gradually extended to other cities, but again this system was not efficient enough to unify the large city. "You can send a letter to Boston, or Albany, or Chicago," a New York writer commented in 1869, "with a tolerable certainty of its reaching its destination. But if you mail a missive from your office in Pine or William Street to your friend in Gramercy Park, or Lexington Avenue . . . the chances of its ever being heard from are slight. The time usually occupied *in transitu* between 'down' and 'uptown' is 24 hours to 24 days." The answer to the urban communication problem was supplied, of course, by the development of the telephone. First demonstrated by Alexander Graham Bell in practical form at the Philadelphia Centennial Exposition in 1876, the telephone remained a scientific toy until it was subjected to a number of improvements and ways were devised to utilize it in a system. The carbon transmitter, the elimination of wire noises by a metallic-circuit system, the central switchboard, and the multiple switchboard were essential for the functioning of the instrument as an urban communication device. In 1880, 148 telephone companies in eight-five cities had obtained only about 48,000 subscribers, but with consolidation of small competitors, the service spread rapidly. By 1900 nearly 800,000 phones were in use—one for every ninety-five persons in the country. The telephone made possible rapid communication throughout the sprawling urban areas and also proved a force in breaking down the isolation of the countryside.

In addition to the fundamental improvements in transportation and communication, a number of other technological developments were significant in shaping the morphology of American cities. Considerable experimentation with paving materials and techniques—including the use of brick, granite blocks, and wood —culminated in the use of efficient asphalt paving, which proved particularly suitable for the bicycle and the automobile. Invention also provided new ways of lighting the city. The electric carbon arc-lamp, utilized as part of an efficient system by Charles F. Brush

163

1879, provided a method of outdoor lighting much more satisfactory than the earlier gas and kerosene lamps. The incandescent electric lamp was demonstrated by Thomas Edison in 1879—one of the best known episodes in the history of American invention. But an even more important step in the development of electric lighting for cities was the establishment of the first central power station at Menlo Park in 1882. Complex new generators, meters, and conductors had to be devised for the experiment; its success demonstrated that electric lighting could be utilized for commercial purposes. Although an improved gas lamp developed in Europe in 1885 and patented in the United States in 1890 gave the gas-light industry renewed temporary vigor, the electric light in the long run proved the satisfactory device for illuminating the large city. The working day in business offices could now be lengthened, factories could be operated around the clock, and the night-time recreational activities of cities could be greatly expanded.

In view of the enormous health problems that resulted from the increased density of population in cities, new methods of removing waste and new methods of ensuring a pure water supply represented one of the more significant areas of technological change. Although the general relationship between unsatisfactory sewage disposal, water contamination and many diseases, such as typhoid fever and cholera, which decimated urban dwellers, was understood by European scientists in the 1860's and supported by many American public-health leaders, these contamination theories and the subsequent germ theory were not accepted widely enough to lead to any public demand for significant changes in methods of waste disposal. People continually complained about dirty water, but the specific health dangers of dirty water were not fully appreciated until the 1890's. The few miles of sewer that had been built in New York, Boston, Chicago, and a few other places proved completely inadequate in the face of the rapid growth of the 1870's. And most cities in the 1870's still used the old methods of private vaults and cesspools. In 1877, for example, Philadelphia had 82,000 vaults and cesspools, Washington had 56,000, and Chicago, despite its sewer system, 30,000. Chicago in 1871 had engaged in a large engineering project, headed by Ellis S. Chesbrough who had studied the sewer systems of European cities, to reverse the direction of the Chicago River, into which the city's sewers emptied, so that it discharged into the Illinois River rather than Lake Michigan. But this project had little effect. "The river stinks," commented the Chicago *Times* in 1880. "The air stinks. People's clothing, permeated by the foul atmosphere stinks. . . . No other word expresses it so well as stink. A stench means something finite. Stink reaches the infinite and becomes sublime in the magnitude of odiousness." Eventually the whole water supply and sewerage system of Chicago had to be drastically re-engineered.

Ironically, much of the advance in establishing better sewage facilities resulted from the agitations of an individual who tenaciously clung to older theories of disease and denounced the scientifically correct germ theory. George E. Waring, Jr., a scientific farmer, writer, and engineer, who achieved national attention as New York's Commissioner of Street Cleaning from 1895 to 1898, launched a crusade in the 1870's against America's inadequate sewerage methods. A contemporary commented that Waring made people so aware of the dangers to health from "sewer gas" that they "feared it perhaps more than they did the Evil One."

Waring was a vigorous anti-contagionist who accepted the idea that disease was the result of filth. He substituted "sewer gas" for the miasma which environmentalists had utilized as a disease-causing mechanism in earlier periods. In an 1878 essay, Waring argued persuasively that not only typhoid fever but most communicable diseases were the result of filth and decay. Outbreaks of disease, he argued, could often be traced to a foul-smelling house drain or the nearness of a drainage ditch. The poison itself might be the result of "the exhalations of decomposing matters in dung-heaps, pigsties, privy vaults, cellars, cess-pools, drains, and sewers; or it may be due . . . to the development of the poison deep in the ground, and its escape in an active condition in ground exhalations." To prevent disease-causing bad air, household sanitary fixtures were necessary, and whole communities would have to be systematically cleansed.

When a severe yellow-fever epidemic struck Memphis in 1878 killing nearly 5,000 people, Waring asserted that the epidemic was the result of the incredibly filthy condition of the city. As a consequence of the attention his argument received, Waring was hired to build a sewer system for Memphis in 1880. His well-advertised efforts in no way prevented yellow fever, which in its etiology is unrelated to filth, but they set off a general campaign in American cities to build sewers. By the earlier years of the twentieth century, especially after the real cause of yellow fever, the last of the mysterious epidemic diseases, had been established by the experiments of Walter Reed and others in Cuba, the germ theory of disease won general acceptance. City leaders, recognizing that typhoid in particular could be prevented, moved to ensure good sewage disposal systems and a pure water supply through tapping distant new sources and through techniques of filtration and purification. By 1910, over ten million urban residents drank filtered water which helped to cut the death rate at least a fifth in New York, Philadelphia, Boston, and New Orleans. Although cities were never able to solve the problem of pollution, at least the danger was recognized, so that technological means could be devised to combat it.

Thus between 1860 and 1910 technology and migration, in a national context of rapid economic growth, had drastically altered the American urban environment. The process of change had called forth corresponding institutional and organizational modication. While the widely advertised cultural institutions of the city— museums, theaters, art galleries—did not change significantly even as their clienteles expanded, the fabric of individual life was rewoven by urbanization as ways of work, patterns of family life, and modes of recreation were shaped to the new environment. Urbanization during these years contributed a a variety of political and social problems which had become national concerns by the turn of the century. In addition, the foundations had been laid for a whole series of new economic relationships, both within the individual cities and among them in the urban network, which were to mature in metropolitan America of the twentieth century.

7

The Web
of Government

Most students have concluded that, judged by standards of efficiency, cost, and service, American cities in the colonial period were well governed. As late as 1830, Alexis de Tocqueville considered local self-government one of the mainstays of personal freedom and independence in America. Lord Bryce, on the other hand, Tocqueville's great successor as a foreign interpreter of this country, argued in 1889 that city government was the one conspicuous failure of the American experiment. Many Americans agreed; cosmopolitan and well-informed Andrew D. White reflected a common view in his frequently quoted remark that American cities were the worst-governed in Christendom. Appalled at the spectacle of city administration and politics, increasing numbers of concerned citizens began to cast about for means of reform. Within a generation they had substantially changed the structure and much of the practice of city government in the United States.

The deterioration which began after the Revolution and the reform movement which began to attract widespread attention in the mid-1880's can both be understood as consequences of accelerating urbanization—and rapid industrialization—occurring in a culture where government was often regarded with suspicion. In part, the problems of city government were simply the result of growth. Governmental structures that had been adequate for cities of 25,000 or fewer inhabitants were strained beyond their capacities as the great nineteenth century urban agglomerations grew. But despite the obvious need there was no real effort to rebuild city government until the end of the century. Meanwhile, municipal administration in the United States which had once compared well with its European counterpart compared badly with that counterpart after a century of growth on both sides of the ocean.

In colonial times the power to incorporate towns and cities had, of course, resided ultimately in Parliament or in the crown. Although this power had on occasion been delegated to proprietors, and had been exercised—with or without delegation—by provincial assemblies, a central authority co-ordinated developments to some extent and might have co-ordinated them still more effectively. In the United Kingdom this was done through the great Municipal Incorporations Act passed by Parliament in 1835. Basic uniformity of administrative structure, along with an important measure of home rule, was thereby assured for British cities. By this time diversity, along with loss of much local initiative, had begun to characterize American cities.

The power to grant municipal charters passed from the British Government into the hands of the newly independent states. No one seriously argued that this power should be given to or even shared with the federal government, either under the Articles of Confederation or under the Constitution. The states delegated no municipal authority to the federal government with the exception of the provision for a national capital. Even in the territories the supervision of new towns was a responsibility of the territorial legislatures and not of Congress. Theoretically, there might have been a question whether the executives or the legislatures of the states would assume this particular power, but in the midst of the revulsion from strong executive authority which accompanied the revolution, the alternatives seem not even to have been discussed, and the legislatures simply assumed the chartering function without contest.

The new city charters in the first two or three decades after independence were somewhat more democratic than the earlier ones in that the last few "close corporations" were abolished in favor of popularly elected councils. In the "close corporation" type of government, which was common in English cities during the colonial period and considerably less common in the colonies themselves, the council members were appointed for life and in some cases could choose their own successors. This arrangement hardly accorded with republican enthusiasm; it was, typically, adjudged "impolitic and unconstitutional" by the legislature of Virginia in 1787, when it changed the charter of Norfolk to provide for election of the city council. Among the other major colonial cities, Baltimore, Philadelphia, and Charleston also experienced the end of close corporation government with the success of the Revolution.

It was not long before the principles of separation of powers and checks and balances, so important to the founding fathers in their deliberations on the forms of national and state constitutions, also began to appear in the government of American cities. In 1796 and 1797, Philadelphia and Baltimore received new charters from their state legislatures which provided them with bicameral city councils. This practice was not universally followed, but it spread widely; Detroit's charter of 1806 (granted by the territorial legislature), Pittsburgh's in 1816, Boston's in 1822, and New York City's in 1830, all included the provision in one or another form. Where it did exist, the bicameral council contributed increasingly, as city governments became more important, to the complexity and inefficiency of those governments.

Sometimes the bicameral institution developed out of pre-existing arrangements; in Boston's case, the lower house took the place of the older town meeting, while the upper house carried on some of the functions of the selectmen. In other cases, however, it reflected deliberate imitation of federal and state models. Its provision in New York City's 1830 charter was explained, in the words of the convention which drafted it, "for the same reason which has dictated a similar division of power into two branches, each checking or controlling the other, in our general government." The same suspicion of government which had led Americans to restrict their national and state authorities with constitutional and institutional limitations re-appeared at the local level, just as the fledgling cities were about to begin careers of rapid and possibly ominous growth.

A further separation of power occurred with the emergence of the mayor as an independent municipal authority. During colonial days, mayors had either been appointed by an authority representing the imperial government, or—as in the close corporations—chosen by the municipal council itself. After the Revolution, elected governors of the states (or in a few cases other state agencies) appointed the mayors, which brought the office somewhat closer to the electorate but not particularly closer to local voters. From the last years of the eighteenth century, the manner in which the mayor was selected began to change, and this led gradually to a change in his role. By 1820 in all the larger cities, he was chosen by the city councils which were, of course, elected locally. In 1822 and 1824, Boston, St. Louis, and Detroit voters were given the privilege of electing their mayors at large. This practice spread rapidly enough that at mid-century it was universal in American cities. By itself it gave the mayors no additional formal powers, but it did make them relatively more independent of the councils. In some places, as time passed, the mayor's powers of appointment and veto were enlarged and the office became one with great potential leverage in city government.

This development was not paralleled, however, by any immediate increase in governmental efficiency. Cities appeared to be losing powers steadily as the nineteenth century wore on. The Revolution had, perhaps ironically, depressed the value of cities' "charter rights;" when the state legislatures took over the power of granting city charters, the charters themselves became mere statutes alterable at will or even repealable by the bodies that passed them. These documents lost whatever "prescriptive" or contractual status they had in the colonial period, and the incorporated cities and towns became simply legal creatures of the state government. As urban populations swelled and demanded more services, the cities found it necessary to ask their respective state governments either to provide the services or else to enable the local governments to do so.

For many years, the first alternative was generally followed and city authorities shared local power with the state capitals.

This sharing of power between local and state agencies became important during the 1830's and 1840's just when the basic principle of home rule had been given to English cities, and also just when a national party system was developing in the United States. The effects of this development on the quality of American city administration cannot be measured in any accurate way, but its importance can be gauged from the fact that home-rule and separation of local questions from national politics were later to become two of the chief goals of municipal reformers. Early in the nineteenth century city government did not impress many citizens as being of any great importance; the states, and even the counties in many places, seemed to bear more significantly upon daily life —to the extent that government at all bore on daily life in the United States. In 1810, New York City with a population of around 100,000 spent only $100,000: a dollar per capita. Voluntary associations took care of poor relief and shared in such an important matter as fire prevention. It would be thirty years before there was a uniformed police force in the United States. To many Americans it was by no means clear that theirs was to be an urban destiny. In the circumstances what one student has called "the petty housekeeping of such small urban communities" held little intrinsic interest for contemporaries.

City offices were not sought for the purpose of carrying out impressive programs of social or economic improvement. For a time after independence they continued to be sought and largely held in the older eastern ports by men of wealth and leisure like Mayor Philip Hone of New York, to whom the holding of public office seemed natural and proper. In the new towns of the interior, these offices were taken over by the entrepreneurs who were promoting the growth of the towns in order to further the interests of their business enterprises. The semi-aristocratic type of public servant in the eastern cities was beginning to be shouldered off the stage by the 1830's with the rise of egalitarian sentiments, and as the interior towns found secure bases for growth, the original entrepreneurs turned aside from public life to pursue their now flourishing businesses. The apparent insignificance of city gov-

171

ernment, changes in the social texture of politics, and the growth of a national system of political parties combined to subordinate local politics to the fortune of the major parties on state and national levels. This subordination along with the weak legal position of city charters made city government, for a considerable time, a kind of forgotten child in the American polity.

It was during the same period that city government became more and more complicated and consequently more and more cumbersome. State interference, the party system, traditional Jeffersonian distrust of concentrated authority, and the lack of any central power to coordinate city development produced complexity and diversity which cannot be described in detail; a few examples must suggest the way in which American city government confronted the voter by the mid-1800's and for a considerable time thereafter. As new urban needs called for new urban services—whether to be provided by state or by local agencies—new offices were created. In many cases these were kept independent of previously existing offices such as the councils or the mayors. The St. Paul, Minnesota charter of 1868 provided that in addition to a mayor and council members, the voters must choose eight separate executive authorities. By New York City's charter of 1867, simplifying the structure which had preceded it, voters elected the mayor, the comptroller, the Board of Councillors, the Board of Aldermen, the supervisors, the corporation counsel, and the Board of Education; the governor, elected by voters throughout the state, appointed the Central Park commissioners, the Board of Health, the police commissioners, the fire commissioners, and the immigration commissioners. In 1885, New Haven citizens had to elect a bicameral city council, a sheriff, a mayor, a treasurer, a city clerk, and an auditor; chosen in various ways (some by the whole council, some by the upper house, some by the lower house, and some by the mayor with the approval of the upper house) were police and fire commissioners, health commissioners, commissioners of public works, a Board of Finance, and several other authorities; meanwhile, the Connecticut legislature appointed city judges for New Haven, who then appointed the city attorney. At one time Philadelphia's government included thirty separate boards to supervise special functions. In the late 1860's there were in New York City four different agencies with power to tear up the streets while there was no agency with clear responsibility for re-paving them.

The impact of state legislative action on city affairs went far beyond naming a few boards or individual officials. The New York legislature, for example, passed more laws for New York City alone in the three years from 1867 to 1870 than Parliament passed for all of the cities in the United Kingdom from 1835 to 1885; in the year 1870, thirty-nine state laws were passed for the city of Brooklyn alone. Jersey City's charter was amended by state action ninety-one times between 1835 and 1875. The date for municipal elections in St. Paul was changed—by the state legislators—three times in four years during the 1860's. An example from Chicago is both dramatic and illustrative: in 1861, the Republican Party won the state elections and the governor appointed a new police board for Chicago, made up of Republicans. Two years later, the Democrats won and reduced the terms of office of the board members, thus making it possible for them to appoint half the board's members. In 1865, the Republicans were back in power at the state capital; they restored the original terms of office for the police board, provided that new members be elected by Cook County voters (rather than by Chicago voters alone, who were characteristically Democratic), and provided also that the city's fire department be controlled by the police board.

State interference in local matters might be justified, and sometimes was, on the ground that the states had a broader tax base available to them and could supply the cities with funds indispensable to the provision of needed services. This was the case in important instances, notably when states granted money to the cities and towns, as they began to do early in the nineteenth century, to aid in the building of public school systems. In such cases, the action initially reflected an actual redistribution of public revenue to the cities' advantage. But the old suspicion of the city and city life played a great part in sustaining the practice of state interference. "It goes without saying," wrote one student of city government in New England in the 1890's, "that country districts are, as a rule, more deserving of political power than are cities. If the judges were locally elected . . . the successful candidates would often be under obligations to elements in the community which are the chief source and nurse of the criminal class." Lord Bryce, although he was English, reflected much American opinion on the matter in describing the influences which made for bad and corrupt government as "far more potent and pernicious in great cities than in country districts." Referring to the immigrant population, the poor, the aloof business men, and the cultivated individuals who disdained politics, he concluded that "in great cities the forces that attack and pervert democratic government are exceptionally numerous, the defensive forces that protect it exceptionally ill-placed for resistance. Satan has turned his heaviest batteries on the weakest part of the ramparts." A prominent and respected New York attorney and public servant, William Marcy Evarts, pointing out the evil effects of state involvement in city administration, actually included among them the proposition that the low character of urban politics was infecting the presumably purer currents of state politics: "The transfer of control of municipal resources from the localities to the capital," he asserted, "had no other effect than to cause a like transfer of the methods and arts of corruption. . . . Municipal corruption, previously confined within territorial limits, thenceforth escaped all bounds, and spread to every quarter of the state."

At the same time that they became more complicated and increasingly subject to state interference, the city governments were of necessity becoming more important. They spent more money in order to satisfy growing needs. The first service to expand noticeably in the nineteenth century was public education. States played a part in this development, but as already noted their function was originally mostly one of supplying additional money to the cities. In the late thirties, the larger places began providing for city school superintendents, and by 1870 every city in the country of any size at all—with the exception of Philadelphia—had a superintendent as well as a school board which in some cases had independent taxing and bonding powers. The degree of state supervision varied, but in most places primary responsibility was left in local hands. From a very early period in the nineteenth century, it was common practice to regard the school boards as "outside of politics;" in many places the practice of dividing board membership even between the parties, regardless of which party controlled the city government, became traditional. Party politics did influence such considerations as the awarding of contracts for school construction, but educational policies and selection of teachers were usually kept free from that influence. The system was flexible enough, with local variations in the manner of choosing the school boards and in their relationships with the rest of the city government, to cope as adequately with the growth of high school education after the 1870's as it had with primary schooling in the earlier years.

Other large responsibilities were presented to city administrations from the 1840's. Water service was prominent among them. New York's needs dictated the building of the great Croton aqueduct beginning in 1846; the same year a large new system of waterworks was begun in Boston, and in the next decade Chicago and Baltimore followed. Until this period, water systems in American cities had been provided mostly by private enterprise, but the large improvements needed by the expanding urban centers were beyond private capacity. The increasing size of the problem and the general feeling that water was so necessary to communities that it should not be a source of private profit led to a spreading movement in the direction of municipally owned waterworks. This added to the financial problems of the cities, since large bonding operations were necessary to build or rebuild the systems. It also added to the need for administrative skill in municipalities; the waterworks as business enterprises—and very large enterprises by nineteenth century standards—were to be run on a self-sustaining basis as well as in the interest of the community.

Another significant expansion of municipal activity in the later nineteenth century was in public health. Here again decentralization and diversity characterized American practice at about the same time that the health activities of English cities were systematized by the Public Health Act which Parliament passed in 1875. There had been boards of health in several American cities much earlier: New York City in 1805, Philadelphia in 1818, and Chicago by the time it was four years old in 1837. But they had no regular staffs and had done very little except during periods of yellow fever, cholera, or smallpox epidemics, when emergency sanitary or quarantine regulations were temporarily prescribed. As a result of the cholera epidemic in 1866 the idea of a more regular service began to spread. In that year the state of New York provided a Metropolitan Board of Health for the New York City-Brooklyn area. It had a permanent force of inspectors and some latitude in prescribing permanent sanitary regulations; after 1870 the board was a municipal agency. This precedent was followed closely by Chicago where a Municipal Board of Health was set up in 1867, and in Boston in 1872. As the boards of health appeared in city after city, their responsibilities increased and they became more expensive. By the turn of the century New York City had almost four hundred health inspectors, Philadelphia and Chicago about fifty each: cities with populations of 50,000 or more were spending around $2,500,000 for their health departments, and between 1900 and 1907 this figure had risen by 600 per cent.

As concern with public health problems grew more widespread, it was associated with concern for living conditions in the growing slums of the cities. These were areas where epidemics might start; statistical correlation between disease and filthy neighborhoods was commonly stressed by those who wanted to correct at least the worst features of life in the slums. New York City led the way in housing reform, as it had in other matters. The first law specifying minimum standards for tenement construction, in 1867, followed closely upon the establishment of the Metropolitan Board of Health and reflected the same impulse. This law was ineffective, and an amendment in 1879 which required a window in each bedroom merely spurred proliferation of the dumb-bell tenements. Other suggested standards—such as some "means of egress" in case of fire—were far from adequate and even so went for the most part unenforced. Amendments to the law, in 1884, were also almost entirely ineffective; meanwhile, the tenement problem grew larger and the sudden burgeoning of interest in contagion and community health strengthened the position of reformers. Under the urging of Lawrence Veiller, a state commission was established in 1900 to study tenement conditions and recommend corrective legislation. Veiller had participated in relief activities in New York during the depression of the mid-nineties and had served two years as an inspector of building plans in the city's Buildings Department. He had devoted a great deal of time to systematic study of urban housing and probably knew more about the subject than anyone else in the United States; appropriately, he was named secretary of the investigating commission and its proposals (along with their embodiment in the law of 1901) reflected mostly Veiller's ideas. Out of the commission's investigations and recommendations, which were well publicized and excited widespread interest, came New York's Tenement Law of 1901. It prohibited future construction of dumbbell buildings and required certain improvements in the thousands already existing; it required courtyards varying in width with the heights of buildings, provided more stringent fire protection measures, and required a separate bathroom for every family dwelling-unit. This was the first carefully drafted building code in the country, and it was also to be the first carefully enforced one. The law provided for a separate Tenement House Commission, which within two years had 166 building inspectors of its own with more than two hundred other employees. In its first twelve years of operation the commission processed nearly half a million complaints of violations. By 1920 at least forty other large cities, usually following the New York model, had acted to tighten up their building codes and to provide improved enforcement machinery. All in all, while this did not solve the social problems of poverty in urban America, it did represent a significant extension of governmental action. As Roy Lubove has commented, "Veiller left as a permanent legacy to the nation the principle of a community's right to high minimum standards of restrictive housing legislation."

Regular police and fire departments constituted part of the growing burden of local government. Modern uniformed police forces began in New York City in 1845, and the example was quickly adopted elsewhere: in Philadelphia, Boston, and Baltimore, for example, before the outbreak of the Civil War. By that time, a strong trend in the direction of state control of large city police forces had set in; the trend probably reflected the exigencies of party politics, and it abated in the 1870's as feeling against state intervention in general began to grow. In the larger cities, the police forces usually came to be supervised by special commissions appointed in a variety of ways, sometimes by state authority and sometimes locally. In 1900 cities with 30,000 or more people were paying for 28,000 uniformed policemen. Fire protection became more expensive and more effective during the same period. The older volunteer fire brigades yielded to regular paid forces during and after the 1850's, at about the same time that fire-fighting equipment, including steam engines and complicated pumping machinery, was becoming more expensive. In the case of fire protection, at least, American cities surpassed their European contemporaries; the New York City and Boston fire departments were regarded by 1900 as the best in the world. Chicago's force had as many men as London's, along with more horses and steam engines, although Chicago was only a third as large as the English metropolis.

Beginning in 1823, the city of Boston took over control of sewage disposal. In 1849 New York did the same and within twenty years had laid almost two hundred miles of pipe for this purpose. Chicago constructed its first public sewers in 1856 and in fifteen years it had built 140 miles. Street cleaning was another municipal function which grew rapidly after the Civil War, associated (as was interest in better sewage disposal) with the public health movement. George Waring's vigorous reforms in the New York City system resulted in the city's employing over 5,000 street sweepers and garbage collectors by 1900 to carry off 3,000,000 cartloads of refuse annually. One of Waring's innovations, which came to be widely imitated, was provision for quick snow removal; John Fairlie, a contemporary political scientist, accurately placed this new practice in the widening category of "increase in the scope of municipal action with a corresponding increase in expenditure."

Public parks came to be regarded as important to American cities partly because of their relationship to community health and partly because it was felt desirable to provide socially wholesome areas of recreation for children and for the poor. Philadelphia bought some land for a small park as early as 1812. In 1851, New York City received authority from the state legislature to acquire land which was to become Central Park; its construction began under the supervision of Frederick Law Olmsted in 1858. Slowly the idea spread to other cities: Baltimore began a 700-acre park in 1870 and in the next twenty years most American cities were looking for land which could be made into public parks. Olmsted's great success with Central Park, along with the planning necessary for Chicago's Columbian Exposition in 1893, encouraged the movement. The parks were ordinarily overseen by special boards created for the purpose, which usually had to share their responsibilities with boards of public recreation and boards of public works.

But by that time American cities should have been used to overlapping authorities. As the governments of the cities became more complicated the need in each city for some coordinating force grew more apparent. To the degree that this need was met at all, it was met by the party organizations. These organizations, while their purpose was to win and retain office and not necessarily to furnish efficient administration, were at least cohesive and provided a measure of discipline—in the sense of predictable behavior—in the ramifying and fragmented structures within which urban public affairs were conducted. In the process whereby the political party became, in E. S. Griffith's words, "the coordinating agency," jobs in the city government became patronage, and contracts or franchises for public construction became graft. In each city the men in the political organizations who could allocate the patronage and the graft most skillfully, with a view to winning elections, reached positions of power. They were called bosses, and although they varied greatly among themselves in characteristic techniques and in personality, still their objective function was the same everywhere: to provide the city governments with at least the minimum of regularity without which the governments could not have functioned at all.

Expanding municipal needs coming in the same period as deteriorating government meant, inevitably, bad local services. Though there were mitigating circumstances and though the picture was not always quite so dark as it was painted, still no serious contemporary could have argued that cities in the United States were well governed in the post-Civil War period. Even in New York, the nation's metropolis, which had pioneered in so many lines of municipal activity, reliable testimony in the late 1870's described an unattractive prospect: "the wharves and piers are for the most part temporary and perishable structures; the streets are poorly paved; the sewers in great measure imperfect, insufficient, and in bad order; the public buildings shabby and inadequate; and there is

179

little which the citizen can regard with satisfaction save the aqueduct and its appurtenances and the public park." In Philadelphia, which had been a model urban community a hundred years
earlier, the situation was no better: "Public work has been done so
badly," stated a bipartisan committee, "that structures have had
to be renewed almost as soon as finished. Others have been in
part constructed at enormous expense and then permitted to fall
to decay without completion. Inefficiency, waste, badly-paved and
filthy streets, unwholesome and offensive water, and slovenly and
costly management have been the rule for years past throughout
the city government."

Expanding needs and deteriorating government also meant expensive government, and herein lay important seeds for later reform. Municipal affairs cost the individual taxpayer more and more
throughout the western world during the nineteenth century. While
the population of Great Britain increased by 300 per cent the
burden of its local taxation increased by 700 per cent. Between
1840 and 1900 the population of France went up only 16 per cent,
while local expenditures went up by 600 per cent; similar figures
characterized the other European countries. The rising incidence
of city expenses and city taxes was just as pronounced in the
United States, and especially in the large cities; between 1850 and
1900 per capita city expenditures in New York, for example, rose
from $6.53 to $27.31.

Two factors especially rendered growing per capita expenses of
city government more burdensome. In the first place, the thirty
years between 1867 and 1897 saw a marked deflation in the general
level of prices. Accompanied as it was by two major depressions,
1873–78 and 1893–97, deflation meant that in spite of the national
economy's growth each individual dollar was harder to come by.
Even during relatively prosperous years the appreciating value of
the dollar along with anxiety about the "business cycle," as it was
coming to be called, lent urgency to demands for retrenchment and
reform. Deflation also meant that measuring increasing city expenditures in dollars understated the real values reflected in the
increases.

In the second place, interest on indebtedness accounted for an
ever larger proportion of these expenditures. In the decade after

the end of the Civil War, when the fifteen largest American cities saw their aggregate population rise by about 70 per cent, the debts of the same cities rose by 271 per cent. This produced a relatively inelastic item of expense—interest on the debt—and as time went on and city debts continued to rise it placed a growing burden of current outgo on each year's budget in addition to casting its lengthening shadow over future generations of taxpayers. St. Louis's revenues, for example, doubled between 1850 and 1858 but during the same years its bonded indebtedness trebled. Interest on the debt of Providence, Rhode Island accounted for 40 per cent of its tax revenues in 1880, and in the same year debt service was eating up an average of 50 per cent of the revenues of cities in New Jersey. At about the same time, one-third of Cleveland's income went to pay interest, and the charges on debts of cities in New York came to more than the whole cost of running the state government.

Much of the debt increase was due to public building programs the costs of which were often under-estimated at the outset. Thus a courthouse in New York City the cost of which had been estimated at $250,000 ultimately came to cost $14,000,000. There were special circumstances, notably the Tweed ring, to explain this spectacular divergence, but elsewhere procedures were similar: a city hall for San Francisco estimated at $1,500,000 actually cost $3,500,000, a market house for Houston estimated at $228,000 actually cost $470,000, and a waterworks for Peoria estimated at $310,000 actually cost $453,000. In many places, part of the debt was due to lavish encouragement to railroads, which stemmed from local rivalries during the booster years; city and county obligations of this kind were conservatively estimated at $185,000,000 in 1870.

Inefficiency and corruption explained some part of the cities' skyrocketing obligations—how much cannot be estimated realistically. The federal census of 1880 brought the figures together in such a way as to impress and even startle many citizens: it triggered an outcry against corrupt city governments. Remarks by a writer in *Harper's New Monthly Magazine* in 1884 were representative: "The story of our political methods for the last twenty-five years is soonest told by the immense increase in our municipal indebtedness." The writer went on to lament that the "best men" in the cities did not interest themselves in public affairs, and were too occupied in "money getting." While these people were politically indifferent, undesirable types were "making their municipal budgets and confiscating their property." But this was, at best, only a partial explanation. The expenses of local government had been rising for at least forty years by 1880: in other words, since the time when urban population growth had begun decisively to outstrip rural. It must be remembered that the expanding services of the large cities made large capital investment necessary in any case; the municipal debts represented the creation in a very short time of what Eric Lampard has called a new "urban infra-structure." The largest payments by American cities toward the close of the nineteenth century were, in order, for public buildings, education, streets and bridges, police and fire protection, and interest on their public debts.

Some cities found themselves unable to pay their debts. Mobile repudiated many of its bonds outright; several other places were forced to suspend interest payments for a period; Memphis, with its problems intensified by nationwide depression and a terrible yellow fever epidemic in 1878 saw the state of Tennessee take over its financial operations in their entirety. In other places, too, states were called on to step in and remedy deplorable urban financial practices although not so drastically as in Memphis's case. In 1872 Illinois enacted strict legislation to control the form and content of city council appropriations, especially in Chicago. Other states enacted constitutional limitations onto the debt-creating power of their cities—limitations which frequently proved ineffective because they were difficult to enforce in court.

A growing number of taxpayers felt that the burden on them, however necessary had been the objectives of expenditure, was unnecessarily high. One of the reasons for this was quickly found in the practices which had grown up in providing for street transportation and later for street lighting. These utilities were different from the water systems, which came to be typically public enterprises. Street railways and lighting systems for the most part were built and operated by private companies which carried on their work under franchises granted by city councils. A franchise was a contract in which the private company's performance was stipulated and its future financial obligations to the city were specified, usually for a given number of years after which the contract could be renegotiated. These franchises were valuable privileges since they conferred a monopolistic or semi-monopolistic position upon the favored company. The growth of the cities insured that there would be increasing business for as long as anyone could predict.

In order to encourage entrepreneurs to build desired street railways, it was generally agreed that franchises should be attractive. Consequently, little thought was taken of the future value of the privilege to the companies and much was made of the present value of the companies to the city dwellers who needed transportation. Franchises were quickly, carelessly, and generously drawn up and passed by city councils, were made to last for long periods, and provided for low taxation on the companies' property. The first street railway franchises were granted in New York City in 1851 and 1852; the companies were allowed to charge a fare no higher than five cents and a vague provision was included requiring them to keep the part of the streets adjacent to their tracks in good condition, but the franchises had no terminal dates at all. Most early franchises were drawn for periods of fifty to a hundred years; Albany granted one for a thousand years and even toward the end of the century Buffalo granted a 999 year franchise.

The circumstances were similar in regard to franchises for lighting the cities' streets. Gas lighting had been introduced in Baltimore in 1816, and lighting became an important urban service after the early 1820's when both Boston and New York City began to use gas for this purpose. In this instance also, the service was ordinarily provided by private companies which needed power to tear up streets or, later, to string wires along them. These companies had positions which were increasingly recognized as monopolistic and they operated under special franchise grants from city councils. When, during the 1880's, cities began using electricity for lighting, the procedures were the same. All these businesses attracted investors in the larger cities; around the turn of the century to consider only privately owned utilities, over $300,000,000 was invested in gas works, about $250,000,000 in electric lighting plants, and over two billion dollars in street railway systems.

183

Utilities other than water service were for the most part privately owned in the larger cities, where they were profitable enterprises. Chicago and Detroit were unusual with their municipally owned electric lighting plants. Philadelphia had a municipal gas works from 1845 to 1899 but then leased it to a private company. Even the Brooklyn Bridge cable car line, owned and operated jointly by New York City and Brooklyn between 1883 and 1889, was leased to a private company in the latter year. Opportunities for profit were not extensive in small cities and towns, and there public ownership was common.

There were rare cases in the earliest days of franchise-granting where the potential problem was recognized and great care was taken in the negotiations. Thus in 1859 Mayor Swann of Baltimore insisted successfully that applicants for a street railway franchise agree to pay the city 20 per cent of gross revenue plus a license tax on each car, and also incorporated a provision that at fifteen year intervals the city might consider buying out the company. But the general trend was different; cities welcomed the companies proposing to supply public utilities in the same way in which the nation at large welcomed railroads, and the history of the relationship between public authority and private enterprise was similar in the two cases. Even in Baltimore a reaction against Swann's cautious policy soon led to much more generous franchises there. New York City's first elevated railroad was built with no restrictions on street occupation; whereas the company had to pay five per cent of gross revenue to the city, later lines were not subjected to this requirement. By the end of the 1880's most city lighting franchises contained no restrictions on rates, and were carelessly or ambiguously worded on the matter of future renegotiation.

Toward the end of the century, public utility companies began to consolidate. Where there had once been thirty street transportation companies in Philadelphia, there was only one by 1895, and a comparable trend was evident in most other cities. Consolidation was in part the result of technological changes which necessitated high capital investment costs, and it brought with it the possibility of sizeable economies of scale. During the 1890's a further stage in concentration took place as control of utility companies in dif-

184

ferent cities was absorbed by holding companies, each of which might own lighting or traction systems, or both, in many places. By the early 1900's, holding companies located in the East controlled the street railway companies of most American cities of over 30,000 population. One syndicate controlled companies in a hundred cities; their aggregate capitalization was around one billion dollars. This trend continued well into the twentieth century, resulting in the huge corporate pyramids of the 1920's associated with such names as Sidney Mitchell and Samuel Insull. One of the nation's best-known corporation lawyers described the Insull empire as "impossible for any man to grasp . . . so set up that you could not possibly get an accounting system which would not mislead even the officers themselves." Financial expansion of the utility companies greatly complicated the tasks of the city governments in dealing with them; when regulation was seriously attempted, long years of litigation delayed it almost everywhere.

One result of the lenient policy in granting utility franchises in American cities was that this country got extensive street lighting and transportation systems much more rapidly than European countries, where more cautious policies were followed. Another result, however, was additional strain and stress on the governing process. The utility problem grew rapidly from small beginnings along with the cities themselves. Brand Whitlock, in his autobiography *Forty Years of It,* recalled from the days of his boyhood the jingling bell of a small horse-car coming long the main street of the town he lived in. The town grew into a middle-sized city; the horse-car line became an electric street railway with vastly increased income. "I ceased to hear of the individual owner any more," Whitlock wrote; "I never saw him in his shirt-sleeves in his little office at the end of the line counting up the nickels of those new families which each meant $73.00 per annum . . . , and it must have been about the same time that I began to hear of the traction company." The line still operated on the original franchise, however, which had given it monopoly privileges and which also assured that the company would be taxed at a very low level. The company, which came to be owned far away in an eastern city, was an important force in city politics because of the franchise which it possessed, the value of which had risen so sharply with

185

city growth. Later on, as Mayor of Toledo, Whitlock found himself struggling almost continually with utility interests which wanted to escape revision of their franchises.

By the time city dwellers realized some of the effects on the finances and the politics of their communities, the problem was already sizeable. As late as 1900 only three cities—Chicago, Baltimore, and Louisville—were deriving any significant revenue from franchise taxation. Private enterprise and public authority were delicately interlocked, and powerful corporations had large stakes in the control of city governments. "My experience in fighting monopolistic corporations as Mayor of Detroit," Hazen Pingree wrote in the 1890's, ". . . have . . . convinced me that they . . . are responsible for nearly all the thieving and boodling with which cities are made to suffer from their servants. They seek almost uniformly to secure what they want by means of bribes, and in this way they corrupt our councils and commissions." A few years later Lincoln Steffens described the city council of St. Louis as totally corrupted by the utility interests, selling franchises and other legal favors to these interests on a carefully worked-out scale on which was computed what each councilman should receive for the votes he cast. The best description of the kind of negotiations Pingree and Steffens singled out for censure was probably given by Theodore Dreiser in two novels, *The Financier* and *The Titan*. Inspired by the career of Charles T. Yerkes, a Chicago traction magnate, the plot details the history of a shrewd and imaginative man (whom Dreiser names Frank Cowperwood) as he becomes wealthy on Philadelphia street railway franchises. Blocked there by misfortunes resulting in a penitentiary term, Cowperwood moves west to Chicago, which was lustily rising from the ashes of the great fire, where he consolidates gas and street railway companies—carefully paying off the important city politicians—into a fortune far surpassing his earlier success in Philadelphia.

As the problem became more obvious and the utility companies drew increasing criticism, reform efforts began to shape a more carefully guarded approach to franchises or the regulation of public utilities. In 1885 the Massachusetts legislature set up a commission to supervise gas companies; two years later it was given the same oversight of the newer electric lighting companies. The commissioners were well paid and protected at least partly by civil service rules; they were expected not to involve themselves in any other remunerative work during their terms of office. No consolidations could be made nor could stock or bonds be issued without their approval; they could disallow any franchise which a city or town proposed to grant. This early example of a strong regulatory agency was not immediately imitated; the notion of public regulation of utilities caught on slowly. A reaction against long-term franchises led to their being limited generally to twenty-five years by the 1880's. In 1889, Colorado restricted all franchises to no more than twenty years, and other states took similar action. In 1907 the state of New York provided for a Public Service Commission to oversee the utilities of its metropolis, and in the same year Wisconsin established a regulatory commission with state-wide authority. By 1920 regulatory commissions were functioning in most of the states, and the most egregious evils of earlier days had been at least partly corrected.

In the meantime, mounting evidence of the extent of corrupt practices, and concern for tax rates which were believed to be needlessly high, led more and more citizens to consider the possibility of general municipal reform. The reform current was weak at first; its beginnings may be traced to the state investigations and the taxpayers' associations of the 1870's. It gathered force, however, so that by the end of the next decade the desirability of reform became almost a cliché. Although the stages of its development were not distinct and the fate of reform efforts varied widely from city to city, certain key elements can be identified. There was a movement away from state interference in city affairs culminating in demands for municipal "home rule." There was a steady tendency toward concentration of executive authority, along with efforts to simplify the organization of the governments. In some places reformers tried to divorce city elections from national and state politics. Toward the close of the nineteenth century separate local reform movements began to try to coordinate their goals and share their experiences. As the twentieth century opened, two wholly new proposals for administrative structure gained popularity: the commission plan and the city manager plan.

While the constitutional status of cities remained unchanged—

187

they continued to be, as they are today, legal creatures of the states
—state legislators in the 1870's began having second thoughts
about continually passing local legislation. States adopted restrictions in this regard which usually took the form of classifying their
cities according to size; general laws could then be made for the
different classes. In Illinois this action, taken in 1870, helped reduce the total number of laws passed annually from about 3,000
to about two hundred. The same state followed its abandonment
of special law-making for cities with a Municipal Corporations Act
in 1872 which broadly outlined the areas in which city governments
might act on their own initiative. New York City was given a
charter in 1870 that abolished state appointments of the boards
in charge of public health, police, Central Park, and several other
local activities. At almost the same time the state constitution of
Virginia was amended to include a model city charter which communities meeting certain size requirements might adopt. The
California constitution's provision, in 1879, represented the trend:
"Corporations for municipal purposes shall not be created by
special laws, but the legislative by general laws shall provide for
the incorporation, organization, and classification in proportion to
population of cities and towns. . . . Cities and towns heretofore
organized or incorporated may become organized under such general laws whenever a majority of the electors voting at a general
election shall so determine." The California legislature soon proceeded to authorize the more populous cities to frame their own
charters subject to its acceptance of the finished products. Missouri
had already provided this privilege, in its 1875 constitution, for
cities with 100,000 or more inhabitants; at the time this applied
only to St. Louis, but Kansas City soon joined the classification
and began its charter-framing history in the late 1880's.

Home rule privileges of this scope were still rare by the end of
the nineteenth century. Only Washington and Minnesota had followed California's and Missouri's far-reaching provisions, although
the inconveniences arising from detailed state legislation were
gradually mitigated elsewhere. As reform sentiment spread and
gathered force, home rule became one of its rallying cries and along
with it were implications at least that the traditional American
suspicion of government was being reconsidered. Frank Goodnow,

a leader in municipal reform movements during the late nineteenth and early twentieth centuries, observed in 1897 that "the fact that a city is an organization for the satisfaction of local needs makes it necessary that its action be determined by local considerations. To this end it must have large local powers." At about the same time, one of Goodnow's fellow reformers asserted that "the most cursory survey of municipal problems will show that they must be such as favor, rather than impede, positive action." Home rule was also promoted as being in the interest of greater democracy; it would, as one writer put it in 1911, make "the people themselves directly responsible for municipal government." At the same time it would remedy the condition in which the "best people" were largely indifferent to local politics. If city administrations were given adequate powers to deal with the problems facing them, reformers urged, "men of ability and patriotism will come to the aid of the city."

The keynotes were clearly efficiency and economy, and swelling demands for these encouraged another development during the same years that saw the promotion of home rule: stronger executive power emerged as a considerable force in the government of cities. This can be traced back to the days when mayors were first popularly elected, but even after that innovation the office typically remained weak for another generation. The tendency toward strengthening the mayor's hand probably reflected growing distrust of the councils, especially in financial matters. It was frequently accompanied by other moves in the direction of budget reform, such as provision for a comptroller more or less independent of other authority whose approval was necessary before any money could be paid out of the treasury. By the end of the century, city councils in many places had lost all power to appropriate money outside of budgets which were submitted by mayors, comptrollers, or other specially designated agencies.

It was after 1870 that the mayor began to acquire important executive authority. His veto power was extended, first in connection with the budget and then over all actions of the council. With demands for economy and retrenchment came realization that the ramifying complications of the various administrative boards contributed to inefficiency and waste; they began to lose powers which were often given to the mayors. One significant power was greatly strengthened when Brooklyn adopted a charter in 1882 which abandoned the traditional requirement that the council approve the mayor's appointment of administrative officials. This was widely imitated; in 1885 Boston took away the council's power to confirm removals from office. The mayor's emergence as a strong municipal power in his own right tended to pose him against the council at moments of crisis or near crisis in local politics. This meant that reformers tied their hopes more and more to the mayors; it also encouraged the tendency in reform thinking to promote executive power at the expense of legislative power, and thus prepared a way for the later commission and city manager plans.

Part of the mayor's growing strength was symbolic: he represented, and might almost come to "personify," the whole city, rather than any special area within it. The special identity of the mayor, wherever it was achieved, stimulated a movement toward what came to be called nonpartisanship in city elections. While political parties provided a degree of coherence amidst the confusion of municipal administrative structures, and thus made those structures at least partly usable, the domination of local politics by the state and national machines of the major parties had tended to obscure legitimate conflict over issues which were really local. Governor Tilden's 1877 commission to study city government and to make proposals for its improvement condemned the intrusion of major party political contentions into city affairs: "There is no more just reason," the commission reported, "why the control of the public works of a great city should be in the hands of a Democrat or a Republican than there is why an adherent of one of the other of the great parties should be made the superintendent of a business corporation."

Some people suggested that local politics ought to generate local parties, unconnected with the national organizations. Something like this actually happened often enough, although on a temporary basis, when successful reform groups were established; they transcended the lines of national party division and carefully avoided use of the words "Republican" and "Democrat." But these organizations were still pitted against regular party machines, whether Democratic as in New York and Chicago or Republican as in

190

Philadelphia, and they did not typically last very long. They did not represent efforts to build durable local parties; most reformers felt that parties by their very nature were an excrescence on the urban body politic. "Whoever heard," asked a prominent reformer in 1895, "of a Republican park or playground, a Democratic swimming bath, a Prohibitionist street cleaning department, or a Populist mortuary?"

Use of nonpartisan ballots, where no party designation was permitted to appear, became possible during and after the 1880's when states began adopting the Australian system of placing the names of all candidates on ballots printed by the government. As a device for separating city affairs from state and national politics its success has been limited, but it was nevertheless widely adopted in American cities during the early years of the twentieth century and is now used in about two-thirds of all communities with populations over 5,000. By 1921, the mayors of almost half of the two hundred largest cities in the United States had been elected as "independents."

Along with this trend came efforts toward civil service reform. Here the federal government led the way with passage of the Pendleton Act in 1883. It set up a commission to supervise certain kinds of jobs, appointment to which came on a nonpartisan basis and only after an applicant had passed an examination. The states of New York and Massachusetts imitated this legislation the following year, and the principle of a classified civil service began very slowly to make an impact on city government. Milwaukee, Seattle, and Tacoma all adopted limited civil service provisions in the 1890's; San Francisco's charter of 1898 applied the principle to a wide range of jobs in the city government. By the 1930's it had been generally adopted in America's largest cities. Its spread reflected partly the reaction against influence of party organizations on city administration, but also—and this became more important as time passed—it reflected a growing understanding of the need for expert knowledge in the increasingly large and sophisticated tasks which the city governments were being called upon to do. By the end of the nineteenth century it was no longer true, if it ever had been, that jobs in the public service were, in Andrew

Jackson's words, "so simple that men of intelligence may readily qualify themselves for their performance."

Toward the end of the 1890's another reform measure appeared on the urban agenda; in the same 1898 charter which had promoted civil service examinations so prominently, San Francisco included provisions whereby citizens might legislate directly. By petition, a proposed law which the city council seemed unwilling to pass could be placed on the ballot at the next general election; it would then go into effect if enough voters supported it at the polls. Similarly, laws passed by the council might be directly repealed by the voters if they saw fit to do so. This was the "initiative and referendum;" in 1903, Los Angeles' charter added provision for dismissing certain public officials by popular vote: a kind of "reverse election" named the recall. Initiative and referendum were quite generally adopted in American city government by 1930; recall did not spread rapidly despite the enthusiasm of its proponents and is possible only in relatively few places. None of these changes had much effect on city government, with the possible exception of the referendum which was used in some cases to invalidate franchises granted by city councils.

Along with concern for the condition of American city governments went growing interest in studying ways in which European cities were run. The impact of this kind of study cannot be determined, but it is evidence of a developing sense that city affairs required professionalism in their handling. European cities, whereas they often experienced just as rapid a growth as American cities and felt as heavily the dislocations of industrialization, had still been administered in political cultures which did not denigrate politics and government as they were denigrated in the United States. In many cases these cities also had histories which went back for centuries into the past and around which clustered traditions of local patriotism and public service. While all of this did not enable Europeans to solve their broad political and social problems any better than similar problems were solved here, it probably did make it easier for them to devise efficient administrative mechanisms. At any rate, Americans increasingly visited Europe with a view to examining different facets of city administration. Thus German public school policy attracted the interest of superintendents of education in Illinois and New Jersey, who visited that country in 1872 and 1877 respectively. Milwaukee and Boston both sent delegations to study the handling of various urban problems in several European countries during the 1880's and 1890's. In park administration, London and Paris proved especially interesting to Americans concerned with that subject. The Chicago Citizens Association, a reform organization, recommended in 1892 that English cities be studied as models of good government in general. The progressives' interest in efficient city government in Europe gradually weaned them from customary American suspicion of public authority. Albert B. Shaw, a prominent progressive editor and journalist, was favorably impressed not only with city government in Germany, but with the philosophy which lay behind it. "The practical management of German cities," he wrote in 1895, "proceeds in harmony with the German conception of the municipality as a social organism. . . . It is enough for us to understand that in Germany the community, organized centrally and officially, is a far more positive factor in the life of the family or the individual than in America. . . . There are, in the German conception of city government, no limits whatever to municipal functions. It is the business of the municipality to promote in every feasible way its own welfare and the welfare of its citizens." The notion of creative government was not immediately welcomed, however, and few of his contemporaries would have gone as far as Shaw in recommending what in the mid-twentieth century has come to be known as a "welfare state."

All the while, as municipal reform became a national movement in the last two decades of the nineteenth century, and as trial-and-error practice built up a growing fund of professional and expert knowledge about the exigencies of city government, agencies to coordinate the movement began to take shape. State municipal conventions appeared first in Iowa in 1877. Early in 1894, a group of Philadelphians invited other organizations elsewhere to send representatives to that city for what should be the first Annual Conference for Good City Government. Out of this convention came a new association in the following year, called the National Municipal League. The League prospered and soon began to issue the *National Municipal Review* in which articles and editorials discussed the administrative problems of many cities. In the last years of the century the League adopted a "model charter," incorporating what its leading experts considered the best proposals for governmental structure practicable at the time. The model charter (which was revised from time to time in future years) called for a strong mayor, an independent comptroller, a large measure of civil service, limitations on franchise granting by the council, and considerable home rule—although there was argument on this point from those who felt that strong state administrative boards were good for city government.

The League was not a leader in municipal reform. It arose rather as a result of maturing reform movements in almost every city in the country. The provisions of its model charter had each been tried out in a variety of ways in individual cities across the land. Most significantly the League did not anticipate (and came rather gradually to support) the two most important of all structural reforms in American cities: the commission and manager plans. But the League's appearance did signal an important stage in the development of American attitudes toward city government. It certified, so to speak, that concern with urban political affairs had become nationalized, and it marked the coalescence of efforts and campaigns that had previously been isolated. "Good government" could now start building its own traditions.

Aside from negative Jeffersonian notions about the desirability of "creative government," theory never played a great role in the shaping of city government in this country. The essentially pragmatic character of reform appears clearly in the emergence of the commission and city manager plans, which stemmed neither from European models nor from doctrinaire considerations of any kind, but rather from special and local circumstances. In 1900 a hurricane and tidal wave struck Galveston, Texas with devastating force. In twenty-four hours one-sixth of the population had been drowned and one-third of the property destroyed. The regular city government proved unable to cope with the terrible emergency and the staggering tasks of reconstruction; the state legislature had to come to the rescue. It did so by appointing a commission of five well-known local businessmen to govern Galveston during the emergency period. The arrangement was extremely autocratic but it also turned out to be highly efficient. The city's affairs were divided into four categories, each with a commissioner in charge; the fifth commissioner was a coordinator and acted more or less like a mayor. So ably was the city administration conducted that the legislature provided for continuance of the new system in a city charter in 1903, according to which three of the commissioners were to be appointed by the governor and two elected locally. This, although it had solid backing in the Galveston business community, was invalidated by the state supreme court, and the legislature then changed the charter so that all the commissioners were to be elected. In this basic form, with many local variations, the "commission system" spread rapidly. One prominent and encouraging adoption was in Des Moines, Iowa where the proposal was successfully promoted as "businessman's government." By 1917 about five hundred communities had adopted the plan (the largest were Memphis and Jersey City), and then its popularity began to wane. In some places people were disappointed to find that the new system did not necessarily eliminate "politics" from city government, nor did it automatically result in increased efficiency—which depended entirely upon finding the right candidates for election to the commission.

Another reason for declining popularity of the commission plan was the appearance of a competitor in the shape of the city manager plan. In the 1890's, while reformers were stressing efficient executive administration and expert knowledge in government, the notion of a "municipal manager" had occasionally been aired, but no effort was made to institute such an office until 1908. In that year the city of Staunton, Virginia hit upon the scheme of having the mayor and council hire a man to control all of the administrative functions of the government, choosing his own assistants who would be the heads of the various departments. This was a way of achieving (or at least aiming at) the kind of simplification and efficiency which were so impressive in the Galveston example, and it would also get around the requirement in Virginia's constitution that cities must have mayors and councils: a requirement that was duplicated in many other states. Staunton's experiment proved that the manager system was workable and in the next four years several other small cities imitated it. Then nature intervened once more in the history of American city government when a disastrous flood hit Dayton, Ohio. There had already been considerable agitation in Dayton (and elsewhere in the country) for adoption of the city manager plan; John M. Patterson, president of the National Cash Register Company with headquarters in Dayton, became a tireless advocate. The flood convinced enough people of the need for unencumbered city administration so that the manager plan was adopted. After Dayton, cities adopted the plan in increasing numbers and by 1923, 310 had done so. In the following year Cleveland decided to try the plan, and in 1926 Kansas City, Missouri and Cincinnati did the same. This seems to have been the high point of the manager system's career; Cleveland abandoned it after a few years and its subsequent slow spread has been among smaller places.

The commission and manager plans were rationalized in classical reform terms: they provided efficient administrative systems and they permitted democracy to function better—the voter could participate more intelligently and effectively in self-government in these relatively simple governmental frameworks. Yet some of their characteristics had other implications. Both plans were frequently compared to the organization of business corporations; much of their success was due to the spread of the idea that city government ought to be conducted on business principles. Bryce, in the 1891 edition of *The American Commonwealth,* had observed that Americans were beginning to draw the lesson that cities "are not so much little states as large corporations." A representative reform view, expressed a few years before the Galveston experiment, had it that "government of cities is business and not politics." Municipal reform, and especially the two innovations just described, represented largely the application of business ideology to city government; most of the support for reform charters came from businessmen and from the professions.

Another important controlling assumption in the movement to reform city government was that expert administrators were necessary and that the voters were not equipped to pass upon the complexities of administrative powers. The tendency of reform was toward relatively unhampered initiative in the hands of the officials, with the voters exercising—in effect—a periodic referendum on the overall results. As an active reformer expressed it, "the details of departmental administration can never be made the subject of intelligent determination by the mass of the electors." The effects of this assumption—the correctness of which in twentieth century conditions need not be questioned—are at best problematic. It is worth noting that the idea of "big government" was assimilated by Americans on the local level before it was assimilated on the federal level.

Much of the history of American city government since the days of Boss Tweed is described unavoidably in terms of bosses *versus* reformers. Without analyzing the implicit value judgments, it may be noted that they can obscure important aspects of governmental development. In the first place, the relationships between bossism and the proposals of reformers have been more complex than is often assumed. Significant measures of administrative centralization and home rule came to New York City in its charters of 1867 and 1870: both of them were secured from the state legislature by Tweed himself, and after his downfall no one proposed to alter their key provisions in later charters. Memphis adopted the commission plan in 1909 and Jersey City followed in 1911; Kansas City, Missouri adopted the manager plan in 1926. Out of the first of these changes arose the machine of Edward Crump; out of the second arose the machine of Frank Hague; and out of the third arose a revivified machine in the hands of Thomas J. Pendergast. Centralization of authority and responsibility was at best a two-edged weapon.

In the second place, there has been one constant factor in the development of city government, quite independent of both bosses and reformers: with mushrooming urbanization, the size, complexity, and cost of city government have grown. In spite of taxpayers' anxieties and in spite of widespread adoption of many measures which undoubtedly increased the efficiency of city government, its cost per capita rose by 53 per cent between 1902 and 1918; this figure does not include interest on indebtedness, and American city debts more than doubled during the same years. In the autumn of 1901, a group of reformers in New York City backed Seth Low, already famous for his fine record as former Mayor of Brooklyn as well as of New York itself, against an incumbent Tammany-supported administration. Low was elected, on a platform calling for "progressive, businesslike, and nonpartisan administration of municipal affairs, with a special view to cutting down public expenses and reducing the present excessive burden of taxation." Many of his backers were surprised when Low's first budget exceeded the estimates prepared by the out-going Tammany mayor by $600,000. An editorial in *The Outlook* magazine noted that it should have been expected: "The more alert the citizenship of a place and the greater their confidence in their city officials the larger is the work the municipality is required to perform for its members." In short, reform was likely to be at least as expensive as corruption.

Regardless of reformers or bosses, there was no way to avoid the increasing range and scale of governmental activity. As early as 1889, the device of the specialized metropolitan commission had been used to provide sewerage facilities in the area of Greater Boston; by the 1920's special commissions dealing with a variety of metropolitan problems had become relatively common. When the five boroughs of Brooklyn, Queens, Richmond, Bronx, and Manhattan were joined into Greater New York City in 1897, the second largest urban agglomeration in the world presented its needs and problems to the new officials. An even more impressive example of the growing size of government in response to acutely felt needs was in the creation of the Port of New York Authority twenty-four years later. New York City and several New Jersey communities had shared the great eastern harbor since their earliest days, but they had not done so with any noticeable harmony. Controversies over navigation, pilot, and quarantine laws, which were different in the two states, marked the relationship from the beginning; in the nineteenth century conflict over railroad rates intensified mutual hostility and rendered interstate cooperation all but impossible. The experience of the First World War brought the basic problem to a head when by 1917, 200,000 railroad cars were backed up in the area around New York City, Hoboken, and Jersey City waiting to be unloaded at the port facilities. The federal government took over the railroads directly once the United States entered the war, but meanwhile the state legislatures of New York and New Jersey had been persuaded to appoint commissions to propose long-term remedies for the port's problems. On their own initiative the two commissions merged into one; after three years' consideration, it recommended creation of a new interstate agency with wide powers over the area's transport and docking arrangements. Both of the legislatures approved measures embodying this recommendation, whereupon it was quickly approved by Congress under the "compact clause" of the federal constitution. The Port Authority grew rapidly because it obviously met a crying need. At the outset its operations were financed by yearly appropriations of $100,000 by each of the legislatures, but its supervision of income-producing facilities enabled it to develop its own bonding program. The first bond issue was for $14,000,000 in 1926; by the early 1960's the Port Authority's outstanding debt amounted to about three-quarters of a billion dollars.

The New York Port Authority has not been directly imitated elsewhere, simply because it was designed to meet a highly specialized problem, but it is an example of needs generated by urbanization that evoke notable extension of public authority. This extension took many forms; during the 1920's, cities in every part of the country were providing new services which ranged from public health nursing and children's clinics to community centers and vocational guidance. It is this perspective which is likely to prove most rewarding in the study of city government. Reform and its antagonists played significant roles, but in a context which embraced both. The pace and character of American urbanization has spawned metropolitan (and even, by mid-twentieth century, "megalopolitan") areas, forced heterogeneous groups of people into close contiguity, and pushed always upon the limits of given stages of technological development. It has at the same time intensified and multiplied needs for community action.

8

Bosses and Reformers

The appearance of "the boss" as a key figure in the American political system was closely related to the cumbersome machinery of city government, physical expansion of the cities, immigration which made them into cultural and ethnic patchwork quilts, and commercial and industrial growth which crowned the efforts of successful city promoters. Inefficient administrative structures encouraged the flow of power into the hands of men who could get things done by cutting corners or even, if necessary, by ignoring the laws. City growth provided an increasing number of tasks which had to be fulfilled. The presence of varying and often mutually hostile linguistic, religious, and racial groups within the urban population complicated the problems of social communication and furnished representative government with a new kind of constituency, one not generally anticipated when the country was founded. The success of urban promotions directed the attention

201

of most businessmen to the management of their private enterprises and away from community problems. Into this gap between the need for government and a growing shortage of volunteers to provide it, strode the professional city politician. People whose exigencies he understood and responded to sustained him at the polls, and when he succeeded in building a reliable voting organization, he was called a boss. The boss, along with his equally typical opponent, the reformer, dominated the urban political scene in the United States for almost three generations.

The boss was stereotyped by the early 1870's, most effectively by the cartoons of Thomas Nast in *Harper's Weekly* during the struggle to oust William Marcy Tweed from the government of New York City. Other cartoonists elsewhere in the country took up similar themes and soon a recognizable, predictable character was sketched out. The boss, in this stereotype, was sometimes snarling, sometimes jovial. He often smoked cigars and wore a derby hat. His face almost always had Irish features. He was usually portrayed with his hand in the public till, surrounded by ill-washed, grinning, and rough-looking cronies.

Like all durable stereotypes, this one has some connection with reality, but it smothers individual differences and ignores context: only one element is singled out and stressed, at the expense of complexity and understanding. Bossism was not a simple phenomenon, but rather a pervasive form of political behavior. It emerged quite naturally in its nineteenth century urban environment, on many levels—from the precinct to the whole city—and with many variations. It can best be understood when urban communities are regarded as partly organic (rather than as mere collections of individuals), such that at stages in their growth they develop needs; these needs can be met, in turn, only by use of the social materials and resources that are available at these particular stages. The different fortunes and the contributions of bosses and reformers alike can be assessed in relation to these needs and resources.

New York City offers an example in Boss Tweed, who bequeathed to his city the best publicized political machine in the United States and whose career excited international comment. It ought to be noted in passing that the city's politics had never been regarded as pure. One editor asked in 1753 "how often have the votes of the people been purchased . . . without the least endeavor to conceal the bribery?" In 1768, a letter in a newspaper described a tavern where "every freeholder or freeman, who was willing to part with his vote, might there meet with a purchaser." It was proposed in 1780—unsuccessfully—to introduce the secret ballot in New York elections, "to prevent men of property, power, and tyrannical dispositions [from] . . . intimidating the electors from a free disposition of their votes."

By the time Tweed reached voting age, in the early 1840's, the Tammany organization was already a considerable power in the city. It traced its origin to a Jeffersonian political club started in the 1790's as the Society of St. Tammany. (The name "Tammany" was probably that of a Delaware Indian chief.) Many such clubs appeared in the United States during these years, as various groups and interests organized to oust the tightly-knit Federalist elite from power. The Tammany club continued to play a political role through the early nineteenth century, without notable success; for example, it fought against DeWitt Clinton's Erie Canal project. It also provided a social center and, like many voluntary associations, burial insurance for its members.

Under the guidance of hopeful local politicians, the Society began in the 1820's and 1830's to back proposals which were to become increasingly popular: abolition of imprisonment for debt and passage of a mechanics' lien law were two of these. During the depression from 1837 to 1842, Tammany officials prominently distributed quantities of fuel, clothing, and food in the poorer quarters of the city. As the modern national party system began to coalesce, Tammany grew into the main agency in New York City for the Democratic Party. As it became consistently (and then officially) Democratic, it also became increasingly popular; its charitable activities and its hospitality to the newly arrived Irish immigrant—along with its staunch opposition to rising anti-Catholicism—made Tammany something of a "poor man's club."

As the party connection became clearer, Tammany also acquired another source of power: patronage. The club was consulted in the choice of candidates, and candidates who won with Tammany's help consulted it about the distribution of city, state, or federal jobs. While federal patronage was not large by modern standards, the New York City custom house did supply a considerable number of opportunities. With the growth of the port, duties collected there became the government's largest single source of income by the 1820's. Between 1827 and 1843 the custom house staff grew from 164 to 503 and its payroll from $112,000 to $489,000. An investigation in 1839 revealed a well-established system of "cut," whereby Tammany got people jobs on the New York customs staff and in return the job holders gave part of their salary to the organization. The same investigation uncovered defalcations by customs officials amounting to a million and a half dollars. Wholesale ballot frauds were common; in the city election of 1844—the first in which Tweed was old enough to vote—55,000 votes were cast; the figure is about 10,000 higher than the number of residents eligible to cast them. Tweed, in other words, did not invent the boss system. The system grew naturally as cities grew.

William Marcy Tweed came from a family of relatively prosperous craftsmen; in his youth he passed through apprenticeship as a carpenter. He was good at his trade and soon owned two shops. Big, full of energy and good will, he was popular with his neighbors and was elected captain of the volunteer fire company to which he belonged. The first time he ran for a ward office he lost, but came back again to win a seat as alderman. Running against a popular Whig, Tweed had persuaded a friend, also a Whig, to enter the race; this split the opposition enough to enable Tweed to get in by less than fifty votes.

On the board of aldermen, Tweed set about centralizing the previously individualistic enterprises of the officials, and raising the scale of these enterprises. By the Civil War decade, political corruption was organized to an impressive degree. Tweed persuaded the aldermen to contract with one man for the entire city's street cleaning, instead of doing it by district as the practice had been. The successful bidder was paid $279,000 for a year's work—and immediately "kicked back" $40,000 from his fee. Again, under Tweed's effective leadership, the city paid $100,000 for a plot of ground for a potter's field; its market value would normally have been $30,000, and the pleased seller gave some of his money from the land sale back to the group of men who had made it possible. At one time the city hall was actually sold to satisfy a claim against the city; it was later bought back for more than had been received at the first sale.

These anecdotes, revealing as they are (and there are many more about the Tweed period), constitute only part of the story. All the while, whatever his reasons may have been, Tweed was seeing that some important things were accomplished. Streets were extended in the sprawling city; franchises were granted for horse-drawn street railways; the planning of Central Park went ahead; a new County Court House was built. Twice during Tweed's public career, New York City's governmental structure was over-hauled in the interests of at least some much-needed efficiency. Tweed favored both revisions; of the second (in 1870) he even said it had cost him $600,000 to get it passed.

It is clear, of course, that the boss could line his own pockets from building, street paving contracts, and franchises, and that centralization of authority through charter revision was likely to strengthen him. Still, the process of urbanization called for these things, and the New York example suggests that in the circumstances corruption was the agency by which they were provided. After his downfall, Tweed remarked that "The fact is New York politics were always dishonest—long before my time. There never was a time when you couldn't buy the Board of Aldermen. A politician in coming forward takes these things as they are. This population is too hopelessly split up into races and factions to govern it under universal suffrage, except by the bribery of patronage or corruption." A recent scholar, Seymour Mandelbaum, has endorsed Boss Tweed's analysis, writing that "only a universal payment of benefits—a giant 'pay-off'—could pull the city together in a common effort. The only treasury big enough to support coordination was the public till."

Tweed and his friends were driven out of City Hall in the fall of 1871, after bankers and others had become seriously alarmed at New York's precarious credit standing in the international money markets. He was indicted on 204 counts, convicted on most of them, and sentenced to jail in a curious, tearful courtroom scene where judge, prosecutor, jurymen, and observers all had recourse to their handkerchiefs. After a dramatic attempt to escape in disguise to Europe, the boss was put in prison where he died after a few years. The end of the Tweed ring and the subsequent history of the Tammany organization need not occupy space here. That bossism as illustrated by the Tweed experience was expensive is beyond dispute. New York City's bonded debt rose, during the two-and-a-half-year period up to September 1871 by around forty million dollars. The total increase covers the refunding of inconvenient short-term bonds into long-term bonds and the conversion of revenue bonds (issued to finance an operation or facility, the income from which is supposed to retire these bonds) into part of the city's general debt; this made the debt more expensive to carry at the same time that the principal amount was increasing rapidly. Moreover, the account books were in an almost undecipherable condition when the reform party came into office. This meant that time had to be spent bringing order into the complicated columns of figures. It also meant that for some time the New York authorities actually did not know how much the municipality owed or to whom; uncertainty about the city's current financial position made accurate budgeting impossible. How much was lost through inflated payments to suppliers and contractors will never be known. Still, the costs of the system could be reasonably assessed only if the likely costs of an alternative system could be computed, and one of the questions at issue is whether there were any real alternatives for the community.

The Tammany organization's long life, along with the almost universal experience of other American cities, suggests that the system was strongly rooted in the conditions of urban growth. A reform coalition drove Tweed and his associates out, but the Tammany-led Democrats were back, victorious, at the next election and held power most of the time thereafter in New York. The organization's features—and over the following two generations, its character—changed; the most flagrant practices from the Tweed period were abolished. But long after the twentieth century began, observers still described the boss system flourishing on its diet of personal influence, patronage, and special favors.

Philadelphia's machine government, during the same period, was in many ways similar to that of New York. The Philadelphia machine, however, was Republican and immigration did not play as large a part in its growth as it did elsewhere: Philadelphia was the most "American" of all the big cities. Moreover, Philadelphia also counted a larger property-owning group than any of the other metropolitan centers in the last third of the nineteenth century. Whereas most city bosses were Democrats and ethnic and class factors were important to them, the system still could flourish in either party and immigration alone does not explain its emergence.

In 1835, a private company began supplying Philadelphia with gas. Six years later the city bought out the company and proceeded to run the gas works as a municipal enterprise. A special board of trustees was set up to superintend the operation. This was done to keep the important utility "out of politics;" ironically, a powerful political machine soon developed in the Gas Trust itself. The trust had the power to contract for construction and repairs and could issue its own bonds, which meant that it could distribute favors and profits to many contractors. It also hired and fired the 2,000 people employed by the gas works, which gave it the largest block of patronage in the city.

Shortly after the Civil War, James McManes began to emerge as the dominant influence in the Gas Trust. Skillful distribution of contracts and jobs gave him and his associates power over most of the city's other activities as well as the gas works. They bought into Philadelphia's largest street transportation company, and this gave them another block of jobs to hand out. Soon McManes had almost absolute control over the Republican Party in Philadelphia, with great influence at the state capital and in Washington as well.

The Gas Trust met and deliberated in secret; McManes kept all payroll and personnel records to himself. City elections were regularly won by the machine. City employees were just as regularly assessed part of their salaries in order to help finance the machine; policemen, for example, had to pay anywhere from ten to twenty-five dollars a year, depending upon how large a compaign effort seemed necessary. Several city government posts provided their holders with sizeable incomes from fees—the Collector of Delinquent Taxes made $200,000 one year—and a share of these incomes was also turned back to the machine.

The system proved expensive in Philadelphia, as it proved in New York; between 1860 and 1880 the city debt increased from $20,000,000 to $70,000,000. This was a powerful influence in the formation of an anti-McManes reform coalition at the beginning of the eighties. A group of the city's best-known businessmen, calling themselves the Committee of One Hundred, of whom almost all were Republicans, cooperated with the local Democratic Party in 1881 to oust the McManes-controlled administration. There followed a wave of legal prosecutions, a thorough paring of the voting rolls which had been heavily padded, and a series of measures to introduce order and accountability into the city's finances. McManes was not indicted, and simply retired to private life. Nevertheless, reform's triumph was short-lived. Within a few years the Committee of One Hundred disbanded, and Philadelphia's affairs again passed into the hands of professional machine politicians. Around the turn of the century, Lincoln Steffens claimed that of all the boss-governed cities in the country, Philadelphia was "the most corrupt and the most contented."

Chicago provides still another example of bossism with variations of its own. Throughout the nineteenth century and well into the twentieth, no single machine controlled Chicago's public life. This may have been due partly to the extremely rapid growth of the place, from next to nothing in 1830 to over a million in 1890. It may owe something to the sprawling geography of the city, from its business heart near the lake in three directions—north, south, and west—to where, as Theodore Dreiser described it in *Sister Carrie,* "narrow board walks extended out, passing here a house and there a store, at far intervals, eventually ending on the open prairie." For whatever reasons, no leader appeared who was able to control enough of the unstable and heterogeneous elements in Chicago's population to dominate the city.

Instead, there were always several machines, sometimes contending, sometimes cooperating, giving the city's politics an inconsistency which made it possible for reform organizations to score more frequent victories than they did in most other cities. Steffens noted that "Minneapolis has cleaned up, Pittsburgh has tried to, New York fights every other election, Chicago fights all the time." There were many bosses in both major parties. Some, like the Carter Harrisons (father and son), Charles Deneen, and William Lorimer, had public appeal and ran their factions from the strongholds of elective office, as mayors or governors or senators. Others, like Roger Sullivan, preferred to move behind the scenes placing men politically indebted to them in the public offices. Each had particular sources of support: Deneen was popular in the middle class residential south side, another faction generally won the northern wards, Sullivan was powerfully entrenched with the utility companies, the Harrisons made great appeal to the Irish Catholics as William Hale Thompson did to the Negroes. "Classes, races, religions, regions," Charles Merriam wrote, "are the background against which the play is built."

In spite of the absence of a central figure controlling the others, Chicago's procedures were like those which prevailed elsewhere. Jobholders in the city government were assessed a percentage of their salaries for the benefit of those to whom the jobs were owed. Boodling—largely the authorizing of franchises in return for money payments to the aldermen—was on a remarkably decentralized basis. At one time, one of the aldermen worked out a scheme for negotiating franchises block by block! During four administrations in the 1890's, there is good evidence that at least fifty-seven of the sixty-eight men who sat as aldermen accepted bribes for their votes.

The universality of bossism is indicated perhaps most forcefully by the experience of the nation's capital in the 1870's. Washington, D. C. was never an industrial city, and its form of government has been unlike that of other American cities. Early in 1871, Congress provided it with a government modeled partly on procedures in the territories. The President appointed a governor and an upper legislative chamber, as well as a board of public works with wide powers to build and to assess costs against the tax-payers. The lower chamber of the council was elected by the city's voting residents; the District was given a non-voting seat on the congressional committee which was responsible for its affairs. One effect of the provisions of the 1871 act was to reduce sharply the power of recently enfranchised Washington Negroes. In a popularly elected city government these people might have played a part corresponding to that of poor immigrants in sustaining bossism in many other cities. As things were, the government of the District of Columbia was not necessarily designed to be responsible to the local popular will.

There was much building to be done. The capital had never

presented a finished appearance and the Civil War years had pushed thoughts of completion into the background. Now, however, progress was in the air. Congress authorized a great new structure to house the State, War, and Navy Departments. Private real estate business quickened as the new form of government went into effect. The role of the Board of Public Works was clearly going to be important.

Very soon the personality of Alexander Shepherd, one of its five members, impressed itself indelibly on the rest of the board. The other board members did what Shepherd told them. He had been born and raised in Washington, and after the Civil War had come into prominence as a highly speculative developer of residential property. Shepherd wanted to move fast in the building of a modern metropolis; he designed and promoted a system of improvements for the city. The political environment for his operations was surprisingly like that in New York, Philadelphia, and Chicago: jobs in the city government constituted patronage for a political machine, but in this case the machine was the national Republican Party under the leadership of President Grant. Shepherd was a friend of Grant's, and this explained his appointment to the board. Later, Grant named him Governor of the District of Columbia.

His program included a new drainage system, the levelling of hills and filling in of depressions, extensive street paving, and provision that views of the Capitol from various points in the city should be impressive. The plan, in the words of historian Constance M. Green, was "calculated to create a city with unrivalled sanitary facilities and clean, well-paved, well-lighted thoroughfares."

It was also expensive, but Shepherd had his way. Over the objections of men who feared the financial consequences—with good reason—he pushed a large bond issue (which did have to be approved by local voters). It passed, helped by Shepherd's judicious distribution of jobs at the disposal of his board, by a twelve to one margin. Within a short time the District's indebtedness had risen to a level where it was surpassed by that of only seven states. References to "Boss Shepherd" began to appear in public print, and critics compared him with New York's Tweed. Still, a cleaner and more attractive city was emerging under the eyes of Shepherd and his critics alike. When his grandiose schemes, along with the panic of 1873, brought Washington to a point where only Congressional intervention could save it from outright bankruptcy, Shepherd lost his job and retired to Mexico.

His public career had resembled Tweed's in many ways: the use of public posts as patronage, graft in the awarding of construction contracts, and the role of financial accounting in bringing about his downfall all testify that bossism flourished in the nation's capital under an explicitly authoritarian government as it did in other cities more responsive to democratic pressures.

Bossism, machine government, and corruption of public officials were typical in American cities during most of the nineteenth century. In Milwaukee a grand jury handed down more than seventy indictments against public officeholders in the year 1903 alone. In St. Louis it was reported that one council member inquired about the possibility of suing a utility official who had offered a bribe but had not paid it. Lincoln Steffens gained his first fame as a journalist going from city to city and describing the bosses and the machines in each for readers of *McClure's Magazine*. Many lesser known writers exploited the same material; few subjects bulked larger in the newspaper and magazine press between the 1880's and the first World War.

There were reformers, of course, and they could count—especially in the early twentieth century—significant victories against the bosses. Moisei Ostrogorski, in his pioneering study of American party organization published in 1902, described what he called "an outburst" of civic reform organizations beginning in the mid-eighties. He concluded that these groups had achieved lasting results; "the aspect of things has changed perceptibly for the better. . . . Municipal reform is not only before the public, but fashionable." Eight years later even Lord Bryce—whose remark that city government was "the one most conspicuous failure of the United States" became one of the frequently quoted sentences on the subject—asserted none could doubt "that things are better than they were twenty-five years ago."

Municipal reform during the late nineteenth and early twentieth centuries usually stressed efficiency and honest accounting in public administration. Its main achievements were structural changes

211

which made those goals easier to achieve or, as many hoped, more difficult to avoid. Home rule for cities, the short ballot, nonpartisan municipal elections, regular independent audits of city accounts, and finally the commission and city manager forms of government, all revealed widespread talent for political innovation and tended to bring government within a more manageable compass. The reformers' analysis of bossism was usually cast in terms of good people *versus* bad people; they argued that undesirable types got into local administrations through the cracks and crannies in the inefficient, obsolete, and impossibly complicated structure of local government. If this was so, then a reform in structure should encourage reforms in substance.

Sometimes another reform dimension was added, when moral crusaders attacked the machines' connection with prostitution, gambling, and bootlegging. The most famous of the crusades during this period was led by a clergyman. In 1894, the Rev. Charles Parkhurst of the Madison Square Presbyterian Church toured some of the more unsavory districts on Manhattan Island and publicized what he learned about police protection of vice. His effective portrayal led to a legislative investigation and roused enough voters to unseat Tammany for two years, during which time some improvements were introduced into police administration by Commissioner Theodore Roosevelt. In the same year, the English journalist William T. Stead published *If Christ Came to Chicago,* which described the same close connections between politicians, police, and criminals in the Illinois metropolis. Seven thousand copies of Stead's book were reported sold on the day of its publication; it triggered a reform movement in Chicago, and continued to attract attention there and elsewhere to the problem with which it dealt.

The structural reforms suggested by political science and the moral ardor usually stemming from religious impulses were not in themselves enough to regenerate any American city. Triumph along these lines was typically evanescent; the reformers captured city hall, fired some policemen, prosecuted some machine public officials, and administered what R. Richard Wohl called "disaster relief" to the city treasury, only to be swept away at the next election by the resurgent power of the bosses. The usual associations of the moral and political reformers were upper-class, native American, and Protestant. They rarely drew any warm response from the cities' poorer masses, many of whom were, of course, immigrants and Catholics. Theodore Roosevelt represented the social philosophy of many reformers when he wrote in 1886, "Voters of the laboring class in the cities are very emotional . . . if a man is open handed and warm-hearted, they consider it as being a fair offset to his being a little shaky when it comes to applying the eighth commandment to affairs of State." A few years earlier, in the wake of Tweed's downfall, a reform-oriented commission appointed by Governor Samuel J. Tilden recommended that voting rights in municipal elections be limited to taxpaying property owners. Inclinations of this kind gave reform a "highbrow" stereotype and made it very difficult for it to find a mass base.

In a few important cases, reform leaders were able to build stable and victorious organizations for themselves—to become, as it might be said, "reform bosses." In these cases, one finds the structural and moral elements included within a somewhat larger program, linking the problems of the city to the more general environment of the American economic scene itself. One also finds the reformer making a deliberate bid for the votes of the common people, attempting to democratize reform out of its long association with upper-class values. The best known examples are Hazen Pingree of Detroit, Samuel M. Jones of Toledo, and Thomas L. Johnson of Cleveland.

Pingree was a well-to-do business man, first elected Mayor of Detroit in 1889; he was successively re-elected until 1896 when he became Governor of Michigan. During his municipal administration Pingree publicized the corruption of Detroit's officials, especially by utility companies. He gained great popularity fighting for carefully restricted franchises for the street railways and gas companies, and managed to have a municipally owned electric lighting plant built. His activities did much to popularize the whole issue of municipal ownership. "Good municipal government is an impossibility," Pingree said, "while valuable franchises are to be had and can be obtained by corrupt use of money. . . . I believe the time has come for municipal ownership of street railway lines, water, gas, electric lighting, telephone, and other necessary conveniences which by their nature are monopolies." This emphasis tended to

213

associate the evils of city government with the larger questions inherent in the relationship between private business and public service.

Samuel Jones, called "Golden Rule" Jones, had made a small fortune manufacturing oil drilling equipment. He became Mayor of Toledo in 1897, remaining in office until he died in 1904. Like Pingree, Jones supported municipal ownership of utilities, and actually became an idealistic kind of socialist. He pushed the development of public playgrounds, free concerts in parks, and free kindergartens in schools. He established an eight-hour day and a minimum hourly wage for city employees. He got a new charter from the state which contained provisions for the initiative, referendum, and recall. Jones broke with the regular Republican organization which had first helped to elect him, and in his three subsequent campaigns he ran as an independent. "The fact of the matter is," he wrote, "there is little hope for improvement, for progress, in the direction of scientific government in our municipalities until we shall first get the people freed from the baneful superstition of partisan politics." Jones's combination of nonpartisan campaigns with a program stressing social welfare suggested that reform itself could be almost unbeatable at the polls.

In Cleveland, Thomas L. Johnson performed comparably as Mayor between 1901 and 1909, when he was finally defeated in a close election. He was something of an inventor, had invested heavily and profitably in steel mills and utility franchises, and was a rich man by the time he was forty. During a train trip one day, he fell into reading a copy of Henry George's economic reform classic, *Progress and Poverty,* and was so affected by it that he began building a second career—this time as a reform politician. With great popular appeal, he served two terms as a Democratic congressman in the nineties, and then turned his attention toward the problems of Cleveland. As its mayor, he broke up the connection between the police and the brothel keepers by promising not to prosecute the madams if they would agree to remain orderly, not to pay anything to policemen, and not to steal from their customers. (A friend of Johnson's remarked that the mayor was not trying to enforce Christianity, but rather to make it possible.)

Like Pingree and Jones, he fought to limit utility franchises, and

214

finally forced the street-railway fare down to three cents, which endeared him to many voters. He was tireless in advocating municipal ownership of utilities. "Only through municipal ownership," he stated, "can the gulf which divides the community into a small dominant class on one side and the unorganized people on the other be bridged; only through municipal ownership can the talent of the city be identified with the city; only by making men's ambitions and pecuniary interests identical with the welfare of the city can civil warfare be ended." At the same time that Johnson fought to bring utilities under public control, he promoted social welfare projects such as municipal bath houses, recreation areas, and careful inspection of meat and dairy products. To help him in the large task he had undertaken he introduced a degree of expertise into his administration, gathering about him a "brain trust" of young men who brought professional scholarship into the practical study of city government. Lincoln Steffens claimed that Johnson made Cleveland the best-governed city in the United States.

These three men resembled one another in that each used some of the arts of the demagogue—each, that is, carefully established his own image as a "friend of the people." At the same time they attacked municipal problems which meant more to more voters than did honest accounting taken by itself. In this way, they gave municipal reform in their own cities a wider and more durable appeal than the Reverend Parkhurst or the National Municipal League or the Committee of One Hundred could supply.

In achieving power by means of broad popular appeals and then using their power to achieve reform goals which included social welfare projects, these three men did not typify municipal reform during the years in which they flourished. Jones's inclination toward socialism especially placed him outside the ranks of representative reformers. For political reform was ordinarily conceived in business, terms, sponsored by successful businessmen, and designed consciously or unconsciously to serve business ends. Pingree, Jones, and Johnson were themselves successful entrepreneurs, but they left their businesses behind them when they turned to public life, and did not regard the latter as a function of the former. The business motivation behind most municipal reform in the eighties, the nineties, and much of the twentieth century reflected the social sources of the reform movements and bore significantly upon the failures and successes of the political reformers themselves.

The boss system arose partly out of universal suffrage and local, decentralized representation in an urban environment. When Tweed explained New York City's political corruption by the diversity of its population, he was largely accurate. Big cities in the explosively industrializing United States in the nineteenth century were governmental units, but socially they were increasingly fragmented as their development proceeded. They became patchworks of neighborhoods which were for most purposes separate sub-communities. Economic and social equality never characterized American cities, but disparities in wealth and status grew wider in the early stages of industrial progress. At the same time, the cities grew so large physically that communication through the ranks in their hierarchies became practically impossible. Men could no longer walk from one neighborhood to any or all of the others at will. In Tweed's day, before the telephone and before rapid transit, it might well have been easier for a man living in Brooklyn to reach another man in Chicago by letter than to reach an administrator in New York's City Hall.

Supposing the physical barriers to communication had been overcome—as they were overcome by invention and innovation—there remained cultural barriers. Cosmopolitan and comfortable George Templeton Strong and the recently-arrived Polish laborer might have had much of interest to say to one another, but how could they have said it? Not only would the languages of the two be different; so would almost all of their basic assumptions about society, wealth, poverty, religion, community and family life, and about what the city was good for. It is most likely, indeed, that neither would have felt impelled to seek out conversation with the other.

Yet they were both New Yorkers. By the mid-nineteenth century the forms and styles of life in New York were various and were becoming more so. On the map, they were distributed into residential districts marked out by class and ethnic lines: rich, middle class, poor, Irish, German, Negro, Jewish, and so on. When Jacob Riis wrote *How the Other Half Lives,* he was able in many cases to mark out the boundaries of the districts by specific blocks and street numbers. In social and cultural life these groups kept largely to themselves. In politics, the system of voting by precincts and wards gave each of them a chance to be represented and to have its imperative needs recognized and discussed near the centers of public power.

At the same time, the system reinforced the physical fragmenta- tion of the cities. From a cost-accounting standpoint it was not an efficient system; there was always the possibility of financial disas- ter, as in the cases of Tweed, McManes, and Shepherd. Moreover, the wealthy groups found that the system made it difficult and sometimes quite impossible for them to assert any control over city affairs. Whether their motives were rooted in public spirit or in anxiety about tax rates, more and more of them grew restive under the restraints and burdens of bossism. Among the better-off busi- ness men were to be found most of the leaders of the spreading political reform movements in and after the 1880's.

This is especially noticeable in movements for the commission and city manager plans. These structural changes proposed to in- troduce the efficiency of the private corporation into the processes of city government. Clinton R. Woodruff's description of the com- mission plan was representative; it was, he wrote in 1911, "an application to city administration of that type of business organiza- tion which has been so common and so successful in the field of commerce and industry." Chambers of commerce almost always led in local efforts to make these changes. Analyzing the organiza- tions which supported charter reform in Pittsburgh in the early 1900's, Samuel P. Hays has found that of the names of 745 mem- bers, almost two-thirds were in social registers and other directories which together included only two per cent of the families in the city. In the forefront of the movement were representatives of the biggest banks and industrial corporations in Pittsburgh.

While the reformers of city politics had to appeal for votes at the polls, and defined their objectives as serving the public in- terest in general, their assumptions about social class and political eligibility were often far from democratic. One spokesman at the National Municipal League's 1907 convention urged that it stood to reason "that a man paying $5,000 taxes in a town is more in- terested in the well-being and development of his town than the

217

man who pays no taxes. . . . Shall we be truly democratic and give the property owner a fair show or shall we develop a tyranny of ignorance which shall crush him?" In 1911, a reform publication contended that "employment as an ordinary laborer and in the lowest class of mill work would naturally lead to the conclusion that such men did not have sufficient education or business training to act as school directors." And in city after city the reformers found most of their voting support in the wealthier wards and very little of it in the poor wards. William Rockhill Nelson's pro-reform *Kansas City Star* was happy to observe, after a victory at the polls, that "it was in the wards where people live the year 'round and own their own houses that the . . . pluralities were the greatest." Nelson, as well as others like him elsewhere in the country, usually claimed that the reform proposals were particularly in the interest of the "middle class" but he was himself a wealthy man, as were most of his associates.

The Chicago reform movement which followed W. T. Stead's revelations is illustrative. In addition to a graft-ridden police force, Chicago was plagued with widespread unemployment during the winter of 1893–94. Stead was able to bring together some of the city's leading business men and labor union representatives to discuss community problems. Out of these meetings emerged the Chicago Civic Federation. Well financed and carefully organized down to the level of wards and precincts, the federation proposed to deal with unemployment relief and labor relations, conditions in the public school system, the problem of gambling, securing honest vote-counting in city elections, street cleaning, and what it called "civic beauty." Over a three-month period in 1894, the federation provided thousands of dollars in work-relief. Applicants were given jobs cleaning streets; they were paid in certificates which they could exchange for necessaries at specified places. Soon the federation was hiring detectives to investigate fraudulent voting; this led to many indictments and convictions. Detailed investigation of Chicago's street railways followed. The federation opposed municipal ownership; it preferred to advocate refinancing of the companies in the interests of cheaper and more efficient service, and its recommendations did produce some improvements. In 1900, an organization called the National Civic Federation came into being, modeled upon the Chicago organization and dedicated to a coordinated attack upon the same types of problems.

But in spite of its impressive record of achievement, the Chicago Civic Federation never had mass support; it never became a "peoples'" organization. Time after time it sought an overhauling of the city's charter along with the taxing system, only to suffer defeat at the polls. The labor union leaders who had at first participated in the federation's activities soon dropped out and left it an organization largely of Chicago's business elite. The Civic Federation's leadership came for the most part from the directorates of the biggest banks and industrial corporations, the Board of Trade, the real estate business, and the insurance companies. The leaders were public-spirited but also conservative in their social philosophies; unlikely to establish warm and lasting relationships with the city's depressed classes, they represented what Daniel Levine has called "the right wing of the reform movement."

The emphasis on business efficiency and the feeling among well-off businessmen that bossism denied them adequate representation in city government help explain one of the most frequent features of municipal reform campaigns: attacks of one kind or another upon the ward and precinct system. Larger electoral units, the reformers felt, would make it more difficult for the bosses to keep their power, which rested on an informal and highly personal kind of politics. If the unit of representation was enlarged so as to include diverse ethnic and economic interests, no one could successfully barter votes in return for simple privileges keyed to the desires of any one group. Wherever the commission or manager plans went into effect, the size of the municipal legislature was drastically reduced and the members represented larger constituencies than had been the case before reform.

In short, while their programs varied considerably and while there is danger in oversimplifying their motives and objectives, it is clear that most of the reformers took a "stake in society" approach to city politics. They believed that ownership of property subject to taxation, experience in business, and educational preparation gave special qualifications for representation and public office. This understandable attitude lent an upper-class connotation to most of their campaigns which was for many years a serious obstacle to their success. In the early years of the twentieth century they began, however, to score increasing victories with the result that the characteristic structure of American city government was markedly different by 1930 than it had been in 1870.

But the successful reformers and periods when they controlled city governments were exceptional, temporarily interrupting the over-all domination of bosses and machines. The urban environment of nineteenth and much of twentieth century America was apparently more stimulating for bossism than for reform. There were several reasons for this, one of which was the general character of the American party struggle. Although many people identified political corruption as an urban phenomenon, it was not; boss rule in the cities was one form which it might take. C. Vann Woodward has described the patterns of corruption and favoritism by which the rural southern states were governed in the post-Reconstruction period. William Allen White recalled in his *Autobiography* how widespread was the understanding, before the turn of the century, that one transcontinental railroad "owned" the legislature of Nebraska and another "owned" that of Kansas. The once popular American writer, Winston Churchill, wrote a novel about the almost unbeatable machine that dominated New Hampshire in the 1870's and 1880's. Adams County, Ohio without a sizable town in or near it, was the scene of astonishing corruption in the early 1900's. A Republican boss controlled the political life of rural North Dakota for over twenty years. The big city bosses represented an urban phase of American politics.

The bosses' power was partly a result of their professionalism; they made the study of politics and political organization a full-time job, which very few other Americans could do or cared to do. George Washington Plunkitt, who made a fortune in real estate during his lifetime as a Tammany official, described the need for professionalism in plain words: "Politics is as much a regular business as the grocery or dry goods or the drug business. You've got to be trained up to it or you're sure to fail. Suppose a man who knew nothing about the grocery trade suddenly went into the business and tried to conduct it according to his own ideas. Wouldn't he make a mess of it? . . . It's just the same with a reformer. He hasn't been brought up in the difficult business of politics and he makes a mess of it every time." And Plunkitt described his own apprenticeship for his interlocutor: beginning at the age of twelve, he progressed up the organization's ladder by making himself useful during every waking hour.

Moisei Ostrogorski repeated a comment made by many observers when he wrote that Americans dedicated themselves to private pursuits: "The desperate race for wealth has absorbed the citizen, and has not left him time to attend to the public welfare; it even encouraged his want of public spirit and converted it almost into a virtue." Businessmen had their own affairs to tend, with little time left over for the demands of politics. The Philadelphia Committee of One Hundred, disbanding after three years, found that it could not keep workers in the field on a purely voluntary basis; "its members became tired of the thankless task of spending time and money in what must be a continuous, unending battle." In New York, Tilden's commission which studied proposals to improve city government noted that most citizens did not expect to be asked to give much of their time to politics. Governments were "contrivances" to protect people earning honest livings: "when these contrivances . . . become themselves the occasion of incessant watchfulness and enormous expense they fail in their essential purposes." Noting the rapidly expanding commercial and industrial life around him in 1871, E. L. Godkin thought it hardly possible "for men to pay any fruitful attention to politics without neglecting their private affairs."

It is not quite accurate to say simply that the businessman's loss of interest in politics contributed to the rise of bossism. It should be noted as well that most people in the changing economy of nineteenth century America had plenty to occupy their attention in their concern with getting a living, or getting ahead. How much time was left over for the ordinary citizen—the clerk, the wage-earner—in which he could consider community policies? There were hundreds of candidates for local and state office; there were highly technical questions about rates of interest, legal and constitutional intricacies, durations of franchises, advantages and disadvantages of various taxes—matters which demanded concentrated study before an informed opinion about them could be offered. It is not strange that only a few people could give much time to city politics. William Allen White was probably too generous when he estimated in 1910 that "in any precinct of two hundred voters . . . not over fifty people in either party paid serious attention to politics." In the circumstances, bosses and their henchmen performed services that few other Americans ordinarily cared to perform.

In the complicated and badly designed formal structures of the city governments, with mayors and councils (sometimes bicameral) supposed to check and balance each other, with independent and partly independent commissions existing beside them, and with lines of legal authority and responsibility hopelessly confused, there was not only opportunity but also need for effective control—which almost had to be informal. This control was provided by the bosses and their machines. At whatever the price, streets did get paved, lighting, heat, telephone and transportation services were provided, and fire and police forces grew. This was done in spite of sets of explicit and legal rules which were such that they themselves tended to prevent publicity and to make any open, systematic attack on these urban problems impossible. Blake McKelvey points out that sometimes the ablest municipal servants "were so eager to press ahead with street paving, sewer construction, and the like that they quickly learned to play politics with jobs and contracts." It was one way, and possibly the most direct available way, to get things done.

A study of Kansas City during the early years of the Pendergast machine shows James Pendergast, older brother of the better-known Tom, supporting bond issues for school and other construction purposes, park and boulevard legislation, and important improvements in the garbage disposal service—the desirability of which was clearly recognized by many of the local anti-Pendergast forces. During the machine's later growth it identified itself even more firmly with the most impressive building programs the city had ever known. Frank Hague in Jersey City, Huey Long in New Orleans, and many other comparable figures could be cited. Building projects, especially, might strengthen the machine's sources of power but this does not affect the proposition that the bosses and the machines supplied an element of vital organization in communities where this might have been difficult to achieve in any other way.

That the bosses found ways to exert authority on their fragmented and legally almost disorganized communities was generally evidence of their superior executive abilities. Bryce, whose sympathies were always with the reformers, had to concede certain virtues to Philadelphia's Boss McManes: "personal capacity, courage, resolution, foresight, the judicious preference of the substance of power to its display." A comparative study of twenty city bosses who flourished during the early twentieth century found one characteristic common to all of them: each had abilities that would have brought success in any regular line of business enterprise. "Have you ever thought what would become of the country," asked Plunkitt, "if the bosses were put out of business, and their places were taken by lot of coat-tail orators and college graduates? It would mean chaos."

The business talents of bosses were also demonstrated in a social context: many of them were immigrants, or sons of immigrant parents, and found through politics secure places for themselves when other doors were not as widely open. Neighborhoods populated by immigrant groups quickly became the most frequently noted sources for the voting strength of the machines, and many observers concluded that there was an organic connection between bossism and immigration. The connection was usually felt to lie in the immigrant's ignorance of the representative institutions and accepted civic practices of his new country. This explanation would not have accounted for the native-born businessmen who were busily financing many of the boss's operations even while the immigrants were voting for him, but it runs through most contemporary comment on the American urban scene.

The connection between bossism and immigration was certainly a close one, but it was more complicated than most accounts have suggested. In the first place, most of the immigrants were poor. They were poor at a time when government was not generally regarded as a social welfare agency. There were no public works programs, free school lunches, food stamps, or social security payments. No progressive income tax modified the market's distribution of wealth. Charitable and other philanthropic enterprises were carried on by private individuals and voluntary associations, and their scale of operation was by no means adequate to ameliorate significantly the lives of the millions of immigrants who added their number to the native urban poor. Much depends upon the definition of "poor;" the word's quantitative and qualitative meanings changed with the uncertain course of the national economy between prosperity and depression. After carefully discounting a multitude of statistical studies, however, Harold U. Faulkner concluded that around the turn of the century "fully eighty percent of the people lived on the margin of existence while the wealth of the nation was owned by the remaining twenty percent." Poverty was a rural as well as an urban phenomenon, but in the cities it concentrated more visibly into growing slums; a large percentage of the inhabitants of these slums were foreign-born or were the children of foreign-born parents.

A man with some influence in the city hall could do much for these people; if he did, his influence could be expected to grow along with their gratitude expressed in votes. In case a poor man found himself in jail, he needed help with the law. In bad times, he needed someone to keep the heat and light in his home from being turned off. He needed assistance in locating jobs for himself and for his children. These services were provided by the bosses. The charitable activity of Tammany representatives during the depression of 1837 was an early example. Boss Tweed's generosity to the needy was better known to them, at least, than his under-cover operations in the city treasury. In the winter of 1870–1871, he gave a thousand dollars to each of the aldermen to use for charity in their districts, and spent $50,000 himself in his own ward. In Kansas City, James Pendergast built up a reputation (and an increasingly powerful machine) by his distributions of jobs and charity where they were most appreciated. In later years the free Christmas and Thanksgiving dinners given by his younger brother, Thomas J. Pendergast, were well-known in the riverfront wards.

The presence in cities of large numbers of immigrant families lent a special dimension to bossism. The foreign-born worker, and in most cases his children, had to contend not only with poverty but also with language difficulties and with attitudes of hostility or contempt on the part of the native-born population. In the

1840's and 1850's, the Irish were described in the newspapers of eastern cities in the same terms which were later to be applied to Negroes. When Italians and Slavic immigrants arrived in this country, they found the same experience waiting for them. Anti-Catholic and anti-immigrant impulses found nation-wide expression in the "Know Nothing" party before the Civil War, in the American Protective Association during the nineties, and more recently in the revival of the Ku Klux Klan in the 1920's.

Most city bosses fought these nativist movements, thereby offering a political and social haven to the immigrants. As part of the developing relationship between bosses and immigrants, the political machine became an avenue of advance—and, quite possibly, of "Americanization"—for many citizens with foreign names. The machine offered more than labor jobs in public or utility construction. For the brighter and more ambitious young men, there were clerical and other white collar positions in the machine itself; such positions represented for many the first step toward middle class respectability. There was opportunism in all of this, for both the boss and the immigrant, but there was more to it than the buying and selling of votes. As Oscar Handlin observes, the boss—himself often exemplifying the success-story of an immigrant boy—represented deeply-felt, if intangible, values for members of his constituency: "Often the feelings of group loyalty focused upon him. He was a member of many associations, made friends on every block. In the columns of every newspaper his name reflected glory on the whole community and he in turn shared its sense of solidarity." Bosses played large roles in the acculturation process which mass immigration rendered necessary in the United States.

It has recently been argued that bossism is disappearing from the American scene. Mass immigration has ended and the third and fourth generations in what were immigrant families have been absorbed into the general American society; they no longer feel special needs because of the spelling of their names. In the wage-earning population, flourishing labor unions now provide the social life and the needed sense of solidarity formerly offered by the machine. The economic policies of the federal government are likely to maintain a widely-diffused prosperity, lessening the number of those whose needs stem simply from their poverty. For the rest, government—and especially the federal government—is now assumed to be a social welfare agency; people in need of help can get it from officially sanctioned sources and do not have to turn to the extralegal money and influence of the boss. There is substance in this argument, and it is certain that the character of city politics has changed in the direction sought by the reformers.

Immigration, however, was important in sustaining bossism predominantly because it presented problems of cultural assimilation. Cultural assimilation is still a problem in American cities and will remain one for some time; it is most visible in the matter of race relations, but exists elsewhere as well. Moreover, some commentators have noted that as government becomes more complex (at the same time that it has more things to offer) there develops a need for people who can explain which door to knock on and which form to fill out. It is not impossible that a new variety of bossism will take shape, to mediate between the citizen in need and the confusing bureaucratic tangle which surrounds him.

In any event, it should be clear that bossism, typifying American urban politics for most of the nineteenth and much of the twentieth centuries, is no simple phenomenon. Any complete estimate of its effects—political, financial, cultural—is, of course, impossible. Bosses capitalized on the in-group feelings of many immigrants as well as upon the needs and the frustrations of the poor. This may have exacerbated these feelings, and prolonged their life. On the other hand, the availability of help and the possibility of advance which the machine offered may well have mitigated ethnic and class conflicts. Even as it marshalled its voters at the polls, the machine did more than buy their votes; it brought them into the body politic, where they probably represented less of a threat to established institutions than they would have represented outside of it.

The effects of bossism upon those who were appalled or shocked by its manifestations is an equally complicated matter. The well-known padding of registration rolls, the falsifying of election returns, the connections between most bosses and certain kinds of crime, the fraudulent franchise grants—these things undoubtedly reinforced the conviction of many Americans that politics was necessarily a dirty game, beneath the concern of respectable people.

226

It might be argued, though, that bossism evoked reform, and also forced it toward more realistic and more penetrating analyses of community life. Part of the great strength of the bosses lay in the fact that they knew their communities as few other men did. They knew what happened in the alleys and the by-ways as well as at city hall, and they put their knowledge to practical use. The political reformers began by regarding the city primarily as a problem of constitutional structure, or as an arena in which good and bad principles came into contention. As the boss continued to dramatize the problematic and threatening aspects of American urbanization, more and more among the reformers came to see a need for broader understanding of the city's life styles. They set about examining the consequences of urban growth. When this happened, the city began to be naturalized in American thought. No longer purely an object of vituperation or celebration, the American city became an object of study.

9

The Urban Community Examined

The pace and the momentum of American urbanization, with its manifold and changing problems, bewildered many observers. Even while city growth was opening opportunities for success and advancement, it made difficult the maintenance of any sense of continuity with the past. Henry Blake Fuller's 1894 novel about Chicago, *With the Procession,* describes not only the emergence of ostentatious luxury and elaborate social rituals in the western metropolis, but also a feeling on the part of several older citizens—who live in wealth and comfort—that Chicago had grown beyond their understandings. In the novel, a wealthy merchant, who came to the city before the Civil War, becomes involved in a misdemeanor case in a municipal court, which he discovers to be dominated by corrupt politicians. Urged to drop the case, he refuses. "I want to see for myself," he says, in anger and frustration, "how things really are. I want to learn what conditions we are

229

living under. I want to understand the things that are really going on about us." A bit later on in the novel, the man's son, a young lawyer, tells him what he will discover: "You'll find a hell-broth: thieves, gamblers, prostitutes, pawnbrokers, saloonkeepers, aldermen, heelers, justices, bailiffs, policemen—and all concocted for us within a short quarter of a century."

In 1888, Dr. Theodore S. Case of Kansas City, Missouri, who had arrived there thirty years earlier when the place had been a raw but optimistic little river town, edited a thick volume of local history. In the introduction he confessed that the steady obliteration of old and familiar landmarks, consequent upon successful city promotion, was confusing to the older settlers; their imaginations could not embrace the progressive alteration of their environment. The newer arrivals had no time for systematic consideration of the city's development: "even the present," Case wrote, "is more than they can keep up with." Another Kansas Citian, surveyor and speculator John C. McCoy, who had come to the spot even before there was any permanent settlement, reflected in the 1870's upon the swift growth of an industrial community of 30,000 people; he concluded that no human will or purpose could have accomplished such a result. It had been dictated by geography; "sheer necessity alone," said McCoy, "caused the upbuilding of the city today." The implication was that cosmic destiny had driven a modern city beneath the feet of startled, if pleased, entrepreneurs.

McCoy's recourse to over-riding determinism, in order to explain phenomena which seemed otherwise to defy rationalization, was by no means peculiar to him; many comparable examples can be found in the local and state histories and volumes of urban reminiscences which appeared in great numbers in the closing decades of the nineteenth century. "New Haven," wrote one of its historians in 1888, "has entered on a new career of civilization as varied as science and as wide as mankind, and . . . its old-time quaintness, simplicity, and homogeneity will be seen no more forever." Whether inspired by nostalgia or progressive optimism, local history flourished in the post-Civil War epoch as it never had before. The National Centennial Fair at Philadelphia in 1876 stimulated its production; a committee which met during the fair devised a standard format for writers and distributed it widely over

230

the country. Individual authors sometimes turned out histories of several places; one indefatigable clergyman named Charles Tuttle published twenty-eight of these during the period 1873–76. John T. Scharf, a Baltimore journalist, turned out a history of that city in 1874, one of St. Louis in 1883, and one of Philadelphia in 1884. Every large city found several chroniclers, amateur or professional, who in the aggregate produced a significant, if not often inspiring, body of writing during the period when Americans were endeavoring to come to terms with their urban surroundings.

While they vary widely in quality, these histories do not typically offer sophisticated case studies in urbanization. They stress picturesque features of the local scene: a visit by the President of the United States, portrayal of a colorful Civil War hero, and interviews with the oldest inhabitant. They generally suppress issues which have divided or embarrassed the particular cities, in favor of optimistic accounts of growth. They include many figures and tables showing the rise in real estate valuation, bank clearings, and commercial transactions. Chambers of commerce sometimes sponsored books of this kind. They were sometimes put together by writers who proposed to sell them by mentioning as many local names as possible; "biographical" appendices running to twice or three times the length of the chronicles themselves were common. Whatever the underlying motives, its great volume, especially between 1870 and 1910, suggests that local history met some needs. It helped to satisfy, however partially, an intense and widespread curiosity about the rise of the city.

Curiosity was stimulated not only by rapid growth, but also by some of its menacing consequences. Violence in a dozen eastern cities accompanying the railroad strikes in the summer 1877, the shock of the Haymarket bomb in Chicago nine years later, the pitched battle between strikers and a small army hired by their employers at Homestead, Pennsylvania in 1892, and the destruction and carnage in Chicago stemming from the Pullman strike of 1894, all seemed to indicate that urban society was vulnerable, that American city dwellers were living on the rim of a social volcano. Charles Loring Brace, a clergyman who dedicated his life to rescuing destitute children from the vice and filth of the streets of New York, described *The Dangerous Classes of New York* in a

231

book with that title which appeared in 1872. Homeless, near the edge of starvation, and disease-ridden, thousands of the city's inhabitants, according to Brace, had no stake in preserving community peace. "Let but Law lift its hand from them for a season," he warned his readers, "or let the civilizing influences of American life fail to reach them, and if the opportunity offered, we should see an explosion from this class which might leave this city in ashes and blood." Increasingly, and in many ways, Americans turned to the examination of their cities, often in the hope that in knowledge they would find power to order the urban environment.

Their studies confirmed much that was shocking and threatening. Some people believed that the problems of urban community life defied solution and that civilization as they had known it was on the road to collapse. Lincoln Steffens exemplified this view. In the years after the appearance of his exposé of corrupt city government, *The Shame of the Cities,* he decided that corruption was a permanent and essential feature of American public life. Since it could not be got rid of, it should be used: Steffens toyed with the notion of achieving good ends by persuading bosses to support them. But nothing came of this, and Steffens finally concluded that the problems of modern life could be met only by a revolutionary dictatorship. Most concerned people were not this pessimistic; appalling conditions revealed by their examinations of urban phenomena ordinarily impelled them to work out ameliorative programs. Community self-study was closely related to reform, and the broadening goals of reform interacted with the broadening scope of the studies that were made.

While Steffens' pessimism was not representative, there was a great deal of anxiety about the consequences of city growth. Henry George, in his widely read *Progress and Poverty* (1879), the book which deeply affected Cleveland's Tom Johnson, noted that "the type of modern growth is the great city. Here are to be found the greatest wealth and the deepest poverty. And it is here that popular government has most clearly broken down." He then epitomized the bosses as the ruling class of the cities; these men "stand to the government of these cities as the Praetorian Guards did to that of declining Rome." Sharing presentiments of Gothic horrors with many other writers of his time, George predicted that unless steps

232

were quickly taken "the sword will again be mightier than the pen, and in carnivals of destruction brute force and wild frenzy will alternate with the lethargy of a declining civilization." Edward Bellamy, author of the popular utopian novel *Looking Backward* (1889), also felt that society was moving toward cataclysm. The hero of *Looking Backward,* a scion of the late nineteenth century Boston aristocracy, recalls for his host in the twenty-first century, "we felt that society was dragging its anchor, and in danger of going adrift. Whither it would drift nobody could say, but all feared the rocks. All I can say is, the prospect was such when I went into that sleep that I should not have been surprised had I looked down from your house-top today on a heap of charred and moss-grown ruins instead of this glorious city." Josiah Strong, a crusading Congregationalist minister whose book, *Our Country: Its Possible Future and its Present Crisis,* was a best seller after it appeared in 1885, wrote that "the city has become a serious menace to our civilization." Urbanization, in his view, threatened to inundate American institutions with poverty, immigration, Catholicism, and socialism.

George and Bellamy were both confident, however, that urban society would reform itself in time, and even Strong felt that the "Anglo-Saxon" genius he so admired would meet the challenge successfully. With the triumph of Christian reform, Strong believed, would come the new city, "the symbol of *heaven*—heaven on earth —the Kingdom fully come." Bellamy's future metropolis on this site of Boston was described as "a great city. Miles of broad streets, shaded by trees and lined with fine buildings, and for the most part not in continuous blocks but set in larger or smaller inclosures, stretched in every direction. Every quarter contained large open squares filled with trees, among which statues glistened and fountains flashed in the late afternoon sun. Public buildings of a colossal size and an architectural grandeur unparalleled in my day raised their stately piles on every side." The narrator soon learns that the amenities of social and individual life in this city are fully worthy of its physical perfection. And it should be noted that Bellamy believed his own prediction; in his words, it was "a forecast, in accordance with the principles of evolution, of the next stage in the industrial and social development of humanity, especially in this

233

country." Bellamy's visionary optimism went beyond that of most reformers; still, intuitions of the good community coexisted in their minds with feelings of disgust and revulsion from the contemporary scene. These sentiments formed the content of many constructive studies of urban life.

That the "good community" seldom resembled existing cities —which certainly impressed their investigators as largely undesirable habitats—has led some students to characterize the urban reformers as basically anti-urban. Traditional agrarian rhetoric often crept into their utterances, and some reform campaigns did posit escape from the streets of the city as essential; but, from the 1880's on, the reformers' program was mainly not to abandon the urban environment but to reshape it. The city as the central fact of American social life was accepted; the argument was no longer over whether or not city development should be encouraged, but over what directions it should be given.

This important change in attitudes toward the city took place gradually. The careers of William Augustus Muhlenberg (1796–1877) and Charles Loring Brace (1826–1890) illustrate its early stages. Rector of New York City's Church of the Holy Communion and deeply committed to the cause of social betterment, Muhlenberg was not instinctively anti-urban. During a trip to England as a young man, he could not repress a sense of boredom in the quiet cathedral town of Ely. "On the whole," he noted in his journal, "I believe I should thrive better, body and soul, amid the rattle and clatter of Sixth Avenue and Twelfth Street!" Back in New York, Muhlenberg threw himself into an effort to provide fresh air vacations for poor children, especially after the 1849 cholera epidemic. As he analyzed the city's spreading slum problem, particularly with respect to its bearing on children raised in slums, he became convinced that it was self-perpetuating; the bad conditions made bad upbringing inevitable for most of the children of the poor: "The noxious physical and moral [influences] are ever acting and reacting with cumulative force." The slum had outgrown men's power to reform it; the evils of overcrowding were "too gigantic for any grasp of reform at all conceivable." Political apathy and the rapacity of slum landlords put legislative action out of the question; benevolent agencies worked with commendable zeal, "but anything like the elevation of a whole locality is beyond their hopes. They cannot remove causes . . . ." Muhlenberg came to believe that the only effective help for children who would otherwise grow up in the slums lay in transporting families to what he called "a Christian industrial community" in which the environment would be planned to encourage spiritual growth. In the later 1860's, with money from wealthy Episcopalian acquaintances, he bought a 500-acre farm on Long Island Sound where he planned such a community for families from the "deserving and industrious poor." It was to include four or five hundred people—tailors, shoemakers, and seamstresses, for example—along with a print shop, a church, and a school. Muhlenberg's project, which he conceived as one of social reconstruction, was never realized, partly because its financial backers regarded its economic communitarianism as a threat to American individualism. The farm on which he had hoped to build a Christian industrial community became first a home for crippled children and ultimately a home for the aged.

During the same years, Brace had promoted a scheme of juvenile reform which was at the outset more anti-urban, and which attracted more attention, than Muhlenberg's scheme. Brace, in whose New England background socially conscious religious ardor was a prominent feature, traveled to England and continental Europe after his college education at Yale and Union Theological Seminary. The reform of juvenile delinquency had attracted much attention in other countries, and Brace was especially interested in German and British organizations which tried to separate children from deleterious urban environments. Back in America, he settled in New York where, in 1853, he and several other ministers founded the agency which was later to adopt the name of Children's Aid Society; he served as its secretary for almost forty years. The organization's main program was to adopt slum children and resettle them in farm or small town homes in the countryside. They should have the benefit, in Brace's words, of "pure country air, instead of the gases of sewers; trees and fields in place of narrow alleys." The idea was not new, even in this country; Joseph Tuckerman had tried it out on a small scale in Boston. But under Brace's direction the program swelled until about 90,000 children had been "sent west" in forty years (upstate New York was actually where

235

most of the children were placed). While it could claim some noteworthy successes, Brace's program drew increasing criticism. Some children failed to adjust quickly to their new surroundings; in these instances Brace was often taxed with exporting New York's problems and thereby "polluting" the country districts. Many Catholics saw his activities as directed primarily against their church. In the 1870's and after, social workers (whose numbers were growing rapidly) argued that attempts to resettle the children simply drew constructive attention away from conditions in the city. Brace continued all his life to defend resettlement, but his own energies went more and more into institutional church work in New York City. Forced, as R. Richard Wohl has observed, to retreat from his original emphasis, "he increasingly geared his activities to the assumption that underprivileged city children would remain permanently in the city."

By the 1870's, a movement which came to be called "the social gospel" was already discernible within the older Protestant church groups in America; Muhlenberg and Brace were among its progenitors. The association of religion with social reform was neither new nor peculiarly American—nor had it ever been especially limited to Protestantism. But between the 1860's and the First World War many Protestant congregations tried to confront some of the consequences of urbanization. The United States had been largely Protestant while it had also been largely rural, and the anti-urban themes of early American culture had influenced the social philosophy of the Protestant churches. American Catholicism and Judaism had grown in America as the cities grew; accordingly, these faiths did not experience as sharply the necessity of intellectual adjustment to the urban environment.

Intellectual adjustment was forced upon Protestant ministers when it began to appear to them that their churches were losing all communication with the rapidly expanding urban population. Washington Gladden, a Congregationalist minister in Columbus, Ohio compared his heavily white-collar congregation with the population at large, and discovered that while about a quarter of the country's population was made up of wage-earners, not more than one-tenth of his membership came from working class districts. At approximately the same time, a Pittsburgh minister took an informal census which showed that businessmen along with salaried and professional workers who made up ten per cent of the local population constituted almost two-thirds of the membership of the city's Protestant churches. In the older eastern cities especially, these churches had included members who, as their early business ventures prospered, became wealthier and moved away from the center of town, while waves of immigrants filled the houses they left behind. On Manhattan Island, the area below Fourteenth Street gained 250,000 people between 1868 and 1888; during the same years it lost seventeen Protestant churches.

It is not surprising, in the circumstances, that some ministers —like Gladden, Brace, Walter Rauschenbusch, and others—sought ways to stem the urban erosion of their clienteles. As early as 1865 delegates from several churches, meeting in Cleveland, formed an evanescent American Christian Commission to study their mutual problem. Churches in the cities, the Commission's first report declared, were hampered by "want of knowledge of [the cities'] moral condition; lack of organization of the wealth, piety and labor which exist there; need of experimental knowledge of the best agencies . . .; and want of trained, tried, permanent laborers in the various spheres of city labor." While it lasted, the commission conducted surveys of poorer areas in thirty-five cities, and on the basis of the resulting data recommended intensive home missionary work; it also set up a committee to study what had been done in European cities. In the following decades Episcopalians, Methodists, Unitarians, Presbyterians, and Congregationalists attacked the slum problem. The "institutional church," with its lodging houses, reading rooms, adult education classes and recreation centers, became a fixture on the urban scene. These projects were often expensive, and wealthy parishioners were asked to contribute heavily. This necessitated a certain amount of educational work by socially-conscious ministers; Muhlenberg and Brace tirelessly assembled data to convince rich acquaintances of the value of their schemes. Spectacular success occasionally crowned their efforts; William E. Dodge, a New York City magnate, contributed $140,000 for an institutional church in the Bowery, and the Chicago Methodist Society raised a million dollars in fifteen years while St. George's Episcopal Church in New York raised two million for the same purpose.

Separate churches found it advisable to cooperate however their doctrines might diverge. Many well-known social-gospel ministers and laymen, including Gladden and Richard T. Ely, helped organize the American Congress of Liberal Religious Societies at the Chicago World's Fair in 1894. Doctrinal controversies retreated to the background as they heard Albion W. Small, the University of Chicago sociologist, argue that all "forms of religion . . . have a common tendency, varying in degree, but essentially social." Interdenominational cooperation for social ends was the main influence in producing the Federal Council of Churches of Christ in America in 1905.

The relevance to American urban history of this widely-studied movement lies mainly in two of its characteristics. First, the social gospel ministers conducted studies, including house-to-house surveys of their neighborhoods, and publicized the results as widely as they could. These surveys played a part in enlightening contemporaries about some of the social characteristics of urban America. Secondly, the exigencies of urban reform led many Protestants further from the old belief that success and failure were the social rewards respectively for individual virtue and vice. Environmentalism began to infiltrate social philosophy at least as early as Tuckerman's reform activities in Boston. Brace had asserted in 1852 that "Material Reform and Spiritual Reform . . . must go on and mutually help one another." A leader of the institutional church movement in New York City conceded in 1893 that poverty lay "very close to the problem of sin." A social gospel minister in Buffalo asserted that if one cared to save the people, who languished "in squalor, poverty, and degradation," he must "exchange their tenements for homes. And to do that," he added, "you must put your finger on legislation. . . . If you wish to prevent the perpetuation of slum life you may as well understand that it will not be done altogether by direct evangelization." The social gospel clergymen were approaching the Salvation Army's inspiring slogan that drowning men needed ropes, not tracts.

Others, in addition to worried ministers, sought to acquaint themselves with their burgeoning urban surroundings, and found acquaintance difficult to gain. "Who shall fathom the vast and deep mystery of a city?" asked novelist Charles K. Lush in *The Autocrats* (1901), a story with a Milwaukee locale. "The city," Lush went on, "is the Dark Continent of this century, into the depths of which have gone many explorers, each returning with but a fragment of knowledge; none with the whole truth." At another point in the novel he notes that "a city is made up of circles, or groups, great and small, divisions and sub-divisions, the members of which have apparently little in common, whose mode of life is dissimilar, and who really know as little of each other as do Hottentots and Esquimaux." In the early 1890's, *Scribner's Magazine* ran a series of articles entitled "The Poor in Great Cities;" "what we need to know," the editor commented, "is what is doing, here and elsewhere . . . and especially, what are the facts with which our own efforts are to deal, and how facts elsewhere compare with them." No source of information could reveal how many people in the United States were on relief. When one of the first systematic analyses of poverty appeared in 1904, its author listed as examples of questions still unanswerable: "how many people in this country are in poverty? Is the number yearly growing larger? Are there each year more and more of the unskilled classes, pursuing hopelessly the elusive phantom of self support and independence?"

The quest for data produced results. Between 1890 and the First World War, a "factual generation"—as Robert Bremner has accurately characterized it—greatly extended the area of available and verifiable knowledge about the conditions of urban living in America. Within a period of about fifteen years books, articles, and government reports (federal and state) poured from the printing presses to enlighten concerned citizens. Since reform sentiments generated these studies, most of the investigating was directed toward the poor and toward the slum. Even so, Ward McAllister's *Society as I Found It,* along with Henry B. Fuller's novels, *With the Procession* and *The Cliff Dwellers,* all of which were published between 1890 and 1894 (and perhaps Thorstein Veblen's *The Theory of the Leisure Class,* which appeared in 1899), enlightened many readers about the behavior of the higher ranks in social life.

The settlement house movement was a logical development of the increasing concern with immigration and poverty that marked the decades after the middle of the nineteenth century. Charity organization societies, institutional churches, and agencies especially interested in living conditions of city children had begun to publicize some of the most painful accompaniments of large-scale urbanization. In the late 1880's, idealistic young people in several of the nation's largest cities began to establish residences in slum districts; these houses, which were called settlements, became centers radiating a wide variety of reform impulses—most of them designed to stimulate community spirit among the poor. A London settlement started in 1884, called Toynbee Hall, caught the attention of traveling Americans; they brought the idea back to this country to adapt it to conditions in New York, Boston, Chicago, and other places. Thus Stanton Coit opened Neighborhood Guild in a noisome New York City tenement house in 1886; it immediately began a program of social and educational events, later changing its name to University Settlement.

Three years later, Jane Addams and Ellen Gates Starr opened what would soon become the best-known settlement in America, Hull House. After a trip to Europe, which included visits to Toynbee Hall, they returned to Chicago excited by the possibilities that city offered for reform. They acquired an old mansion on South Halsted Street, in the middle of an immigrant neighborhood. Contributing their own money and raising more from contributions by rich Chicago matrons, the two young women began with a kindergarten for the small children in the neighborhood. They added clubs for the older children, a day nursery to help working mothers, and an employment bureau. A series of adult education courses and lectures by visiting speakers soon developed into one of Hull House's most popular features.

The early settlements were widely imitated; by 1895 there were at least fifty of them in the country and the number continued to grow. Their significance has had many facets; particularly important was their role in clarifying the picture of the city, in adding to the systematic data which was available to Americans seeking to understand the urban milieu around the turn of the century. People who participated in settlement work became tireless agitators —partly in their need to raise money from the better-off sections of the cities—carrying their descriptions of life among the poor to other quarters of the community. In 1895, a New York publisher brought out *Hull House Maps and Papers: A Presentation of Nationalities and Wages in a Congested District of Chicago,* a series of essays and carefully prepared data gathered by the Chicago group. Men and women active in the settlements often became public officials, as state and local governments added social welfare agencies to their functions. Florence Kelly and Julia Lathrop, again from Hull House, served respectively as chief factory inspector and on the board of charities of the State of Illinois. The programs of the successful settlements served, in fact, as pilot projects which local governments took over once the need had been sufficiently publicized. As Ray Ginger has observed of Hull House, "if an enterprise proved its worth, the next step was to convince the city to enter the field. The playground, the public bath, the kindergarten—such projects instituted by Hull House were year by year taken over by the city." This testified to the effectiveness not only of the specific reform enterprises but also of the educational campaigns carried on by the settlement workers.

As the settlement houses were appearing in city after city, and at the same time that discussion of the germ theory of contagion stimulated interest in public health, Jacob Riis published *How the Other Half Lives;* a detailed description of New York City's immigrant neighborhoods, it quickly became popular and was influential in the growing movement for housing legislation. It was, so to speak, a book whose time had come in 1890; its popularity reflected increased interest in the city which was in turn encouraged by studies of depopulated rural counties in many parts of the United States, anxiety over the social effects of immigration culminating in movements to restrict it, and widening consciousness that "the frontier"—in the sense of free land in the West—was gone. Riis had grown to early manhood in a small, closely-knit Danish town where he had become a carpenter. Emigrating to the United States in 1870, he held a succession of jobs, coming finally to journalism. Thirteen years as police reporter on two New York dailies sharpened his prose style and gave him a great amount of poignant and colorful data, which his own background as an immigrant enabled him to use sympathetically. After *How the Other Half Lives* catapulted him into prominence, especially in reform circles, he promoted the idea of reconstructing decayed neighborhoods by developing recreational and adult educational activities in the public schools. His success was limited by the fact that neighborhood reconstruction came to be mostly in the hands of the settlements and also by the steady turning of reformers' attention toward housing codes as a weapon against the slum.

Congress itself authorized an investigation in 1892, "relative to what is known as the slums of cities." The language suggests a tentative approach to a new and still only dimly-perceived phenomenon, and the investigators found it difficult to define slums. These, "according to the dictionaries, are dirty back streets, especially such streets as are inhabited by a squalid and criminal population; they are low and dangerous neighborhoods." To avoid ambiguity, the investigators decided to confine their attention to the very worst areas, "concerning which there can be no difference of opinion as to whether or not they are slum districts." Led by Carroll D. Wright, Federal Commissioner of Labor and one of the early systematizers of social statistics, the team carried out what could only be regarded as a preliminary study. Coverage of the slums in the nation's sixteen cities with populations over 200,000 had been projected, but the $20,000 Congress appropriated sufficed only for a survey of four cities which were considered as representing different types. New York, Philadelphia, and Baltimore were all seaports; New York was regarded as primarily commercial, Philadelphia as more heavily influenced by manufacturing, and Baltimore as "the most typical southern business city in the Union." For the fourth, "Chicago, as a great inland city with all its varied interests of transportation, manufacturing, and general commerce, and the varied nationality of its population, was naturally selected." The neighborhoods to be studied were chosen after consultation with local authorities; their aggregate population of 83,000, Wright insisted, did not comprise the whole slum population of the four cities, but only that part of it over whose slum characteristics no one could possibly disagree.

There were few surprises in the report. Curiously, its careful house-to-house survey found no greater incidence of disease in the slums than in the cities at large; Wright suggested this might be owing to the surveys having been conducted in the healthiest part of the year, late spring, when "people were living with open windows and thus not subjected to the foul air which might be found in the winter." The slum was better equipped with saloons than the rest of the city; arrests for crime were more frequent there; illiteracy was higher. Foreign birth or parentage was much more common in the slum than elsewhere; the report included the interesting information that the foreign-born constituted between forty-four per cent and sixty-two per cent of the voting population of these districts. Working hours, wage rates, and living expenses were touched on rather lightly. The most significant feature of the report was neither in its contents nor in any direct consequences attendant upon its publication—in fact, there seem to have been none. It did represent, however, an important stage in the identification and the emergence into community thought and discourse of an urban problem. More graphic and exciting data could be found in Riis's book and in other privately sponsored examinations of the urban scene which were beginning to appear in rapid order.

The campaign for improved housing legislation, which matured in New York City in the 1890's and then spread to other cities, provided additional impetus to the process of community self-study. Lawrence Veiller's work on the various public and private tenement house commissions during the decade was especially significant. Veiller's most striking contribution to the urban education of his contemporaries was made in 1900, when he and his associates were nearing the successful conclusion of their effort to get the New York legislature to adopt a practical tenement housing code. Working, as he later recalled, six hours a day for months (in addition to many other responsibilities), Veiller constructed a three-dimensional exhibit to clarify the tenement house problem. He made a model of an actual tenement block out of cardboard and papier-mâché, around which he assembled hundreds of photographs, charts, and tables which detailed the characteristics of slum housing. There were many correlations of disease and crime with tenement housing; Veiller added comparative data from other cities both American and foreign. Ten thousand visitors saw the exhibit in February and March, 1900; it was then sent on a tour to other cities and proved to be an attraction at the Paris World's Fair in that year. Most of the data which had gone into the exhibit appeared three years later in *The Tenement House Problem,* a two-volume report of the state tenement commission prepared by Veiller and Robert W. DeForest. Veiller's work, of course, was crowned with success in the passing of the 1901 New York Tenement Law, and this added to the importance of his close and systematic study of life in the slums. It seemed to prove, in Robert Bremner's phrase, that "the path to reform lay through research."

The research itself became more systematic. In 1905 a Charities Publication Committee, including both Riis and Jane Addams, was formed and began quickly to plan comprehensive surveys of urban social problems. The magazine *Charities and the Commons* served as the committee's organ; in 1905 and 1906, two special issues— one on "The Negro in the Cities of the North" and the other, entitled "Next Door to Congress," on Washington, D. C.—attracted much attention. The committee then launched an investigation of Pittsburgh, Pennsylvania on such a large scale as to dwarf anything that had come before it. Money was contributed by the Russell Sage Foundation (then headed by Veiller's one-time associate, Robert W. DeForest), a staff of trained social workers headed by Paul U. Kellogg was assembled, and two years of field work got under way. The condensed results began to appear in print in 1908, but full publication of the Pittsburgh Survey took five years (1909–1914) and six large volumes.

The Pittsburgh Survey defined its subject as a complex of pressing social problems; the satisfactions of life in the steel city were not analyzed or described. This definition simply emphasized the close relationship between the development of social studies and urban reform. The underlying inspiration of the Survey, and much of the research that preceded and followed it, was to attack social waste and social dangers armed with knowledge about their causes. What the Pittsburgh study added to its predecessors was its scope: no single "problem" monopolized its pages but rather many problems were seen as interrelated. Crime, prostitution, city politics, housing, the labor of women and children, wages and hours, the family as an institution—all of these were given exhaustive treatment.

The survey idea spread rapidly, and maintained its close connection with reform-minded groups. The Sage Foundation sponsored surveys in six other cities from Atlanta, Georgia to Topeka, Kansas. Other communities organized their own self-study programs; *Charities and the Commons* changed its name to *Survey.*

Although they were concerned with politics, administration, and especially finance, the appearance and rapid spread of the municipal reference bureaus deserves mention as part of the deepening current of community self-examination. The first one was established in New York in 1906; by the 1920's most of the big cities had them. They carried different names, and bore different relationships to the governments of the cities; some even had tax support. Most were organized by business groups in the interests of efficient and economical city government; the major functions of these agencies were to study local financial operations in great detail and to publicize the results of their studies. Their typical concerns were therefore quite different than those of the social investigations, but still the objectives were often cast in broad terms. The language of the Bureau of Municipal Research in San Francisco suggested that the concept of efficiency, which it sought to promote, was a wide one, including "development of a constructive programme for the city that shall be based upon adequate knowledge and consideration of community needs . . . ." In their investigations of local government economy, the bureaus frequently studied public education and recreation programs, as well as the operation of city housing commissions and health departments, which brought them into areas where their concerns were shared by the social workers.

All the while, books and articles about the ills of urban society were published in ever-growing numbers. The year 1899 alone saw W. E. B. Du Bois' *The Philadelphia Negro;* Robert Woods' description of poor neighborhoods in Boston, *The City Wilderness;* and Algie M. Simons' description of the stockyards area in Chicago, *Packingtown.* These were followed by Robert Hunter's *Tenement Conditions in Chicago,* in 1901, and his classic study including all of the larger cities, *Poverty,* in 1904. Roy Lubove cites no fewer than nine published investigations of the standards of living of workers between 1904 and 1911.

At about the same time, city governments began to establish municipal welfare departments. Kansas City, Missouri was the first to do so, in 1910, and the operation of its department demonstrated the connections between social gospel, community self-study, and urban reform. In the background of its establishment had been an investigation into unemployment in the city during the winter of 1909. The report of the investigation related unemployment to other social problems, and recommended the new governmental agency to plan not only for the unemployed but also for the sick and for those in the city's correctional institutions. The emphasis was to be preventive: "we believe," the authors of the report said, "that poverty, disease, and crime should not be accepted as a matter of course, but should be recognized as results of conditions . . . subject to control." The Welfare Department's first superintendent was Leroy Halbert, a young graduate of Chicago Theological Seminary who had served as assistant pastor to Charles Sheldon, author of the famous social gospel tract, *In His Steps.* Halbert exemplified his generation's passion for the facts of urban living when he proposed a local survey which, had it ever been carried out, would have gone well beyond the Pittsburgh Survey. "The only way to really measure the city's problem," Halbert wrote, "is to establish in the city a thorough system of sociological record keeping. . . . Every family is as worthy of record as every lot is, and every individual should be as carefully accounted for as every dollar is." Study of "the entire population" was not practicable at the time, but Halbert instituted a research bureau in the department which did make a complete card-catalog of one depressed area in Kansas City, calling attention to "the immediate need of socializing efforts" there and in similar neighborhoods.

The explicit motives of urban reformers embraced practical as well as humanitarian considerations. Reform, it was argued, was necessary to the good order or even the preservation of the community; at the very least, its accomplishment would save money and trouble. As early as 1857, a special committee of the state legislature investigating New York City's housing reported that "had the evils which now appall us, been prevented . . . by wise and simple laws, the city . . . would now exhibit more gratifying bills of health, more general comfort and prosperity, and less, far less expenditure for the support of pauperism and crime." After the Civil War, reformers recalled the 1863 draft riots which had cost many lives and almost paralyzed the metropolis for several days;

the mobs which participated in them "were gathered in the over-crowded and neglected quarters of the city." The urban slum was a sore on the body social from which infection, in the forms of disease and crime, could spread into the quarters of the middle and upper class districts. Alfred T. White, who tried to develop model low-cost housing as a private enterprise in the later nineteenth century, described the tenement areas in 1879 as "nurseries of the epidemics which spread with certain destructiveness into the fairest homes . . . hiding-places of the local banditti . . . cradles of the insane who fill the asylums and of the paupers who throng the almhouses; in fact [the tenements] produce these noxious and unhappy elements of society as surely as the harvest follows the sowing."

Warnings such as these seemed to imply a corollary proposition that a changed environment would result in more desirable in-dividual character. Those who called for the abolition of the slum moved steadily toward a consistent environmentalist theory of per-sonality development. Henry George, while not specifically an urban reformer, expressed the emerging view in his *Progress and Poverty:* "How little does heredity count," he wrote, "as compared with conditions. . . . Change Lady Vere de Vere in her cradle with an infant of the slums, and will the blood of a hundred earls give you a refined and cultured woman?" In the first half of the nine-teenth century, most urbanites regarded slums, along with poverty and failure in general, as evidence of personal shortcomings and vices; drink was the favorite explanation offered. But by the end of the century the more common view was coming to be that slums and poverty were active causes while personal shortcomings and vices were results. Two generations of concern for the effects of city living especially on children had been the main influence in bringing about the change. Jacob Riis spoke for many people when he maintained in 1893 that "as we mould the children of the toiling masses in our cities, so we shape the destiny of the State . . . ."

By the 1880's and 1890's, reformers almost without exception assumed that the large city was permanently on the social scene. They aimed at mitigating the harsh impact of urbanization on those who had fewest advantages in the struggle for existence and improvement, but they did not doubt that the city was and would continue to be the locale of their major endeavors. In his introduction to the final report of the Country Life Commission in 1909, President Theodore Roosevelt expressed the dawning notion that however farming might be encouraged, "city life is advancing more rapidly, because of the greater attention which is being given by citizens of the towns to their own betterment." Harvard economist Thomas Nixon Carver wrote in 1910 that while "the cry 'back to the farm' may possibly check the migration from country to city, it will not be able to stop it completely. We must expect, as far in the future as anyone is able to see, that the stream of migrating youths will continue to set cityward."

This recognition, accompanied by the development of environmentalist interpretations of personality and behavior, encouraged the growth of the notion that society is organic: that communities constituted living, unified organisms of which each individual was a member in the sense that fingers are members of the physiological body. Individual fates and lives were vitally interlaced, so that the unfolding of each bore directly on all the others. By the first decade of the twentieth century, most of those who studied city life were concluding that its very nature, compelling—as one of them wrote in 1910,—"manifold cooperations," was forcing the individual to "conform his acts in an ever increasing degree to the will and welfare of the community in which he lives." A contemporary writer stressed that "the life of the individual must be brought into organic and vital touch with the life of the community. The citizen must think of the city as far more than a protector of life and property." Efforts to rebuild neighborhood life, such as those backed by Riis and the settlement workers, were thought of as promoting healthy social organisms. Jane Addams noted that the people at Hull House were forced "to regard the entire life of their city as organic . . . and to protest against its over-differentiation." One of the best-known urban reformers, Frederick C. Howe, who had worked with Mayor Tom Johnson in Cleveland, stated simply in 1915 that "the city has destroyed individualism."

Theories of organic society and their possible application to the problems of city life deeply influenced the development of urban studies in American universities, which were just beginning, toward the close of the nineteenth century, to develop social science graduate programs on the German seminar model. Beginning in the 1880's and 1890's, the city came increasingly under scholarly examination. As early as 1883, Herbert Baxter Adams had begun encouraging his doctoral candidates at Johns Hopkins to produce historical studies of American cities and towns; these generally focused on political institutions and administrative structure. In 1899 at Columbia University, Adna F. Weber published the first comprehensive statistical analysis of European and American urbanization. By that time a sociology department had been initiated at the new University of Chicago, and almost immediately concentrated its attention on urban problems.

The University of Chicago sociologists were well acquainted with Jane Addams, Graham Taylor, and other settlement workers; scholars and reformers mingled inside and outside of the classroom. In fact, the early history of scholarly urban study cannot be understood apart from its close relationship with reform. Sociologist Nels Anderson observed retrospectively in 1929 that "we cannot separate the beginnings of urban sociology from the perennial battle to wipe out the slum." To many teachers and students, it appeared that the close study of urban society was primarily an effort to give a rational and systematic basis to philanthropy.

Under the direction of Albion W. Small, William I. Thomas, Charles R. Henderson, and Charles Zueblin, graduate students in the Chicago department began to use the city about them as a laboratory for social science. The first serious attempt to elaborate a theory of urban life came out of the "Chicago school" in 1915, when Robert Park published his essay, "The City: Suggestions for the Investigation of Human Behavior in the City Environment." Park had begun his adult life as a newspaperman in Minneapolis. His inclination, however, like Lincoln Steffens's, was to generalize upon his observations; he went to the University of Michigan, to Harvard, and then to Europe, trying to work out a satisfactory philosophy of journalism. Returning to the United States, Park joined the already flourishing sociology department at Chicago and began to analyze urban neighborhoods as "natural areas" of communication. The key fact about urban society was precisely that it was complex; its shape resulted from the dynamic equilibrium and tension among the many different groups, or sub-communities, which made it up. People congregated in neighborhoods (which Park sometimes called "moral areas") as they were impelled together by similarities in culture, language, economic status, and temperament. Thus the city should be studied as a developing organism whose parts were neighborhoods; on this premise Park and his associates began a long series of investigations into Chicago's characteristics and problems. Books with titles such as Louis Wirth's *The Ghetto* (1928), Frederick Thrasher's *The Gang* (1927), and Harvey Zorbaugh's *The Gold Coast and the Slum* (1929), indicate their lines of investigation and also reveal a close parallel in subject matter with the earlier writings of Veiller and the authors of the Pittsburgh Survey.

In 1923 a Social Science Research Committee was established at the University of Chicago to coordinate research activities. In quest of an organizing framework for research, which would enable various scholarly projects to reinforce one another, committee members concluded that the city at their doorstep was, as Charles Merriam wrote, "an ideal scene [for] cooperative investigation. . . . It becomes increasingly important to understand as nearly as possible the inner nature of cities and find the key to the understanding of their problems." A new dimension was added to concerted urban study when the committee decided to sponsor a detailed history of Chicago. Bessie L. Pierce was invited to the university in 1929, and commenced work upon the history with the help of a research staff and financial backing from the university and from foundations. Scholars had interested themselves in the history of cities on earlier occasions, but the initiation of the history of Chicago project marked urban history's coming-of-age as a recognized field for research.

Meanwhile another landmark in the sociological examination of American cities was in preparation, as Robert and Helen Lynd moved into Muncie, Indiana with a team of helpers, to live there and gather data for two years. The Lynds were trained in sociology at Columbia University; Robert Lynd also had a degree from Union Theological Seminary, which suggests latter-day echoes of the social gospel movement. Their object was to describe the effects of industrialization on the social structure and institutions of an urban community. Muncie was chosen partly because its modest size and almost entirely native-born population seemed to render it a manageable subject for a small group of scholars; after 1929, when the Lynds published *Middletown,* the Indiana city found itself attracting more intellectual attention than it ever had. *Middletown's* conclusions were neither startling nor wide-ranging; a community culture, largely bourgeois in its leading features, embraced both the business and working classes, but people on different rungs of the social ladder responded to the culture with varying degrees of warmth. Muncie was a business-dominated city, and the Lynds found interesting indications that the elements of business culture "filtered down," as they put it, "through various intermediate levels," to sustain a sense of community across class lines. Nevertheless, the main lesson they drew from their studies of Muncie was that of "the extent and complexity of the task confronting social science."

Even as it became more sophisticated and more scientific, urban study did not completely lose its connection with urban reform. In his foreword to *Middletown,* the noted anthropologist Clark Wissler asserted that the book "should enlighten the conscientious citizen and serve as a suggestion as to what information is needed by those who attempt to direct the affairs of an American town." Earlier, Robert Park had written that the basic problem of urban society was "the problem of achieving in the freedom of the city a social order and a social control equivalent to that which grew up naturally in the family, the clan, and the tribe." The examination of community life was posited, for scholars as well as others, on the assumption that knowledge is power. Understanding the city would lead to improving it.

Notions of the urban community as organic (at least from some points of view) and of the desirability of consciously shaping the urban environment have always been present in American thought. The Puritan doctrine of soul-liberty in the "city on a hill," William Penn's careful planning for Philadelphia, and James Oglethorpe's commodious design for Savannah, reflected the view that the good life can be achieved in a properly laid-out city. The best known expression of this conception in the early experience of the United States was, of course, the planning of the nation's capital. Most people assumed from the beginning that Washington would soon become a great city; southerners (often stereotyped as "anti-urban") were happy to see it located between Virginia and Maryland where they hoped it would stimulate the economy of the whole region. Patriots felt that the capital should embody the grand ideals of the republic: it should be stately, magnificent, and proud. Many decades passed before any such adjectives could be applied, for the city did not grow as rapidly as had been anticipated, even though ten years of planning preceded the installation of the government in Washington in 1800.

Locating the permanent seat of the national government occasioned sporadic debate for seven years after the treaty of peace was signed with the British in 1783. The constitution adopted in 1789 authorized Congress to govern whatever site, not exceeding ten miles square, might be selected. In 1790, Congress passed the Residence Act, providing that the President should choose a location somewhere along a specified stretch of the Potomac River; he was also to choose three commissioners, along with surveyors, charged with responsibility to prepare the capital for occupation by the end of 1800. Early in 1791, the president selected a location adjacent to Georgetown and named the commissioners; he appointed Andrew Ellicott to survey the boundaries and Major Pierre Charles L'Enfant to prepare drawings of sites which might be convenient for public buildings. L'Enfant, born in France in 1754, had been educated as an engineer and architect; he had volunteered for military service with the American revolutionaries and bore wounds received in their cause. He soon acquired a reputation as a designer of buildings, and when New York City was chosen as the first seat of the federal government, L'Enfant was picked to remodel the city hall into a national capitol. Ambitious, idealistic, and possessed of vision, he wrote President Washington offering to plan a permanent capital city; he urged that the plan "be drawn on such a scale as to leave room for that aggrandisement and embellishment which the increase of the wealth of the nation will permit it to pursue at any period, however remote." L'Enfant stressed "magnificent distances:" broad avenues radiating from central squares, leaving great empty spaces which could only be filled in as the city grew up to his plan. There was a brief conflict between L'Enfant and Jefferson, who favored a compact rectangular plan. But Jefferson yielded, and the Frenchman developed his grandiose ideas for the next year and a half with little hindrance, although Washington added a few modifications of his own as the planning went on. Capacious squares to be adorned with statues and obelisks, sites for educational institutions, a broad garden-lined boulevard along the river, five large fountains—even a plan to divert the river, making it flow toward the capitol whence it would be routed over a forty-foot waterfall and back to its original course —all of these went onto the increasingly detailed maps which L'Enfant prepared.

Planning, as L'Enfant undertook it, was a slow process, whereas the President, the commissioners, and others wished quickly to start selling some of the government's land in the District of Columbia. Otherwise, the privately owned land there would be offered and bought for building purposes in the new city, and the government's revenue would suffer accordingly. L'Enfant refused to produce a properly engraved plat which could be distributed to advertise land sales, for he feared that hasty real estate promotion would impair the integrity of his plan. He also balked at accepting the supervisory authority of the three commissioners. A series of increasingly ill-tempered disputes led to his dismissal in 1792. He was then consulted by Hamilton on the latter's projected industrial town at Paterson, New Jersey, and later designed a great house in Philadelphia for the famous banker, Robert Morris. L'Enfant had never learned to take care of his own financial affairs, however, and his pride had induced him to refuse compensation for some of his works. In the early 1800's, Benjamin H. Latrobe, another architect and urban engineer, described his French predecessor as almost starving; L'Enfant and his dog walked through the streets of the slowly rising capital city each day, while governmental parsimony, the momentum of real estate development, and the ideas of other urban designers eroded detail after detail of his original plan. He died in 1825 on the estate of a Maryland farmer who had offered him a home.

L'Enfant's baroque vision, as sketched out in his design for the capital, was widely copied as other cities in the early and middle nineteenth century sought grandiose effects; John Reps has found at least two dozen city plans modeled in part on the early one for

253

Washington, including those of Buffalo, Indianapolis, and Detroit. The current of romantic thought and feeling, however, soon began to alter typical projects of the well-ordered city. Trees and extensive floral designs became more prominent in the thinking of those who influenced the shapes in which cities grew. By mid-century Andrew Jackson Downing noted the vogue for large, sylvan cemeteries which were by then to be found in all the bigger cities. Many people regarded them more or less as parks, and thousands of visitors enjoyed the rural surroundings of Philadelphia's Laurel Hill, Boston's Mount Auburn, and New York City's Greensward. Downing urged that the obvious lesson should be drawn from these cemeteries, and that the cities should establish regular public parks on similar plans. "The true policy of republics," he wrote, "is to foster the taste for great public libraries, sculpture and picture galleries, parks and gardens, which *all* may enjoy, since our institutions wisely forbid the growth of private fortunes sufficient to achieve these desirable results in any other way."

As New York's growing population crowded onto Manhattan Island in the 1840's and 1850's, the idea of a great park simply to make the city livable was more frequently discussed; and in 1853 the state legislature authorized the beginning of work upon what became Central Park. Three years later, the commission in charge of the park's development chose Frederick Law Olmsted to superintend it. Born in 1822, Olmsted had traveled extensively and had made a name as a writer on agriculture. At the time of his appointment, most of his experience had been as a gentleman farmer on Staten Island, highly attentive to efficiency and conservation of resources. Working with Calvert Vaux, a former partner of Downing, Olmsted conceived a grand design for Central Park that emphasized the topography of the area. Natural features would soon be obliterated elsewhere on the island, and the planners thought it desirable to interfere with the park's "easy, undulating outlines, and picturesque, rocky scenery as little as possible . . . ." The hope was to preserve rural nature in a close relationship to the city. Olmsted pointed out that such a design would be less costly than any which proposed large-scale alteration of the topography, but it is clear that he considered the aesthetic advantages most important. Explaining his ideas, he wrote in 1870 that

254

the object of city parks was to bring natural beauty to bear upon city life—"the beauty of the fields, the meadow, the prairie, of the green pastures, and the still waters." In summary he remarked that "what we want to gain is tranquillity and rest to the mind."

There was nothing "anti-urban" in this. In the same 1870 article, Olmsted pointed out that urbanization would continue and that it was closely related to advancing concepts of freedom, culture, and general prosperity; the city was not only inevitable, it was also basically a good thing—one which could be made better, especially if people would "prepare for a continued rising of the townward flood." Parks, in Olmsted's mind, were means of strengthening community feeling in urban centers: they would preserve the health of the body social. He recalled seeing fifty thousand people at one time in Central Park. Where else, he asked, could so many be found together, "with an evident glee in the prospect of coming together, all classes represented . . . each individual adding by his mere presence to the pleasure of all others . . .?" Olmsted's insistence on a rural environment in his parks derived from his insight into its urban usefulness. "By making nature urbane," Lewis Mumford accurately observes, "he naturalized the city."

The success of Central Park was quick and impressive; it commanded emulation and within twenty years a dozen other cities had summoned Olmsted for help in designing their own parks. He urged them to create whole systems of parks, connected by broad and tree-lined boulevards; even the city's business and industrial areas would then be within reach of the fresher air and the soothing colors of rural nature. Other men studied Olmsted's methods and objectives, and the notion of closely juxtaposing urban and rural environments, in order to improve the former, generated a park and boulevard movement in the United States beginning in the 1870's. One of its most important propagators was Henry W. S. Cleveland; like Olmsted, he had taken an early interest in scientific farming, but Cleveland was also a trained surveyor and civil engineer. He designed cemeteries, estates, and public parks in cities and towns in New England, the South, and the Midwest. In his book, *Landscape Architecture as Applied to the Wants of the West,* which appeared in 1873, Cleveland warned growing cities that they should acquire tracts of land for park systems before private real estate development made it impossible. Proposing a system of parks and boulevards for Minneapolis, he wrote in 1884: "look forward to the time when the city has a population of a million, and think what will be their wants." In Kansas City, Missouri George Kessler produced a scheme for parks and boulevards in 1893, which the city began almost at once to construct. Kessler pointed out the need for quick action while desirable land for parks was still available—"lands that, in addition to serving the purpose of local recreation grounds or parks, would permit of retaining for all future time some of the characteristic features of our natural scenery, and would protect localities that possess especially fine views."

With all its emphasis on the virtues of rural surroundings, the vision of these men was essentially urban; they prescribed a measure of ruralization as antidote for city disorders. Although they were usually called landscape architects, they were in reality city planners. Sylvester Baxter, who played the leading part in designing Boston's metropolitan park system, described what he called "an ideal city" in 1893; the aesthetic features of natural topography would be preserved, and open spaces would alternate with residential and business areas. "A city planned in this way," he continued, in language reminiscent of Bellamy's, "besides its frequent great parks and its water-side esplanades, would probably have its houses so arranged around pleasant garden-like open spaces . . . that every dwelling would face upon a pleasure ground of some kind." Cleveland predicted the results of adequate park and boulevard planning in immense detail, stressing that all of the city's functions would be enhanced. In order to secure "the full enjoyment of its theaters, museums, libraries, lectures, and social pleasures," he wrote, "it is essential that the means of access to them should be rendered not only easy, and free from danger or discomfort, but attractive and elegant . . . ." Inhabitants of the slum and tenement districts of cities did not escape the attention of the landscape architects. Baxter was actively involved in housing reform in Boston. Cleveland indicated the advantages of a sound park system for the "education of children who are born and bred in the crowded tenement-houses which are the (so called) homes of thousands of the inhabitants of every city." Olmsted told residents of Detroit that good park planning would "divert men from unwholesome, vicious, and destructive methods and habits of seeking recreation." Kansas City's Kessler gave sharp expression to the urban intuition of the landscape architects when he wrote that a program of beautification through parks and boulevards "would not only make this a beautiful city but would give the city a special character and beauty of its own." It would "create among our people warm attachments to the city, and promote civic pride."

During the same period which saw the widening influence of the park and boulevard movement, another approach to community planning was on the way to disaster. Planned manufacturing towns in America dated back to the efforts of New England industrialists to attract laborers to their water-power mills after 1815; they were also trying to avoid the horrifying social conditions with which their observations of English factory cities had acquainted them. The best known example of their urban enterprises was, of course, Lowell, Massachusetts, but private town planning in the interest of industrialism reached its high point later in Pullman, Illinois.

George M. Pullman, the railroad car innovator, had directed the Pullman Corporation so successfully that by the mid-1890's its capitalization amounted to $36,000,000 and its assets to $62,000,000. Pullman, who single-handedly dominated the operations of his company, came from a poor family in up-state New York. Talent, determination, and no doubt some luck had made him by 1880 one of Chicago's most successful business men. In the words of Almont Lindsay, "he was brusque, unapproachable, and domineering;" his politics were Republican and his attitude toward organized labor was one of unyielding hostility. Nevertheless, Pullman had a considerable measure of social imagination, and he resolved to create a model industrial community in which his workers might live. This, he hoped, would soften the bitter antagonism which wage-earners often felt toward their employers, and would enable him to attract a stable and highly competent labor force; it would also earn six per cent on the money invested in it.

In 1880 he chose a spot which was still open prairie just south of Chicago, where he built his factory and the town of Pullman. There were impressive experiments in company towns in England, France, and Germany, which Pullman may have studied; they were widely publicized during the Gilded Age when urbanization seemed to be offering society an almost insoluble problem in labor-management relations. In any event, George Pullman's company bought 4,000 acres of land on Lake Calumet; an architect and a landscape engineer were retained to draw up a plan, and early in 1881 the town of Pullman was in full operation. Difficult problems of sewerage and water supply were ingeniously surmounted, streets were carefully macadamized, and terraced front yards sloped back to rows of neat, clean houses. A large Arcade Building contained a shopping center; near it were the Florence Hotel (named for Pullman's wife), the Pullman Post Office, and the Pullman Bank. A luxurious library, an even more luxurious theater (which, according to one newspaper report equalled "the most elegant theaters in the country in point of architectural beauty and artistic design"), a church, and a school provided for a complement of social and cultural institutions. The town had neither saloons nor brothels.

Pullman's population reached 12,600 just before the onset of the depression of 1893. An International Hygienic and Pharmaceutical Exposition, held at Prague in 1896, considered it the best town in the world from the standpoint of public health. Visiting speakers and artists offered a varied program of entertainment and adult education. Until 1889, Pullman was legally governed by the Village of Hyde Park, within whose boundary it lay. In that year Chicago annexed Hyde Park, but effective control of the model town lay always in the hands of George Pullman. He named a "town agent" to supervise the community's affairs, somewhat after the manner of a city manager. These affairs were run well; while rents averaged higher in Pullman than in nearby places, its tenants had generally better quarters and more efficient services than were available elsewhere. A writer in *Harper's New Monthly Magazine* commented in 1888 that Pullman was "The only city in existence built from the foundation on scientific and sanitary principles. . . . Its public buildings are fine, and the grouping of them about the open, flower-planted spaces is very effective. It is a handsome city with the single drawback of slight monotony in the well-built homes."

Still there were rumblings of criticism from the beginning, and Pullman was never the idyllic community which its owner had projected. There were serious strikes (broken by the company) in

1882, 1884, 1886, 1888, and 1891. Some attentive visitors to the town reported much discontent among the residents. Richard Ely, the well-known economist and student of municipal reform, described Pullman as embodying ideas foreign to democratic America: "It is not the American ideal. It is benevolent, well-wishing feudalism, which desires the happiness of the people, but in such a way as to please the authorities." The absence of any local participation in government contributed, according to some observers, to a lack of civic pride; and over all, there seemed to hang a blanket of suspicion and hostility.

The violent Pullman strike in 1894 focused much unfavorable attention on the model town. To many, it proved that paternalism had failed to solve the problems of urban communities. In 1898, the Illinois Supreme Court ruled that the Pullman Company's charter did not authorize its community enterprise; within another decade the company had divested itself of its town property and Pullman simply became a part of Chicago. Little regret was expressed at the passing of this urban experiment; most opinion seemed to agree that its paternalism, its "feudalism," ought not to have been applied to an American community. Pullman was the last impressive effort to build a satisfactory industrial community on the company town model. City planning was evolving only slowly and uncertainly in the framework of voluntary business and political action across the nation: there was much waste and much left undone. But the Pullman experience suggested strongly that authoritarian direction would produce no better results.

Meanwhile, landscape architecture and city planning were being fused into one concept by the Chicago World's Fair of 1893–94, called the Columbian Exposition, which celebrated the four hundredth anniversary of the discovery of the New World. The idea of having the celebration had been discussed intermittently in the 1880's, somewhat prominently at a session of the American Historical Association's convention in 1886. Congress provided official sanction in 1890, and after considering the spirited rivalry of many cities that wanted to host the exposition, it chose Chicago. Especially in view of Chicago's resurgence from its own ashes after the fire of 1871, this choice was appropriate, and great enthusiasm gathered around the planning and construction of the fair. The most active supervisor was Daniel H. Burnham, a well-known Chicago architect with talents for organization and propaganda; "beauty," he once said, "has always paid better than any other commodity and always will." He consulted Olmsted on the choice of a site, and brought together many architects, landscape planners, engineers, and sculptors to participate in building the fair. After one joint consultation, Augustus St. Gaudens remarked to Burnham that it had been "the greatest meeting of artists since the fifteenth century."

The scope of the project meant that in order to hold the fair at all a brand new city must be built. As the grounds were laid out and the white buildings rose on every side—even a canal was cut through the Jackson Park location to enhance the fairgrounds— water, sewerage, transportation facilities, police and fire protection, in short a whole complex of urban services, had to be provided. Burnham oversaw the labors of seven thousand workmen, seventeen of whom died from accidents which were frequent during the frenetic activity. The fair opened in May 1893; on the first day almost half a million people swarmed onto the grounds, and by the time the Columbian Exposition closed in October more than 27,000,000 admissions had been counted.

People began calling the fairgrounds "the White City," and realized quickly that it constituted an unparalleled example of building a city to a pre-established plan. The fair's success stimulated intense enthusiasm for city planning. The president of the Fair Commission anticipated this in 1893, saying that "as an educational force and inspiration, I believe the buildings, their grouping, and laying out of the grounds will in themselves do more good in a general way than the exhibits themselves." A character in Fuller's *With the Procession,* returning to Chicago in 1894, met with "the universal expectation that the spirit of the White City was but just transferred to the body of the great Black City close at hand, over which it was to hover as an enlightenment—through which it might permeate as an informing force." In later years, the reputation of the Columbian Exposition as the great generator of subsequent city planning became distorted, obscuring the significance of the park and boulevard movement that had preceded it. Nevertheless, the symbolic value of the magnificent fair can hardly

260

be overstated; it encouraged people to think about their cities as artifacts, and to believe that with sufficient effort and imagination they could be reshaped nearer to images of civilized living.

The first important application of the principles both explicit and implicit in the White City came in Washington, D.C. Once more an anniversary helped focus attention: in 1900 Washington would celebrate its centennial. Beautification of the capital city had always excited thought in some minds; in the early 1850's Downing prepared a plan for that purpose, and in the 1870's Alexander Shepherd had refurbished much of the city in the ambitious building program that ultimately ruined him. In 1900, the American Institute of Architects devoted its convention (held in Washington) to consideration of improving the city's design. The architects' interest was encouraged by Senator James McMillan of Michigan, who pushed a measure through Congress directing the District of Columbia Committee to take the matter up officially. The committee called for advice upon several men who had been active in developing the Chicago fair: Burnham and Charles McKim were among them, and Frederick Law Olmsted's son was also included. This group drew up a plan centered upon reconstructing L'Enfant's project for a great mall between the Capitol and the Potomac River; additional historical monuments were to be built, and Rock Creek Park was to be completely landscaped. McKim, Burnham, and their associates prepared an exhibit consisting of hundreds of drawings, models and photographs to clarify their ideas to President Roosevelt and other government officials. Agreement with the president of the Pennsylvania Railroad made it possible to eliminate a railway station blocking the mall, and piece by piece the plan, in its essentials at least, was carried out.

The notion of city beautification received added impetus from the improvement of Washington. Burnham popularized beautification tirelessly, carrying his contagious enthusiasm to every part of the country, and finally back to Chicago. Here, with the backing of the Commercial Club, he and an associate, Edward H. Bennett, launched the Chicago Plan of 1907, in which the expansive and carefully laid out lakefront had its origin. Describing the plan for Chicago, Burnham and Bennett revealed how the ideas of the romantic park and boulevard landscape architects had blended with

261

the ideal of magnificence which recalled the name of L'Enfant's plan for the District of Columbia. But along with the magnificence, Burnham and Bennett wrote, recourse to nature must always be available. "Natural scenery furnishes the contrasting element to the artificiality of the city. All of us should often run away . . . into the wilds, where mind and body are restored to a normal condition, and we are enabled to take up the burden of life in our crowded streets and endless stretches of buildings with renewed vigor and hopefulness. . . . He who habitually comes in close contact with nature develops saner methods of thought than can be the case when one is habitually shut up within the walls of a city." Appropriately, they referred to Chicago's Latin motto, *Urbs in horto:* a city in a garden.

By the time of the Chicago plan, the "city beautiful" movement had fully matured, and discussion of rebuilding cities and parts of cities in these terms was common. Early in the 1900's, planning agencies—usually with little independent power—were appearing in city governments, with New Haven in 1907 and Chicago in 1909 offering two of the first examples. City planning had spawned its own profession: the American City Planning Institute met for the first time in 1916; by that date the subject's literature was already large.

The landscape planners and the proponents of the "city beautiful" movement met with frequent criticism; their aesthetic notions were often naïve or old-fashioned. Still, their activities were essential in promoting the growing self-awareness of America's urban centers. They took the city's existence for granted; "the tendency of mankind to congregate in cities," wrote Burnham, "is a marked characteristic of modern times." They believed that planning could ameliorate the dangerous and ugly consequences of rapid urbanization; to quote Burnham again, "the slum exists today only because of the failure of the city to protect itself against gross evils and known perils, all of which should be corrected by the enforcement of simple principles of sanitation." They were inspired by striking vistas of the urban future; Charles M. Robinson, a Rochester architect and propagandist for the "city beautiful," reflected this when he wrote in 1918: "When the heavens rolled away and St. John beheld the new Jerusalem, so a new vision of a new London, a

262

new Washington, Chicago, or New York, breaks with the morning sunshine upon the degradation, discomfort, and baseness of modern city life. There are born a new dream and a new hope."

Robinson's evangelical optimism about the city's future would have been shared by few of his contemporaries, but there was no serious doubt by the time of the First World War that the city dominated the economic, social, and cultural life of Americans. Their novelists, short story writers, and poets may have helped them reach this conclusion, and in any event fully shared it. As an environment for life and conflict, the city had been naturalized in American letters by the turn of the century. William Dean Howells, with his Ohio small-town boyhood, could still regard the metropolis as something of a curiosity, but his two greatest novels, *The Rise of Silas Lapham* (1885) and *A Hazard of New Fortunes* (1895), unfold their plots in Boston and New York, respectively, with no suggestion that these cities are in any way unusual settings, or that they threatened moral destruction to individuals any more than other settings might do. All of Henry James's major writings have big city locales: Venice, London, Paris, and again New York and Boston in the United States. The characters in these stories reflect conflicting social values, along with representative human vices and virtues, and there is in both Howells and James much implicit protest against social or cultural conditions which they deplored. Still, their criticisms are directed largely against capitalism or materialism, and not against the city itself.

One of the themes inherent in American urbanization which attracted late nineteenth and twentieth century writers was the enthusiasm of town promoters. Mark Twain satirized it in *The Gilded Age* (1871), recording the lugubrious collapse of the plans of Colonel Beriah Sellars, who had described a future metropolis on the banks of a Missouri creek-bed in terms which Jesup Scott or Robert Van Horn would have found familiar. But the later chapters in *Life on the Mississippi* (1883), with their approving descriptions of the urban progress along the river from St. Paul to New Orleans show that Twain wrote sympathetically of Sellars, and regarded the unfortunate booster as naive and caught up in the machinations of others rather than as a man who was basically reprehensible. A short passage catching the spirit of the promoter in Stephen Crane's story, "The Blue Hotel," has been less noted. A Swedish immigrant arrives in a rough and tough Nebraska town in the 1870's; he has heard blood-curdling stories about the cowboys and villains of the American West, and fears for his life. When he tells the owner of the hotel (one of the town's leading citizens) that he expects to be killed, the owner replies: "Why, man, we're goin' to have a line of ilictric street-cars in this town next spring. . . . And there's a new railroad goin' to be built down from Broken Arm to here. Not to mintion the four churches and the smashin' big brick school-house. Then there's the big factory, too. Why, in two years Romper'll be a met-tro-*pol*-is." The booster-promoter does not appear frequently enough in works of fiction to be called a stock figure, but authors did find him useful. Finally, in Sinclair Lewis's *Babbitt* (1924), he became a hero. George F. Babbitt is a real estate developer in the city of Zenith, who becomes confused by the social and cultural diversity of his city; after a series of mis-adventures (two of which were later cited by W. Lloyd Warner for the accuracy of Lewis's sociological insight) culminating in a love affair with an artistically bohemian woman, Babbitt comes to understand that his proper place in the scheme of things is found in his office and his home. In order to write *Babbitt,* Lewis toured midwestern cities, staying for weeks at a time in Indianapolis, Kansas City, and other places, to get material with which to construct his synthetic Zenith; he subscribed to several real estate journals in order to familiarize himself with the business; with the help of his wife, he even constructed a three-dimensional model of Zenith, naming the streets and buildings, and carefully following his characters on it as he caused them to walk or drive through the fictional city. *Babbitt* became a best-seller in the 1920's, and although it was at first widely misunderstood, it ranks near the top of any list of serious urban fiction in America.

Another theme which authors elaborated upon was the lure of the city: the magnetic power urban centers exerted on people of imagination and ambition. Willa Cather described the lure with intense pathos in her story, "A Wagner Matinee," which appeared in 1903. A young Boston resident learns that his old aunt who has spent most of her adult life on a Nebraska farm which he had long ago left, is to visit him. He remembers that in his boyhood

264

this aunt had taught him something of literature and music, and hopes that an afternoon at the opera will please her. She listens to the music entranced, and memories of her earlier hopes of being a musician come flooding back into her mind. When the concert is over, the two remain in their seats until everyone else has left; the aunt finally "burst into tears and sobbed pleadingly. 'I don't want to go, Clark, I don't want to go!' I understood. For her, just outside the door of the concert hall, lay the black pond with the cattle-tracked bluffs; the tall, unpainted house, with weather-curled boards, naked as a tower; the crook-backed ash seedlings where the dish-cloths hung to dry; the gaunt, moulting turkeys picking up refuse about the kitchen door."

The city's lure was often sentimentalized, even by first-rate writers. Theodore Dreiser exploited it in *Sister Carrie* (1900) in lachrymose terms: "The city has its cunning wiles, no less than the infinitely smaller and more human tempter. There are large forces which allure with all the soulfulness of expression possible in the most cultured human. The gleam of a thousand lights is often as effective as the persuasive light in a wooing and fascinating eye. . . . Unrecognised for what they are, their beauty, like music, too often relaxes, then weakens, then perverts the simpler human perceptions." But the net result for Carrie of her migration to Chicago and later New York is a life of fame and wealth as an actress. Southerners felt the same urban attractions, even though many of them denied it. George Washington Cable and Walter Hines Page found it impossible to live in southern or rural environments in the later nineteenth and early twentieth centuries and sought the northeastern cities. A generation later Thomas Wolfe gave poetic expression to the drawing power which Boston and New York exercised on a young North Carolinian: "the city would always be the same when he came back. He would rush through the immense and glorious stations, murmurous with their million destinies and the everlasting sound of time, that was caught up forever in their roof—he would rush out into the street, and instantly it would be the same as it had always been, and yet forever strange and new."

Authors described the overwhelming poverty and filth of the slums much as Riis and Veiller had done; indeed, the coinciding of the work of those writers with several works by Crane and

Dreiser testifies once more to the insatiable curiosity which American urban development had aroused by the twentieth century. Crane's *Maggie: A Girl of the Streets* was not widely read in this country until thirty years after it was written; when it appeared, in the 1890's, it was still too realistic for most editorial taste in the United States. Briefly, Crane tells the story of a girl brought up in one of New York City's tenement districts; she is "ruined" by a faithless lover, becomes a prostitute, and ultimately jumps in the river. As an episode in *How the Other Half Lives,* Crane's story would have fit perfectly. He describes a tenement house in memorable words: "a careening building, a dozen gruesome doorways [giving] up loads of babies to the street and the gutter. A wind of early autumn raised yellow dust from cobbles and swirled it against a hundred windows. Long streamers of garments fluttered from fire-escapes. In all unhandy places there were buckets, brooms, rags, and bottles. In the street infants played or fought with other infants or sat stupidly in the way of vehicles. Formidable women, with uncombed hair and disordered dress, gossiped while leaning on railings, or screamed in frantic quarrels. Withered persons, in curious postures of submission to something sat smoking pipes in obscure corners. A thousand odours of cooking food came forth to the street. The building quivered and creaked from the weight of humanity stamping about in its bowels." In another story, probably written about the same time, called "The Men in the Storm," Crane describes a crowd of men waiting outside a charitable establishment where they can have a bed for the night and something to eat next morning for five cents. A blizzard descends upon the city, and the men crowd and fight to get in when the doors open. "The tossing crowd on the sidewalk grew smaller and smaller. The snow beat with merciless persistence upon the bowed heads of those who waited. The wind drove it up from the pavements in frantic forms of winding white, and it seethed in circles about the huddled forms passing in one by one, three by three, out of the storm." Dreiser described almost exactly the same kind of institution in *Sister Carrie,* as George Hurstwood steadily descends the social ladder in New York until he reaches the bottom on Blackwell's Island—where he is buried with other paupers.

266

This kind of literature was often regarded as unacceptable. Both *Maggie* and *Sister Carrie* were suppressed for some time by publishers, whereas Riis, Veiller, and the Pittsburgh Survey authors were read widely and taken to heart. Why the novelists and the housing reformers had such contrasting receptions, when their material and often their language was so similar, is difficult to explain. But it must be remembered that Dreiser and Crane did not offer their descriptions of the seamy side of urban civilization wrapped about in the mantle of reform. It may be that artistic portrayal of observed truth was felt to have less justification than portrayal of the same truth when offered as a spur for social improvement.

However they used the urban environment, the writers sought the values that it embodied. The city represented power; Frank Norris, in *The Pit* (1902), described Chicago as "the Great Gray City, brooking no rival, [imposing] its dominion upon a reach of country larger than many a kingdom of the Old World. For thousands of miles beyond its confines was its influence felt. Out, far out, far away in the snow and shadow of northern Wisconsin forests, axes and saws bit the bark of century-old trees, stimulated by this city's driving energy. Just as far to the southward pick and drill leaped to the assault of veins of anthracite, moved by her central power. Her force turned the wheels of harvester and seeder a thousand miles distant in Iowa and Kansas. Her force spun the screws of . . . innumerable squadrons of lake steamers crowding the Sault Sainte Marie. For her and because of her all the Central States, all the Great Northwest, roared with traffic and industry; sawmills screamed; factories . . . clashed and flamed; cog gripped cog; beltings clasped the drums of mammoth wheels; and converters of forges belched into the clouded air their tempest breath of molten steel." Dreiser, looking backward to earlier days, wrote in 1931, "I loved Chicago. It was so strong, so rough, so shabby, and yet so vital and determined. It seemed . . . like a young giant afraid of nothing, and that it was that appealed to me."

In addition to representing power, the city also represented freedom. Even writers who later on described the large cities as corrupting influences and compared them invidiously with the small towns of their youth had left those small towns in order to find

267

literary careers in the urban centers. For Dreiser's Frank Cowper-wood, in *The Titan* (1914), Chicago represented escape from ruin; after his jail term in his native Philadelphia, Cowperwood had to find a new field in which to rebuild his life. Chicago, "a seething city in the making," offered the necessary opportunity: "Why it fairly sang! The world was young here. Life was doing something new." For Hart Crane, a young poet with consuming ambition to compose the great American epic, New York City, with its great symbol, Brooklyn Bridge, stood for nothing less than the spiritual integrity of modern man. In his "Proem: To Brooklyn Bridge" (1930), Crane invoked the spirit of the Roeblings' masterpiece; he found myth-sustaining intimations of divinity in the vaulting curves of the bridge rising above the swarming city. The quest for positive and creative values implicit in urban life could hardly be carried further. By the time of the Great Depression, Americans had examined their cities closely and had accepted their urban destiny for better or worse. The city was to be the theater for their cultural, political, and social dramas; the city's priorities would shape their thoughts and their actions.

10

The Emergence
of Metropolis

Informing much of the late nineteenth century examination of the problems and the prospects of the American city was the view that city and country represented distinct environments, opposed ways of life. This view would continue to influence the character of popular argument—especially in political debate —until at least the 1950's. But an occasional observer around the turn of the century recognized that the conception of city as one thing and country another—a conception which had such deep roots in western culture—could no longer be applied to American society. The city by this time had enormously extended its spatial area and its influence. There was often difficulty in physically distinguishing city from countryside, for the two often blended together in sprawling urban regions. The country no longer represented an independent community, since it was affected in hundreds of economic and social ways by the city. "The city has become the

269

central feature in modern civilization and to an ever increasing extent the dominant one," wrote the municipal reformer Frederic C. Howe in 1906. "This rural civilization, whose making engaged mankind since the dawn of history, is passing away. The city has erased the landmarks of an earlier society. Man has entered on an urban age."

In a general way, Howe was describing an aspect of the phenomenon of "metropolitanism,"—the extension of the influence of the large city over enormous hinterland regions. A few years later, the phenomenon received more explicit demographic recognition in the statistics presented in the federal census of 1910. As early as 1880, the census bureau had provided data for the metropolitan district of New York and its suburbs. Aware of the inadequacy of the customary urban classifications (populations of 8,000, 4,000, and 2,500 had all been used), demographers now applied the statistical notion of the metropolitan district to the whole nation. Twenty-five metropolitan districts were identified ranging in size from New York (including Newark) with its 616,927 acres of land and 6,474,568 people to Portland with its 43,538 acres and 215,048 residents. Through this device it was possible to indicate the unity of such urban areas as the twin cities of Minnesota, the cities on San Francisco Bay, and the two Kansas Cities along the Missouri-Kansas border. Also evident was the importance of the clusters of suburban communities around the large eastern cities of New York, Boston, and Philadelphia. Through continued growth over the next half century, these cities and their suburbs would come to constitute a kind of continuous metropolitan region which may represent a new stage in urban organization—the megalopolis.*

The growth of the metropolis constitutes the central theme of twentieth century American urban history. For the 1950 census,

---

* The term "megalopolis" was devised by Jean Gottman and is generally applied to an urban region that contains several metropolitan centers. An alternative term "conurbation" implies an urban region formed from the fusion of several earlier cities. It has more application in Europe than in the United States; the cities along the Ruhr River in Germany and the Amsterdam-Haarlem-Leiden-The Hague-Rotterdam-Utrecht complex in the Netherlands supply examples of this kind of urban development. The term "metropolis," as is evident from Chapter One, acquired a different meaning in the twentieth century than it had historically.

demographers devised a more sophisticated device than the metropolitan district to assess the importance of the rise of metropolitan regions. This was the Standard Metropolitan Area (renamed the Standard Metropolitan Statistical Area in 1960), which was defined as a whole county containing a central city of 50,000 or more, plus any adjacent counties that appeared to be integrated to the central city. For overall examination of twentieth century metropolitan growth, it is perhaps most convenient to use the principal S.M.A.'s (those with 100,000 or more population at a given census), which the Census Bureau has "retrojected" to past census periods. But whatever measuring scheme is employed the trends are evident.

First, there was a great increase in the number of metropolitan areas and in the total population that lived in these areas. During the period from 1900 to 1950, the total United States population increased from 76.0 million to 150.7 million, while the number of principal S.M.A.'s increased from 82 to 147 and their total population from 24.1 million to 84.3 million. This represented a percentage change in the metropolitan population from 31.9 per cent of the nation's total to 56.0 per cent.

Second, for the entire period the growth rate for the principal S.M.A.'s was substantially higher than for the country as a whole: 32.6 per cent as opposed to 21.0 per cent from 1900 to 1910, 25.2 per cent as opposed to 14.9 per cent from 1910 to 1920, 27.0 per cent as opposed to 16.1 per cent from 1920 to 1930, 8.3 per cent as opposed to 7.2 per cent from 1930 to 1940, and 21.8 per cent as opposed to 14.5 per cent from 1940 to 1950. For every decade in the period except 1900–10, when it was 15.0, the growth rate for nonmetropolitan areas of the country was substantially below ten per cent.

Third, there has been a tendency for rapid growth to take place in the outlying areas of metropolitan centers at an accelerating rate. After 1920 metropolitan "rings" grew much faster than "central cities" themselves, by the 1940–1950 decade nearly two and a half times as fast (34.8 per cent as compared with 13.7 per cent). During the first decade of the century, metropolitan rings claimed only about one-sixth of the total United States population growth

271

(15.7 per cent); in 1940–50 this figure had risen to nearly one half (48.6 per cent).

The metropolises of the twentieth century, whose growth constituted the most dramatic demographic development to be found in statistics of United States population, were much more than greatly enlarged traditional cities. Involved in the concept of the modern metropolis are complex changes in function and structure within the city and its suburban areas—decentralization of numerous activities, separation of areas of residence and work, and a high mobility over greatly extended spatial areas. Also involved are many relationships with other cities and areas outside the immediate limits of the urban region.* The sociologist R. D. McKenzie in his pioneer study of metropolitan communities in the early 1930's argued that these considerations were so striking that the huge city of the twentieth century with its surrounding suburban towns and cities and its far reaching economic relationships ought to be considered as "practically a new social and economic entity." A few years earlier N. S. B. Gras had examined the existence of a world-wide metropolitan community and the intricate relationship of world cities of various sizes within that community. "We may think of metropolitan economy as an organization of people having a large city as nucleus," Gras wrote. "Or we may put it this way, metropolitan economy is the organization of producers and consumers mutually dependent for goods and services, wherein their wants are supplied by a system of exchange concentrated in a large city which is the focus of local trade and the center through which normal economic relations with the outside are established and maintained."

"Just as villages remained when town economy prevailed," Gras continued, "so do towns remain when metropolitan economy comes

---

* The terminology relating to the metropolis is confusing. Some writers use the term "metropolitan community" to designate the area where population is integrated on a daily basis to the locale, that is, pretty much the commuting area of a metropolis; the term "metropolitan region" can then describe the larger area of more indirect influence. Employing the latter concept, it would be possible to divide the whole nation into a number of extended "metropolitan regions." But there is little consistency in the use of metropolitan nomenclature, and we have not attempted to be unduly precise here.

into existence. Towns remain, but in economic subordination to the metropolis. They continue to play a part, but as tributaries to a larger center. A closer examination of these dependent towns would show different types performing different functions, but all subordinate."

Gras' conception of "metropolitan dominance"—the control of the huge city over vast surrounding areas—influenced much of the subsequent study of the metropolis. Yet, as Gras himself recognized, "dominance" alone supplied an insufficient explanation. Not only were outlying areas of the metropolis dependent upon the city, but the city in turn was dependent upon its hinterland. In fact, the whole series of relationships within a metropolitan area was so complex that the biological term of symbiosis was often employed to indicate their nature. The twentieth century metropolis provided a new system of social and economic organization—a distinctive social configuration. As Leo F. Schnore observes, the metropolitan area cannot profitably be conceived of "as a simple two-part arrangement of center and ring, a large city with its adjacent territory. . . . The metropolitan community must be viewed—in organizational terms throughout—as a highly specialized mosaic of subareas tied together into a new functional unity. Moreover, it is to be viewed as a multinucleated territorial system. Within these broad areas, the large centers are marked by functional diversity, while the smaller places, many of them formerly independent cities in their own right, tend to be narrowy specialized. At the same time, however, the main centers are specialized in the coordinating functions of administration and control."

The rise of the metropolitan region is often associated with the introduction of the automobile. Up to a point this is accurate. Statistically, if all American cities are considered together, the great jump in suburban population occurred in the 1920's when the automobile became the main device of urban transportation. Nevertheless, it is clear that the process of population decentralization—a fundamental aspect of the rise of the metropolis—had begun for some cities and in some regions of the country in the latter part of the nineteenth century. Schnore, one of the few contemporary urban sociologists to undertake detailed historical analysis of urban demography, has provided an ingenious study of

A History of Urban America

decentralization of population in ninety-nine metropolitan central cities that had a population of at least 100,000 at some point in their growth. His study, which takes into account annexations and the persistence through thirty-year periods of decentralizing patterns, indicates the early tendency of a number of individual cities to grow more rapidly in their peripheral areas than at their centers. New York began decentralizing as early as 1850. Nine other cities had begun to decentralize by 1900; another thirteen cities were added to the list during the first decade of the century. The process speeded up after 1920, of course, and fully sixty cities began to decentralize between 1920 and 1940. In short, suburbanization, although it greatly accelerated in the twentieth century, is a trend in American urban development that extends back at least a hundred years. In Philadelphia, to cite an extreme example, the population movement away from the center of the city was proportionally greater in the fifty years between 1860 and 1910 than in the half century between 1900 and 1950.

The basic economic institutions that enabled larger cities to develop highly specialized metropolitan functions within a network of varying sized towns and cities also had nineteenth century origins. The techniques of modern merchandising—with their emphasis on trade over vast regions—were fully developed by the end of the century. In the 1860's, Marshall Field's in Chicago combined the features of a number of large stores in Paris and New York—a fixed price system, large display advertisements, and numerous special departments—to establish the modern department store. The Great American Tea Company was organized in 1864 in New York; five years later it became the Great Atlantic and Pacific Tea Company. It began to establish branches throughout the country and became one of the first major chain stores. Frank W. Woolworth opened his five-and-ten at Lancaster, Pennsylvania in 1879, established branches at Harrisburg and Scranton, and within a decade owned stores in a number of localities. Modern advertising techniques, low-cost mass insurance, mail-order stores, centralized stock exchanges, and specialized banking were examples of other metropolitan activities that developed in the latter part of the century. Technological innovations in printing—new presses, linotype machines, improved halftones—permitted city newspapers greatly

274

to expand their circulations. This provided one of the most important means through which the influence of the metropolis was extended. In the early work of American urban sociologists, measurement of newspaper circulation provided a convenient way of estimating the range of metropolitan influence.

Another significant aspect of metropolitanism with nineteenth century origins was industrial suburbanization—the growth of "satellite cities," as Graham Taylor termed them in one of the first investigations of manufacturing communities on the outskirts of large cities. Although this aspect of decentralization has not received as much attention as the creation of the residential "dormitory" suburbs, the suburbs of employment and production have been equally important in shaping the character of the modern metropolis. In the late nineteenth century, the substitution of electric power for steam in industry and improvements in transportation made it possible for manufacturers to move away from central cities, and they were encouraged to do so by a number of factors: the need for vast amounts of cheap land to build factories incorporating all stages of large-scale complex production, lower taxes, and freedom from regulation in regard to smoke and noise. Early attempts to build industrial communities in America had been influenced by conceptions of social control. Through the establishment of small carefully planned rural manufacturing towns, it was hoped that America might escape the abuses of the European manufacturing city. But after the disastrous Pullman Strike of 1894, which stemmed in large part from the system of paternalistic control instituted in George Pullman's planned community, American manufacturers abandoned social planning in setting up their decentralized manufacturing centers. To the extent that they had to provide housing and urban facilities for workers, they did so in the simplest and most economical manner and as quickly as possible got out of the business of managing communities.

Gary, Indiana, the largest city ever built by an American manufacturer, illustrated the new approach. In 1905, the United States Steel Corporation, as part of an effort to expand and consolidate portions of its vast productive facilities, purchased eleven square miles of empty land below Lake Michigan on the Calumet River in Indiana. While new mills were being constructed at the site, the corporation, through its subsidiary Gary Land Company, constructed a system of basic utilities for a city of 200,000, platted out streets and lots on the simple, efficient gridiron design, had houses built through private contractors, and sold these to incoming workers on long-term contracts. Eugene J. Buffington, who managed the U.S. Steel operation at Gary, reflected the new outlook of American manufacturers when he stated that "the most successful attempts at industrial social betterment in our country are those farthest removed from the suspicion of domination or control by the employer. . . . Gary is nothing more than the product of effort along practical lines to secure right living conditions around a steel manufacturing plant." Gary was organized as an ordinary municipality; aside from trying to restrict the sale of alcohol, the Gary Land Company made no attempt to impose controls on workers. U.S. Steel's experiment in decentralizing manufacturing was strikingly successful. Gary was well located in relation to the railroads and the labor market of Chicago, and in a few years, a vast suburban industrial complex, "the cities of the Calumet," had developed in the region.

Occasionally in the founding of smaller twentieth century industrial communities—such as Morgan Park, a suburb of Duluth built by U.S. Steel, or Goodyear Heights, developed by the Goodyear Rubber Company outside Akron—the utilization of techniques of planning did help provide a desirable environment for living and working. But more often than not, the industrial satellites had dismal slums right from the start. Many areas in the manufacturing complex that grew up across the Mississippi River from St. Louis—including the communities of East St. Louis, Granite City, Madison, and Venice—lacked even elemental urban services. Particularly miserable was Granite City, where 65 per cent of the 8,500 workers in a granite processing factory lived; a large densely settled slum area known as "Hungry Hollow" remained a part of Granite City for several decades. Norwood and Oakley, outside of Cincinnati; Lackawanna built in a swamp outside of Buffalo; and South Omaha were other early twentieth century industrial suburbs that demonstrated the deleterious effects of the absence of planning and control.

Even though U.S. Steel provided satisfactory urban services at the beginning, and later financed a number of recreational and educational projects, Gary, too, developed many of the problems of the large manufacturing city. The first construction workers at the site had lived in tents and various thrown-together shacks of tar paper, tin, and board. The area was allowed to remain for a time, and the structures became homes for many of the unskilled immigrant laborers in the mills. The company also built dormitories for unskilled workers; they were soon overcrowded, and the area where they were located deteriorated into a slum called "Hunkeyville." When the temporary camp area was finally cleared, many of the workers moved into a section south of Gary called "The Patch," where developers had thrown together ramshackle housing outside the control of Gary municipal officials or the company. When, as part of a clean-up attempt, the company forced the tenants out of the Hunkeyville housing, most of them also moved to The Patch. Although skilled workers were able to obtain adequate living quarters, this was not possible for the unskilled. The slum areas around Gary soon developed the customary problems of alcoholism, prostitution, and crime, although, owing primarily to a good natural water supply, they were not struck by serious epidemics.

The building of industrial towns and cities in the early part of the twentieth century reflected a general pattern of decentralization clearly indicated in statistics of manufacturing. A Census Bureau study of twelve of the thirteen largest "industrial districts" showed that from 1899 to 1904 the number of persons employed in industry in central cities increased by 14.9 per cent while in the outlying zones the number increased by 32.8 per cent. From 1904 to 1909 the increase in central cities was 22.5 per cent while in the surrounding zones it was 48.8 per cent. For the decade, the growth rate was over two times as great for the suburbs—97.7 per cent to 40.8 per cent. This trend toward industrial decentralization became even more pronounced with the general acceleration of suburbanization after 1920. In 1919 eleven central cities in the country's forty largest manufacturing counties still accounted for 85 per cent of the manufacturing workers; by 1937 this percentage had fallen to just under 60. The number of wage earners in the eleven central cities during the period declined from 2,045,789 to 1,808,692 while in the outlying areas of these cities the number increased from 365,403 to 1,218,465. In addition to the decentralization of manufacturing, many of the commercial functions of the nineteenth century city showed a marked tendency to decentralization, again particularly after 1920.

Cheap electric power and the telephone were important in the decentralization of economic activities. Also important was the mobility of labor permitted by the trolleys and inter-urban railroads. But the most significant development stimulating rapid suburbanization was the automobile, and to a lesser extent, the motorized truck. In the early 1890's, mechanics in the United States and in Europe had put together workable automobiles. But until the turn of the century they were built on individual order and were largely a toy of the rich, with only 8,000 vehicles registered by 1900. During the next decade actual manufacturing began. By 1910 the number of motor vehicles had risen to 468,500, and in 1915 to 2,490,932. Then came the tremendous post-First World War expansion of the industry: motor vehicle registration jumped from 9,239,161 in 1920 to 19,940,724 in 1925 to 26,531,999 in 1930. In spite of the depression of the 1930's, the number of motor vehicles still increased by nearly a third during the decade reaching a total of 32,035,424 registrations in 1940; by 1950 the number had grown to 48,566,984.

In addition to the obvious effects of increasing the mobility of workers and consumers and facilitating the movement of goods and materials in cities, the general use of motor vehicles also modified the spatial pattern of the metropolis. In the late nineteenth and early twentieth century, cities spread out along the lines of trolleys and inter-urban railroads. The suburbanized parts of the metropolis resembled tentacles extending from the central city in radial fashion. Highways, particularly in older and larger cities like Chicago and New York, first tended to follow the railroad lines. The new suburbs made possible by the automobile became part of the older pattern of growth. Gradually, however, as road building greatly expanded after the passage of the Federal Highway Act of 1916, the interstices of the metropolitan area began to be filled in. Complicated lateral movements of traffic became a defining characteristic of the metropolis. Newer cities, such as Los Angeles, that experienced great growth in the twentieth century spread out along highways and did not develop the clearly defined central business districts of older cities. The transportation systems of older cities, even after the automobile came into general use, still tended to funnel traffic into the center, greatly intensifying the problem of congestion.

During the 1920's and early 1930's, engineers perfected and governments adopted the various devices that were part of a high speed system of motorized transportation—grade separation of highway from city street, traffic circle, divided dual highway, and synchronized stop lights. These techniques, along with new bridges such as the George Washington in New York and the Camden-Philadelphia, and an innovation such as the Holland Tunnel under the Hudson, permitted easier movement of automobile traffic through the huge, sprawling metropolitan region. But just as in past eras, the rush-hour, weekend, and holiday traffic jam was an all too familiar aspect of urban life.

The expanded economic opportunities created by the automobile stimulated an urban land boom that radically inflated property values in American cities. Particularly where automobile routes tended to follow older fixed forms of urban transportation, considerable expansion took place in central business districts. This expansion contributed to an optimism that caused property values to rise, and as Homer Hoyt has dryly observed, "In each successive land boom there is a speculative exaggeration of the trend of the period." In 1920, the total value of land in American cities of over 30,000 population—only about one-fifth of one per cent of all the land in the United States—was estimated at $25 billion; by 1926 this figure had doubled to $50 billion. During the same period the value of American farm land dropped from 55 to 37 billion dollars —a figure 33 per cent less than the value of land in cities above 30,000. Real estate on Manhattan Island was assessed at over five billion dollars in 1930; this was more than the value of the farm land in 23 states in 1925. The corner of State and Madison in the heart of Chicago's loop was leased during the decade at a rate of $50,000 a front foot, a rate equivalent to $21,789,000 an acre. One small holding at 1 Wall Street in New York City sold for $100,000 a front foot, a rate of nearly $44,000,000 an acre.

Inflation of downtown land values and the post-First World War prosperity of many sections of the economy stimulated the great era of skyscraper building in American cities. For twenty-five years after Jenny's initial efforts, architects experimented with the new building form; the Woolworth Tower of New York completed in 1913 established a standard style. Chicago's group of towers along the Chicago River built in the early 1920's differed little from the new "Woolworth Gothic" skyscrapers that sprang up in New York. Cleveland, Pittsburgh, San Francisco, and Kansas City developed the jagged sky lines characteristic of the twentieth-century American city. By 1929, American cities had 377 skyscrapers of more than twenty stories in height, largely built without concern for the character of the surrounding urban space and without concern for the patterns of traffic created by the buildings. Even in the cities of the plains the skyscraper was as much demanded as on the tight plots of lower Manhattan Island. Many of the nation's tallest buildings were begun in 1928 and 1929 and only completed after the depression. The most famous skyscraper of all, the Empire State Building, was finished in 1930 and for many years was a white elephant in a city which during the depression had more than enough office space. Not until the late 1950's were the pressures of urban growth great enough to stimulate another era of skyscraper building.

Although architects criticized the skyscraper for its lack of esthetic distinction and planners criticized it for contribution to intense traffic congestion, it was through the jagged towering skylines of great cities that many observers perceived the character of the new metropolitan civilization. The German director Fritz Lang was inspired to make his classic motion picture "Metropolis" with its striking vision of the urban future after a visit to Manhattan in the mid-1920's. The French historian, Bernard Fäy, who visited New York late in the decade, echoed the sentiments of many travelers to the city in finding the mass of skyscrapers an appropriate symbol of a new order:

The very thing which I admire most in New York is its adaptation to the continent. In this sense, its architecture is intellectually reasonable, logical, and beautiful. Skyscrapers are the dwellings of the supertrusts; they are Eiffel Tower cathedrals which shelter Mr. Rockefeller, the Emperor of Petroleum, or Mr. Morgan, the Czar of Gold. . . . Some say that New York crushes them—and not without reason; the individual is overwhelmed by these great buildings. This is not an architecture for men, like the Parthenon or the châteaux of the Loire and Versailles. It is an architecture for human masses. Such buildings do not shelter or isolate men as do those of Europe. They gather and shuffle them. Often more than five thousand persons are united under one roof. . . . The New York skyscrapers are the most striking manifestation of the triumph of numbers. One cannot understand or like them without first having tasted and enjoyed the thrill of counting or adding up enormous totals and of living in a gigantic, compact, and brilliant world.

As cities went upward, they also went outward. The introduction of the automobile launched a great era of suburban building. The 1920's saw the complete emergence of modern residential suburbs and this was reflected in spectacular percentage growth rates during the decade for some of the more famous of them: Beverly Hills, 2485.0, Glendale, 363.5, Inglewood, 492.8, Huntington Park, 444.9 (suburbs of Los Angeles); Cleveland Heights, 234.4, Shaker Heights, 1000.4; Garfield Heights, 511.3 (suburbs of Cleveland); Grosse Pointe Park, 724.6, Ferndale, 689.9 (suburbs of Detroit); Webster Groves, 74.0, Maplewood, 70.3, Richmond Heights, 328.3 (suburbs of St. Louis); Elmwood Park, 716.7, Oak Park, 60.5, Park Ridge, 207.9 (suburbs of Chicago). Numerous new towns and villages appeared around large cities, as demonstrated in the incorporation statistics for the decade. Of the thirty-eight new incorporations in Illinois, twenty-six were located within the metropolitan regions of Chicago or St. Louis; of the thirty-three in Michigan, twenty-two were suburbs of Detroit, and of Ohio's fifty-five incorporations, twenty-nine were near Cleveland. Cities in the 2,500–10,000 bracket showed a rapid growth rate for the period, chiefly because so many of them were located on the fringes of metropolitan areas.

In addition to all their other effects, the urban transportation devices of the twentieth century added new dimensions to one of the oldest economic activities associated with American urbanization—town promotion. No longer could promoters create great cities in the wilderness through the winning of railroads, but they could build highly profitable suburbs on car lines and highways. Early in the century, promotion was tied to the trolley and the inter-urban railroad, and as in past eras, the activity occurred in all sections of the country. Before the First World War, New Orleans interests, through the able use of trolley lines, built a number of profitable suburbs along the Mississippi River and on the north shore of Lake Pontchartrain. Similar communities sprang up around Shreveport when the Shreveport Railway Company and the Gladstone Realty Company joined their operations. Another Louisiana real estate firm, the Kent Company of Alexandria, gained control of the Alexandria Electric Railway Company and used the line to develop a suburban area. The company provided a typical inducement when it promised free street car rides for three years to anyone who bought a new lot in its subdivision.

In southern California, Henry E. Huntington through the use of these methods enlarged the family fortune and set off a land boom comparable to that of the 1880's. In 1901 he incorporated the Pacific Railway Company and began building a network of electri-fied inter-urban lines around Los Angeles that by 1913 had reached forty-two incorporated cities within a radius of thirty-five miles. In virtually all instances, Huntington's railroad building was tied to the promotion of suburbs. One of his more spectacular successes involved his development of Redondo Beach along Santa Monica Bay. Within a few weeks after the project got underway, he was able through the sale of lots to regain what he paid for the inter-urban line leading to the area and for the land picked as the site of the suburban community. By persuading the president of the Los Angeles Metropolitan Water District to join his enterprises, he was even able to set off a boom in the waterless San Fernando Valley. As a result of Huntington's promotions, some thirteen new cities were incorporated from 1910 to 1920, all except one of them located on his lines. The Huntington Land Company, which he had formed with a capital of $100,000 in 1902, had increased its value in the meantime to $10,000,000 in 1912 and to $15,000,000 in 1917. Huntington got out of inter-urban transportation in time to avoid the crash in the business caused by the introduction of the automobile. Even during their heyday, inter-urbans often did not make a profit in hauling passengers, but when tied to real estate ventures in suburban communities, as they generally were, they could be spectacularly successful.

One of the most famous examples of this kind of suburban development was Shaker Heights outside of Cleveland. Shaker Heights attracted attention by demonstrating how new planning conceptions could be applied to real estate development. The community served as a model for hundreds of less successful experiments in suburb building. Shaker Heights was the creation of two business-tycoon brothers, Oris P. and Mantis J. Van Sweringen who had started out as office clerks in Cleveland, had briefly owned a bicycle shop, and had become interested in real estate at the turn of the century. After success in buying a tract of land beyond the Cleveland street car line and then persuading the local company to extend its track to their property, the two promoters purchased 1,400 acres of country land, which had once been the site of a Shaker religious community. Their plan was to develop a rigorously controlled residential suburb containing separate sections of homes in various price categories so that cheaper houses would not depress the prices of the more expensive ones. The Van Sweringens employed many of the features of suburban residential development that were to become standard: abandonment of the traditional gridiron and the substitution of curving and semi-elliptical roads running from main automobile boulevards; the preservation of natural park areas throughout the development; and strict architectural and decorating requirements. With the opening of a rapid-transit system to the community in 1920, Shaker Heights began to boom. From 1919 to 1929, nearly 300 new houses were built each year; the community's population jumped from 1,700 to 15,550. The price of one-hundred-foot lots rose from $20 a foot to over $200 a foot in some sections of the community; by the end of the decade the valuation of the property had climbed to $80,000,000. The Van Sweringens used their profits from real estate to engage in some of the more grandiose railroad speculations of the 1920's, and until their pyramid of holding companies collapsed in the 1930's, they occupied a high rank among American corporate leaders.

The use of the automobile greatly enlarged opportunities in suburban promotion; the new era in town booming began in spectacular fashion with the Florida land boom of the 1920's. With the building of highways, tourists from the northeastern seaboard, by driving south for only a few days, could escape winter temporarily. During the early twenties, people flocked to Florida in ever increasing numbers. Hundreds of promoters and salesmen went to work selling lots—usually on option through a "binder"—and advertising new town sites. Much of the boom went on in Miami, which grew from 30,000 in 1920 to 75,000 by 1925. But, as on so many past urban frontiers opened by transportation, fabulous claims were advanced for fabulous new cities—Silver Heights, Coral Gables, Picture Bay, Montezuma Manors, Sea Cove Crest, and Biscayne Bay. The number of lots platted in Florida during the boom, according to some estimates, reached 20 million, which with a little overcrowding would have been sufficient to house the entire population of the United States. Large profits were sometimes realized in series of frenzied property transactions. Before the boom, a New Yorker bought a stretch of land in West Palm Beach at a low figure and sold it for $800,000 in 1923. The tract was then turned into city lots that sold for one and a half million dollars; by 1925 the tract was valued at four million dollars. One Carl Fisher bought a tract in Miami Beach for $8,000,000, paying $3,000,000 down. Two weeks later he had sold it for $11,000,000, collecting a down payment of $4,000,000. The boom continued through 1925; early in 1926 it began to fall off slightly as fewer people appeared in Florida for the winter. A severe hurricane which struck the state on September 18, 1926 turned many of the shoddily constructed developments to ruins, ended the boom, and wiped out virtually all the ambitious speculators. Although in the long run a good share of the land involved in the boom was utilized as urban property, as late as ten years afterwards the bulk of the lots were weed-grown or under water.

The Florida land boom is often considered as another bizarre episode of a decade of excess. Yet it was part of a pattern of over-development of land for urban purposes encouraged by the use of the automobile. Portions of Los Angeles County experienced sub-division development similar to Florida; 75 per cent of the total platted area of Burbank, California, for example, was vacant in the early 1930's. In 1929, 175,000 of Cleveland's 375,000 lots were empty; over sixty-five per cent of the lot area in Duluth, fifty per cent in Portland, Maine, thirty per cent in El Paso remained un-used a few years later. Similar premature subdivisions occurred in the metropolitan area of New York. The announcement of plans for the George Washington Bridge set off a boom in Bergen County, New Jersey, characterized by many of the same features as the Florida boom. A large section of farm land was platted and divided by paper streets; lots were sold at auction, through high pressure mail campaigns, and by newspapers as part of their sub-scription efforts. But little of the area was actually developed. Dur-ing the 1920's lots sufficient for all the inhabitants of the five boroughs of New York were platted on Long Island. By late in the decade, nearly half the lots had become county property owing to unpaid taxes. The chaotic development of subdivisions in the 1920's greatly complicated the problems of urban leaders in trying to provide municipal services over vast thinly settled areas and in attempting to impose some degree of social order on the rapidly burgeoning American metropolises.

In the twentieth century, expansion upward and outward modi-fied the morphology of American cities. In addition the character of urban population and its distribution throughout the areas of the city also changed. The decade of 1900–1910 was the last in which foreign migration contributed substantially to the growth of American cities. In 1907, the high year for the decade, 1,285,349 immigrants arrived in the United States. With the outbreak of war in Europe, the number fell to 326,700 in 1915 and reached a low point of 110,618 in 1919 with European immigration constituting less than 25,000 of this total. Immigration revived in the early 1920's reaching 805,228 in 1921, but the legislation establishing a quota system passed in that year and revised in 1924 reduced annual immigration to around 300,000 in the years from 1925 to

1929. During the depression of the 1930's it dropped even more drastically and not until 1946 did the annual figure again rise above 100,000.

With immigration from abroad sharply restricted, cities grew largely through internal migration down to the 1940's when the birth rate of urban dwellers began to rise substantially. One of the most significant aspects of this rural-urban migration was the movement of southern Negroes to the cities of the East and Mid-west and on a lesser magnitude to the cities of the South. From 1820 to 1910 the urbanization of the white population of the United States had always been at a more rapid rate than that of the Negro. But failures of the cotton crop in the south in 1915 and 1916 and the demand for industrial labor caused by the war reversed this pattern in the next decade, as the percentage of native white population classified as urban increased by six while that of Negroes increased by 6.7. The trend was intensified during the next decade, with the percentage of native white population classi-fied as urban increasing by 4.9 while that of Negroes increased by 9.7. In 1910, eighty-nine per cent of all Negroes lived south of the Mason-Dixon line; as a result of the migrations, by 1930 twenty per cent of the Negro population lived in the North East and Middle West with eighty-eight per cent of this group classified as urban. This was primarily a movement to the larger cities and it continued unabated during the years of depression. Between 1930 and 1940, for example, the Negro population of Chicago in-creased by more than 43,000, an increase of 18.7 per cent. During the whole period from 1900 to 1950 the percentage of Negroes outside the South increased from ten per cent to thirty-two per cent and the percentage within cities rose from seventeen to forty-eight per cent.

Urbanization of the Negro population modified the social pat-terns of larger cities. The older ethnic colonies had always con-tained a fair number of people not of the predominant group. In addition, these colonies had been relatively impermanent with one ethnic group succeeding another in a given area. The Negro colonies in northern cities were much more homogeneous, and, as time proved, much more permanent. Wards in New York and Chicago had percentages of Negro population that approached 95 by 1930. To a large extent cities within cities had been created. "Black Metropolis is the second largest Negro city in the world, only New York's Harlem exceeding it in size," wrote St. Clair Drake and Horace Cayton in their 1945 study of Negro life in Chicago. "It is a city within a city—a narrow tongue of land, seven miles in length and one and one-half miles in width where more than 300,000 Negroes are packed solidly. . . . Walk the streets of the Black Belt and you will find no difference in language to mark its people off from others in the city. Only the black and brown and olive and tan faces of Negro Americans seem to distinguish it from any other section of Midwest Metropolis. But beneath the surface are patterns of life and thought, attitudes and customs, which make Black Metropolis a unique and distinctive city within a city. Understand Chicago's Black Belt and you will understand the Black Belts of a dozen large American cities."

As Drake and Cayton's account so clearly indicated, the Negro ghetto intensified old urban problems. Racial segregation drastically limited the possibility of upward mobility by individual or group. The black metropolises of Chicago, New York, Cleveland, and Detroit were areas where few could benefit from the economic and cultural advantages of the city but where all the long-standing urban problems of crime, poverty, and disease existed in aggravated form.

The urban segregation of the Negro reflected a general tendency to increased economic and cultural segregation in the twentieth century metropolis. The wealthier and more powerful members of the community steadily moved to the outer zones of the city and to the new suburban areas. A study of over 2,000 substantial Detroit families in the early 1930's demonstrated a striking de-concentration of that city's elite. In 1910 nearly fifty-two per cent of this group still lived within a three-mile radius of the main business center of Detroit, and only 9.7 per cent outside the municipal boundaries. By 1930 these percentages were nearly reversed with only 7.5 per cent of the substantial families near the business district and fifty per cent in suburban areas. Numerous studies of economic zones within cities and of spatial zones away from the center made by the urban sociologists of the 1920's and 1930's demonstrated clearly the cultural advantages and the greater sta-

287

bility of the outer regions of metropolitan centers. Crime, the need for public welfare, and infant mortality decreased radically in the outer areas and usually in direct proportion to the distance of the area from the center of the city. In the past, many had resented the city because its extremes of wealth and poverty seemed a denial of American equalitarian beliefs. In the twentieth century metropolis these inequalities appeared more obvious, more rigidly confined, and more permanent.

The rise of the metropolis presented a whole new set of considerations to those concerned with ordering the urban environment. But despite the complexity of the twentieth-century supercity and its tremendous influence on society, much of the debate about the city in America was still conducted in terms of the old country-city polarity. The effort to restrict foreign immigration, the crusade for religious fundamentalism, the prohibition movement, and the election of 1928 were aspects of national history influenced by the traditional defense of the values of the country and the traditional attack on the values of the city. People could still accept at face value the famous photograph of President Calvin Coolidge seated on a hay wagon with rake in hand, his clothes spotless, while in the rear his assistants stand by an automobile waiting to whisk him back to the city. Writers of popular fiction in the twenties and thirties still employed the nineteenth-century imagery of the soulless city. To find "real values" one had to flee the city. "I have had to do many things, terrible things, things no decent man should have done," says a hero of a 1925 *Cosmopolitan* short story who finds peace in the wilderness. "Thank God that's all behind me now. Out here I can be a real person again." On a higher level, twelve southerners in their notable manifesto *I'll Take My Stand,* published in 1929, defended an idyllic rural life that probably never existed. "Back to the land," a position popularized by Ralph Borsodi who established a subsistence homestead outside New York City in 1920 and preached the virtues of the Thoreauvian way of life, became an organized movement that influenced federal policy during the depression of the thirties. Its disciples offered a classical Jeffersonian defense of the agrarian ideal. "The farms have always produced our great leaders in finance, industry and statesmanship," a witness testified before a House committee in the early 1930's. "The vast population must depart from the congested industrial centers and cities and once again become self-sustaining on our vast and fertile farms, pasture, and prairie lands. Herein lies the real hope for the bright destiny of America."

Despite the persistence of these old ideals, many thinkers and reformers abandoned the simple notion of country versus city and began to develop new conceptions of the social environment that emphasized the community, the neighborhood, the region. The old problems that had special urban dimensions—health, poverty, and the slum—had not disappeared, and housing the poor of the cities continued to be one of the principal concerns of urban reformers. But the complexity of the new metropolitan communities forced consideration of ways of reordering the whole urban environment. Proposals for new kinds of cities and for comprehensive plans that encompassed whole urban regions now became part of the discussion of the future of American cities. Writing in 1922, Lewis Mumford, who was to become one of the better known students of urban civilization, reflected the urgency of the new point of view: "Our metropolitan civilization is not a success. It is a different kind of wilderness . . . but the feral rather than the humane quality is dominant; it is still a wilderness. The cities of America must learn to remould our mechanical and financial regime; for if metropolitanism continues they are probably destined to fall by its weight."

As had so often been the case in the past the inspiration for new ways of dealing with urban problems came from Europe. Particularly influential was the Garden City idea of Ebenezer Howard, a London court reporter and reformer. Drawing on the nineteenth century British tradition of community planning, which had earlier influenced American experiments, Howard proposed a new kind of community that he hoped would combine the best features of town and country. The size of the Garden City would be limited to 30,000 people. A permanent greenbelt would surround it, and enough industry would be developed in carefully specified areas to ensure the community's self-sufficiency. The land on which the city was built would be owned by the community as a whole and administered by a public authority. All leases would contain specific and detailed building requirements and areas of greenery would be preserved throughout the city. The profits of growth would go to the community rather than to the speculator, since only limited dividends could be paid to the original investors in a Garden City project. This would also ensure that there would be no temptation to modify land use or increase the planned density of the city. Howard foresaw Garden Cities being founded throughout England, providing a way of checking the continued growth of the huge, congested industrial cities. The successful establishment of the first Garden City of Letchworth, England, begun in 1903, led to a world-wide Garden City movement; interest was reinforced by the start of a second community called Welwyn in 1919. Letchworth and Welwyn were the only two cities built in accord with Howard's overall plan, but his ideas influenced a number of American planners and architects. Although they seldom embodied the significant aspects of Howard's conceptions of a new kind of community, "garden villages," "garden suburbs," and "garden homes" became the fashion of the day after about 1910.

Forest Hills Gardens on Long Island, financed by the Russell Sage Foundation and designed by Frederick Law Olmsted, Jr., was completed in 1911, and the project, though it became simply a suburb for well-to-do commuters, demonstrated the possibilities in carefully planned housing developments. Many of the conceptions that were part of Garden City and other plans for new-style towns and cities were initially applied by businessmen who were not unduly concerned with creating a good community but who foresaw large real estate profits. The term "garden city" was often used to describe any planned new community that preserved a natural setting; the Van Sweringens in promoting Shaker Heights utilized the appeal of Howard's conception. Torrance, California—one of several of the small planned suburban industrial communities developed in the early years of the century—was labelled by its founder, the industrialist Jared Sidney Torrance, as the "greatest and best of the garden cities of the world." In 1914 the limited-dividend principle, which had been a fundamental part of Howard's plan, was employed in the development of a suburban area of Boston called the "garden suburb" of Billerica. Nowhere, however, was more than a portion of Howard's plan utilized during this first period of enthusiasm; often in the 1920's, "garden city" became a description of any suburban housing project.

Utopian city proposals that required a drastically new conception of the rights of landed property—as Howard's plan did—could not be expected to make much headway in a nation committed to traditions of individual enterprise. Yet the planning and zoning movement, which flourished between the First World War and the depression, reflected to a limited extent the same concern with the whole environment of metropolis that motivated Howard. In part, the vogue for planning had its origins in the City Beautiful movement, but it also drew support from the popularity of the Garden City idea. As a result of the interest in planning, the number of planning commissions and planning boards had grown from seventeen in 1914 to over 735 in 1930, and although they remained primarily advisory agencies, their powers tended to increase.

Closely related to the establishment of planning commissions was the passage of zoning regulations, for zoning was ordinarily a part of plans for city redevelopment and growth. The techniques of zoning had initially been applied in German cities beginning in 1900, but in the United States zoning was largely a development of the post-war period. Before 1916 only five American cities had zoning regulations, but New York's adoption in that year of a zoning law for the entire city popularized the approach. Between 1916 and 1920, twenty-five cities passed zoning laws, and by 1930 the number of zoned cities had risen to 981. After several years of litigation, the United States Supreme Court finally upheld this type of governmental regulation in 1926. The earliest zoning ordinances in the United States were designed mainly to keep residential areas free from business and industry and only regulated land use in various districts of the city. The laws passed after 1925 tended to be more comprehensive and regulated not only land use but the height and bulk of buildings as well. A study in 1929 indicated that of the 754 municipalities with zoning, 475 had comprehensive ordinances controlling the use, height, and area of buildings. Measures requiring set-backs on the upper portions of taller buildings contributed to the uniformity of the tower skyscrapers of the 1920's, and in general led to more consistent building styles in American cities.

Although zoning and planning was advocated by urban reformers who were genuinely concerned with trying to make cities better places in which to live, the movement to some extent merely intensified certain problems of the metropolis. Building requirements often contributed to the segregation of groups within the city on the basis of wealth. Many residential suburbs, for example, were kept as enclaves of wealth through rigorous zoning requirements. Until they encountered court difficulties, early zoning measures in southern cities were rather frankly aimed at maintaining the segregation of Negroes. It has been argued that zoning requirements represented an effort by older inhabitants of cities to maintain control of the downtowns they were abandoning. In this way, they protected their investments at the same time they kept newcomers to the city confined.

Business interests often supported planning and zoning, not out of an altruistic concern to improve the quality of urban life, but rather because they recognized that these programs would make cities economically more efficient and easier places in which to do business. Powerful support for the basic New York zoning law of 1916 came from Fifth Avenue merchants, who were distressed by the encroachment of garment industry plants into their shopping district. The reports that preceded the law appealed to this kind of sentiment. "The natural result of a poor utilization of its land areas by a city is high rents for occupiers and low profits for investors," stated the New York Committee on Building Heights in 1913. "It may seem paradoxical to hold that a policy of building restriction tends to a fuller utilization of land than a policy of no restriction; but such is undoubtedly the case. The reason lies in the greater safety and security to investment secured by definite restrictions."

The relationships between planning and zoning, new conceptions of community, and business profit are clearly illustrated in the career of Jesse C. Nichols, a leading spokesman of real estate men in the 1920's and 30's whose Country Club District of Kansas City, Missouri attracted international attention. In his real estate operations, he was concerned with making a profit but he was also genuinely concerned with establishing new patterns of business and residential location that would alleviate some of the problems of the sprawling metropolis. Nichols grew up on a farm near Olathe, Kansas, graduated from the University of Kansas, and studied economics at Harvard University, where he wrote a thesis on land development. On a visit to England during his student days, he was impressed by the parks, lawns, and gardens of the smaller English cities and later maintained that the notion for the Country Club District was conceived at that time. After leaving Harvard, he got his start in business building houses for workers in Kansas City, Kansas. With capital accumulated from this venture, in 1905 he began buying property south of Kansas City, Missouri. The residential district he established was a success from the beginning. It was eventually to cover 6,000 acres, one-tenth of the area of the city.

In the 1920's Nichols' Country Club District became one of the most extensive restricted residential developments in the country, and the techniques he employed were widely copied by real estate men elsewhere. On all property sold by the Nichols company, comprehensive deed restrictions controlled land use, minimum cost of buildings, open space, set-back lines, and sales to Negroes. The Nichols company was probably the first to employ the device of self-perpetuating deed restrictions. These were automatically continued unless a majority of the owners in an individual subdivision moved to change them at least five years before the expiration of the usual twenty-five-year term of initial subdivision deeds. Nichols also sponsored the formation of self-governing Homes Associations, which received charters from the state. These Associations, which had grown to twelve in number by 1926, levied assessments on residents and provided a variety of governmental, cultural, and recreational services such as garbage and snow removal, lawn contests and flower shows, and maintenance of parks and playgrounds initially provided by the Nichols company. Students of the city, including a number of English visitors who made comparisons with the Garden City, pointed to the Homes Associations as a desirable system to promote the spirit of neighborhood in the impersonal metropolis. City planners from as far away as South America and Australia visited the Country Club District. The British planner Charles Read echoed their reactions when he commented that no man in the world had done as much as Nichols "to carry beauty and comfort into everyday life."

Nichols also won attention for his development of the first large decentralized shopping center in the United States, the Country

Club Plaza Shopping Center, begun in 1922. In the early 1920's, he visited the garden cities of Welwyn and Letchworth and also toured Spain to get ideas for the project. His carefully planned and controlled shopping center successfully harmonized Spanish-style architecture with the natural setting of the district. The design for the center was widely copied by suburban developers, but few other planners were able to preserve the harmony and architectural integrity that Nichols insisted upon.

Owing primarily to the attention his Country Club District received, Nichols became a national leader in the real estate industry. In his speeches he consistently defended zoning and planning. Zoning, he suggested, could provide a means of ensuring "air, light, sunshine, and decent surroundings" for the laboring man as well as for the owner of the large estate; it would bring "order instead of chaos into American building." Lack of planning intensified the problem of the automobile; traffic congestion was largely the result of "stupid application of the conventional checkerboard scheme without regard to grades or traffic needs." In addition to pointing out that planning could make cities more livable, Nichols always emphasized to business audiences that planning could also be profitable. "City planning," he told the Kansas City Chamber of Commerce in 1921, "is based on love, ambition, and profit. . . . If you are ambitious for the growth of your business, your institution or your city, if you believe in its future growth, you plan for healthy expansion."

Nichols, like many less practical theorists of the city, was acutely sensitive to the ugliness of the new metropolitan environment that was rapidly being created in the 1920's. In a 1926 essay on shopping centers, he developed this theme:

> In American cities of any considerable size our new outlying business centers frequently are becoming the ugliest, most unsightly and disorderly parts of the entire city. New traffic throats of congestion are being created that will sooner or later call for the expenditure of gigantic sums of public funds to relieve. Buildings of every color, size, shape, and design are being huddled and mixed together in a most unpresentable manner. A mixture of glowing billboards, unsightly rub-

294

bish dumps, hideous rears, unkempt alleys, dirty loading docks, unrelated, uncongenial mixtures of shops of every type and use, with no relation to one another; shacks and shanties mixed up with good buildings; perfectly square, unadorned buildings of poor design, are bringing about disorder, unsightliness, and unattractiveness that threaten to mar the beauty and good appearance of the residential regions of American cities. . . . The abandonment of formerly beautiful residential areas, neglected and blighted former business sections, should arouse in everyone a determination to protect the appearance of his city as well as the property values themselves.

Nichols was aware of the problems of metropolis and attempted to do something about them. His innovations helped to provide a better way of life for many city-dwellers. But not everyone could benefit from the amenities of Nichols' Country Club District. Deed restrictions kept out Negroes, a practice not invalidated by the Supreme Court until 1948. Construction requirements assured that lower income groups would not live there. By the 1930's, the area contained a homogeneous population of upper-white-collar and professional families. The Country Club District reflected the difficulties in private efforts to develop new living patterns in cities. Well-planned industrial villages and luxurious residential suburbs did virtually nothing to provide housing for the poor. And this was one of the most significant problems of the metropolis. Real estate men like Nichols frequently accepted the need for government regulation of urban expansion through city plans and zoning laws. But they did not, of course, advocate any significant departure from the established practices of private ownership and private development of land in cities. It remained for reformers outside the real estate business to argue the necessity for more drastic approaches to the problems of the metropolis.

Much of the agitation for new policies toward cities stemmed from a very old urban problem—inadequate housing. The new restrictive codes popularized by Veiller improved the quality of housing but did nothing to provide homes for the poor. The shortage of housing for low income groups became so serious during the First World War that it interfered with production, and as an emergency measure the federal government instituted a program of public housing. Through two agencies, the United States Shipping Board's Emergency Fleet Corporation and the Department of Labor's United States Housing Corporation, the government built, sponsored, or controlled a number of housing projects for war workers. Developments like Yorkship Village (later the Fairview Section of Camden, New Jersey) and Union Park Gardens near Wilmington, Delaware provided reasonable, attractive, and well-designed housing. The projects also permitted American architects and planners—many of them imbued with Garden City concepts—to experiment with urban design, including curvilinear street systems, the row house, and balanced residential neighborhoods. Despite protest, as soon as the war ended Congress liquidated the program as quickly as possible. But the experiment could be pointed to as a precedent for government action in housing.

The acute housing shortage that followed the armistice indicated the need for new policies. Shortages of capital and inflated construction costs checked the anticipated resumption of normal building, which had helped to justify quick termination of the government programs. Building increased after 1921 and was one of the factors sustaining the mixed prosperity of the 1920's, but expansion was accompanied by a highly disproportionate rise in building costs. Rents also rose much faster than wages. Moreover, there was considerable deterioration in the older tenement districts. Well before Franklin D. Roosevelt's second inaugural address, there was recognition that one-third of the nation was ill housed. The 1930 census indicated that more than 6,000,000 homes in cities, over twenty-five per cent of the total, did not meet minimum standards. Because of the seriousness of the problem, much of the early twentieth century discussion of the future of cities had housing as its central emphasis. City planners and housing reformers generally agreed that private builders operating within a free market were simply not able to provide satisfactory low-cost housing. As a result of their agitation, there were efforts after the First World War to encourage the establishment of limited-dividend and cooperative housing projects. A precedent-breaking Wisconsin law of 1919 permitted counties and cities to purchase stock in cooperative housing companies; a Milwaukee cooperative company with support from the city, erected 105 houses, at alleged savings of $1,500 a house. Other private housing cooperatives, totalling forty in number in 1925, were organized, virtually all of them in New York City. The New York State Housing Law of 1926 provided tax exemptions to limited-dividend housing projects, permitted municipalities to exempt the projects from local taxes, and set maximum rents for authorized projects. Two cooperatives and one limited-dividend company built a total of six projects in New York City under the law. But these private and public efforts to supply low-cost housing before the New Deal period were so restricted that they had no effect, virtually, on the general problem. Nevertheless, there was increasing recognition of the fact that some type of government intervention in housing had become a necessity.

A group particularly influential in establishing this point during the 1920's was the Regional Planning Association of America, an informal association of planners, architects, social theorists, and housing experts who began meeting in 1923. The organization included many of the leading students of city problems. The RPAA evolved from other groups concerned with the postwar housing crisis, and good housing for the poor remained a dominant concern of the organization until it broke up around 1933. But the group went much further and attempted to formulate ways to plan whole metropolitan regions. Their program emphasized the development of a new kind of regional city, which would preserve small towns and villages and renew metropolitan centers through a comprehensive, flexible ordering of the relationships between population, resources, and institutions.

As part of their effort to develop more reasonable and more livable urban communities, the RPAA turned to Howard's Garden City as a beginning. In 1923, Clarence Stein, an architect who had been most responsible for the formation of the group, convinced Alexander M. Bing, a New York real estate man, to support RPAA plans for building residential communities along Garden City lines. Bing sponsored the formation of a limited-dividend housing company, the City Housing Corporation; between 1924 and 1928 the corporation built the first of its two garden-city-style communities, Sunnyside, New York. Sunnyside was located on a seventy-acre tract in the borough of Queens on land purchased from the Pennsylvania Railroad. Unable to obtain modification in the existing gridiron plat for the area, Stein and Henry Wright, an expert on housing costs and site planning, nevertheless laid out an attractive development of row houses and apartments enclosing large central gardens. Contrary to the hopes of its founders, the project did not supply housing that accommodated low income groups. Even though the dividends of the City Housing Corporation were limited to six per cent and certain economies in efficient site planning were realized, Sunnyside did not provide housing that was competitive with that built by large-scale, private speculative builders.

The RPAA's most significant effort—and one of the most significant housing efforts of the early twentieth century—was carried out in New Jersey on a 1,258 acre site some seventeen miles from New York. Sunnyside had been a kind of trial run; Radburn, New Jersey was to be a real Garden City of 25,000 people. Before the project could be completed, the depression hit; Bing's corporation was thrown into receivership; and Radburn remained a town of about 1,500. But in the period between 1928 and 1931, Radburn was considered the closest approximation to a Garden City in America, and was internationally hailed as a "town for the motor age." Radburn had no unique features of building or design, but it artfully synthesized most of the proposals for planned communities in the 1920's—the 40-acre superblock, interior parks, curvilinear streets, and, perhaps most significantly, a system of roads that separated the automobile from the pedestrian. Benton MacKaye's 1930 plan for the "townless highway," which anticipated most of the features of the modern turnpike, was suggested by the Radburn experiment. But Radburn was at most only a limited success. Because of high land costs, no greenbelt was provided, and the founders were never able to attract industry as they had hoped. Rather ironically, in the 1930's Radburn became a suburb of white-collar commuters instead of the self-sufficient, neighborly community that the RPAA leaders had hoped to establish within the modern regional metropolis.

The coming of the Great Depression ended the expectation that private experiments could substantially modify the character of the urban environment. The Depression Era marked a new stage in

American urban history, as the national government became a significant force in shaping the quality of life in cities. Until this time federal policy had only occasionally and only incidentally influenced the course of city growth; urbanization had been a dimension of the national experience independent of events and decisions in Washington. The planning and building of the national capital, the information gathering of the census, and the First World War housing experiments nearly exhaust the examples of federal involvement in urban life before the 1930's. The National Resources Committee, a New Deal agency, argued in its 1937 report on "Our Cities" that "widespread neglect of the cities as a major segment of national existence" had been one of the major sources of urban problems. "Indicative of this neglect," the Committee declared, "is the fact, although the United States has been a predominately urban nation for more than two decades, this report . . . is the first inquiry of national, official, and comprehensive scale into the problems of the American urban community." But under the impact of Depression and New Deal, this all changed; henceforth concern with the city and attempts to order the urban environment would be a persistent feature of American national policy.

The general impact of the Depression on the great cities—mass unemployment; malnutrition, disease, and even starvation; the exhaustion of relief funds—is a well-chronicled subject in American history. But the Depression did have special urban aspects. Housing in cities had always been inadequate, and for a century housing reformers had been demanding changes. Now conditions suddenly worsened. Building nearly came to a halt. Repairs were not made. Slums expanded. Between 1928 and 1933 construction of residential property fell ninety-five per cent; the amount spent annually on housing repairs dropped from fifty million to half a million dollars. In 1932 273,000 people lost their homes, and during the next year a thousand homes a day were being foreclosed. "The literally thousands of heart-breaking instances of inability of working people to attain renewal of expiring mortgages on favorable terms, and the consequent loss of their homes, have been one of the tragedies of this depression," wrote Herbert Hoover.

Much of the early legislation designed to cope with the problem of depression in the cities was of an emergency nature: raise relief funds, provide employment, check foreclosures. In July 1932, at the urging of President Hoover, Congress had established twelve Federal Home Loan Banks to lend funds to building and loan associations, banks, and other mortgage agencies whose credit had been nearly exhausted. But the program, which was tied fundamentally to the operation of the inadequate private housing market, had only limited success. The Roosevelt administration continued this policy and supplemented it with the Home Owners Loan Corporation in June 1933 which refinanced individual mortgages of homeowners at long terms and low interest and permitted needed repair costs to be added to the loans. During its period of operation ending in June 1936, the HOLC extended over a million loans and assumed about one-sixth of all home-mortgage indebtedness in cities. Largely as a result of this policy, foreclosures by 1937 had fallen to half of what they had been in 1933.

This program assisted the relatively well-to-do middle classes— those who could afford to buy houses in the first place. The same point could be made about a more permanent New Deal program enacted in June 1934 that created the Federal Housing Authority. This agency was authorized to insure loans made by private agencies for the construction, repair, and improvement of houses. In the long run, its activities, in addition to raising standards of construction, brought about significant changes in the system of financing American residential building: the length of mortgage loans was greatly extended, down payments were drastically reduced, the second mortgage was generally eliminated, and the single monthly payment on a mortgage covering amortization of the loan, taxes, and insurance became common. These new procedures—particularly during the boom in housing after the Second World War— extended the possibilities of home ownership to a wider group in society and added impetus to suburban growth.

Concern with the cities was also reflected in the early stages of the recovery program. The Reconstruction Finance Corporation established during the Hoover Administration had power within its broad lending authority to make loans to private limited-dividend housing corporations. Although this program had little effect, its approach was continued during the Roosevelt administration by the Housing Division established in the Public Works Administration—a basic recovery agency of the early New Deal. The National Industrial Recovery Act of June 1933 establishing the PWA authorized the agency to provide for "low rent housing and slum clearance projects." Initially, the Housing Division, reflecting the conservative cast of many New Deal efforts, attempted to carry out these programs through private enterprise. But owing in large part to the efforts of real estate interests to unload undesirable property in cities at high prices, only seven of the five hundred applications from limited-dividend corporations were approved by the government. Forced to abandon this method, in February 1934, the Housing Division moved directly into the management of slum clearance and low-cost housing projects. This effort encountered bitter resistance from private real estate interests. A federal circuit court decision in Kentucky in 1935 found the direct condemnation of property by the federal government an unconstitutional extension of the right of eminent domain. The decision forced the Housing Division thereafter to manage its projects through state or municipal authority, foreshadowing the character of the eventual permanent federal housing policy.

The Housing Division during its four and a half years of operation did engage in a number of significant individual projects. Eleven slum blocks in Atlanta were cleared and became the site of Techwood Homes. Lakeview Terrace succeeded Cleveland's Whiskey Island tenement house area. Brooklyn's Williamsburg Houses replaced twelve slum blocks with modern apartments for 6,000 people. But on the whole this program represented a minimum effort. The PWA built or started forty-nine projects with less than 25,000 units. Overall, this did relatively little to alleviate the problem of housing for the poor; administration leaders did not consider the program a success. "From what I saw and heard," Harold Ickes, head of the PWA, confessed in his diary after a tour of Chicago projects, "I was very much disappointed with the progress that has been made. There isn't any doubt that something is wrong in the Housing Division, in fact, has been wrong for a long time. We are not getting results."

During the course of the New Deal, federal policy embodied, on a limited scale for the most part, virtually all the approaches to housing that had been suggested by urban planners and reformers during the preceding twenty years: the conservative policies of mortgage insurance and loans to limited-dividend housing companies, as well as relatively more radical approaches of slum clearance and garden cities. Roosevelt himself, although quite willing to cultivate an urban constituency, had little interest in the programs of housing reformers concerned with the slum and improving cities, and showed more sympathy to the decentralization schemes of those who wanted people to get back to the land. In 1913 he had suggested that farms in the suburbs ought to be provided for city dwellers so that city life could be improved and cities made places "where people will be pretty proud to hail from." It is doubtful that he ever substantially modified this outlook, which after all was compatible with one important urban reform tradition represented by Brace, Olmsted, and many of the intellectuals in the Regional Planning Association of America. Rexford G. Tugwell, a Roosevelt "brain truster" who headed the Resettlement Administration, recalled in the fifties that Roosevelt "always did, and always would think people better off in the country and would regard the cities as rather hopeless."

Accordingly, although Roosevelt eventually came to its support, the major piece of New Deal housing legislation, the National Housing Act of September 1937 (the Wagner-Steagall Act), was not really an administration measure; it was supported by reformers in Congress concerned with housing, notably Senator Robert F. Wagner of New York. The United States Housing Authority created by the act took over the PWA projects and was authorized to make sixty-year loans at low interest to local public agencies for slum clearance and housing projects. Through this measure, the slums of Chicago, San Antonio, Memphis, New Orleans, and a number of other places, came under attack. Of all the New Deal measures, this one may have been of most benefit to the urban Negro. Gunnar Myrdal declared, in his monumental study of Negro life, *An American Dilemma,* that the USHA gave Negroes "a better deal than has any other major federal public welfare agency." By 1941 the agency had made contracts for 511 low-rent public housing projects providing a total of 161,162 units. Although the administrator of the USHA optimistically proclaimed in 1939 that "for the first time in a hundred years, the slums of America ceased growing and began to shrink," it is doubtful that New Deal public housing did more than ameliorate somewhat the problem of the slum. As with many of the earlier private efforts to provide better living conditions for the urban poor, many of the New Deal projects themselves rather quickly deteriorated into slums. But the act had established the precedent for action, and a permanent policy for urban renewal along these lines was provided in the Housing Act of 1949.

The counterpart of slum removal was planned suburban development. Tugwell indicated the relationship when he wrote early in 1935: "My idea is to go just outside centers of population, pick up cheap land, build a whole community and entice people into it. Then go back into the cities and tear down whole slums and make parks of them." The presence of this viewpoint among government planners led to the most significant of the New Deal experiments involving urban life—the greenbelt towns. "In world-wide influence," writes Paul K. Conkin, "they rank high among New Deal accomplishments; in the field of public works they are hardly excelled, even by the Tennessee Valley Authority, in imagination, in breaking with precedents, and in broad social objectives. They represented, and still do represent, the most daring, original, and ambitious experiments in public housing in the history of the United States." The greenbelt towns were an attempt to create the Howard-type garden city in America. But as it developed, the greenbelt program drew on the whole nineteenth century American tradition of suburb and park planning plus, in Tugwell's view, the demographic evidence of suburban growth. The greenbelt towns were to be decentralized communities of varying size and function, located outside of metropolitan centers, designed in accord with the best theories of professional planners, sustained by preservation of a natural setting, built by the government, but leased to local cooperatives made up of residents. Supporters of the greenbelt towns argued that they would not only help solve the housing problem of the city but would also help provide an answer to the problem of the urban slum. Tugwell optimistically hoped that 3,000 of the communities could be built in America. After initial study by the Resettlement Administration, which had been established in June 1935, twenty-five cities were selected for location of the towns. Roosevelt approved eight projects, but congressional cuts in appropriations reduced the number to five. A St. Louis greenbelt town was eliminated because of opposition from a local housing commission. A New Jersey project called Greenbrook, designed by Henry Wright of Radburn as a self-sufficient industrial community and closest of all the towns to the Howard ideal, was stopped by injunction proceedings in the courts. In the end, three greenbelt towns were built: Greenbelt at Berwyn, Maryland seven miles from Washington; Greenhills near Cincinnati; and Greendale outside Milwaukee. Limited funds hampered the establishment of the communities; none of them was as large as planned. They were continually fought by real estate interests, and after the decision involving Greenbrook, such a threat hung over them that it was clear that no more projects could be initiated. They were denounced as "communist towns" and were perhaps one of the most bitterly hated New Deal experiments. They proved expensive, noncompetitive with private housing, and after the Second World War were sold at a great loss by the government. Yet, during the late New Deal period, for those concerned with the quality of urban life they provided a vision of a better future that might lie ahead if only systematic planning could be applied to the town, the city, and the region. They were visited by 1,200,000 people during the first year of operation, and European planners consistently praised them. A government housing expert, Tracy B. Augur, conveyed the enthusiasm of those associated with the project when he remarked that the greenbelt towns signalled "the birth of an urban nation."

But providing an attractive environment for only 2,267 families can hardly be considered that significant, and perhaps the greenbelt towns only suggested what might have been. The American tradition of private property, so fundamental in shaping the history of American cities, had once again defeated attempts to provide a better kind of community. The same point might be extended to the whole of the New Deal program in so far as it dealt with cities, for its accomplishments in improving urban life were singularly limited. In the end, perhaps what was most important during this era was the recognition in federal policy that the city was here to stay and that it could be a positive force in American culture. "Surely in the long run," asserted the National Resources Committee, "the Nation's destiny will be profoundly affected by the cities which have two-thirds of its population and its wealth. There is liberty of development in isolation and wide spaces, but there is also freedom in the many-sided life of the city where each may find his own kind. There is democracy in the scattered few, but there is also democracy in the thick crowd with its vital impulse and its insistent demand for a just participation in the gains of our civilization."

Much of the New Deal's planning in regard to cities was based on the view that urban population in the future would be stable or would even decline. Scholars who influenced national policy argued that the falling birth rate of the 1930's combined with the increasing proportion of people in cities meant that city growth could no longer be sustained by migration from the farm. But the prediction, although it was based on a mass of statistical evidence, proved dead wrong. With the end of the Second World War and the continuance of a long era of general prosperity, American cities once again began another great period of growth. Contemporaries found the effects of urbanization so dramatic in this period that they began to speak of urban explosions and suburban revolutions. A whole new vocabulary—"megalopolis," "polynucleated urbs," "cities as long as highways," "the symbiosis of urban and rural"—was coined to try to describe the character of the larger urban agglomerations of the 1950's; continuous urban settlements—first noticed by airline pilots—seemed to be developing from Boston to Washington, from Cleveland to Milwaukee, from San Francisco to San Diego. But how revolutionary this was could still be debated. It was not clear whether "Megalopolis" represented a new form of urban organization or simply an overlapping of extended metropolises that had been shaped much earlier. In any event, the trend toward the super-city had long been present in American life.

Two-hundred and fifty years of American urban history suggested that a number of viewpoints about the city and contemporary urban life might easily be questioned. Expanding cities were portrayed in vivid metaphors of voraciousness—destroying, swallowing, devouring the countryside. Yet cities at mid-century

305

still represented a spatially concentrated form of human settlement; "urbanized areas" of the United States, which included cities of 50,000 or above and their seemingly vast environs, still occupied less than one per cent of the land in the continental United States. Theorists argued confusingly that the values of the suburb now threatened the values of the city, yet from the beginning the suburb had been an enduring feature of American urban life—a constant in the process of urbanization. As Olmsted and Cleveland had so clearly indicated, the values of the city could not be pitted against the values of the suburb; they were inseparable in American culture. Reformers portrayed the "Negro cores" of great cities as a new dilemma of American society. Yet, for over a hundred years, urban critics, Tuckerman, Riis, and Hunter among them, had portrayed the slums of great cities in precisely the same light; the slum lord was a favorite target of Muhlenberg. Aside from the social tensions engendered by race (and how these might differ from the ethnic tensions of another day was still problematic), it is doubtful that Negro cores represented anything new in urban sordidness and misery. The urban juvenile delinquent became a stock figure of the new era, but a host of nineteenth century reformers such as Muhlenberg and Brace had been exercised by exactly the same problem. Intellectuals harangued Americans to abandon the myth of the evil city, but if belief in the evil city had ever been important in American life it had always been balanced by belief in the good city as Scott and Gilpin had so clearly demonstrated. And such ambivalences are not the stuff of social myth. Planners denounced the automobile and the expressway as the source of urban problems and insisted upon the return to older systems of transportation. Yet traffic congestion had been a feature of urban life for a hundred years, and the critique of planners missed the point that changes in transportation were not the result of caprice but of response to the almost deterministic necessities of the city. Observing the destruction of old buildings and often whole neighborhoods which lay in the path of urban redevelopment, traditionalists and others with a strong attachment to the past sought to preserve structures which had been historically significant. Yet the thrust of American urbanization has always destroyed the old to make way for the new; urban development has always involved "urban redevelopment." Urban politicians demanded renewal of American cities, yet few of them seemed willing to confront the question of private use of urban land, which had been so fundamental in shaping the whole nature of what they putatively attacked. Change and continuity are both exhibited in the course of American urban history, but too much of the contemporary analysis, through lack of historical understanding, emphasized only the change. In 1940, Louis Wirth, one of the Chicago sociologists who had done so much to promote systematic study of the city, commented vividly on the contemporary meaning of urban society. "What we call civilization," he wrote, "as distinguished from culture has been cradled in the city; the city is the center from which the influences of modern civilized life radiate to the ends of the earth and the point from which they are controlled; the persistent problems of contemporary society take their most acute form in the city. The problems of modern civilization are typically urban problems." This was true in 1940, at the start of a great era of urban growth. In many senses, it had always been true, and would be true in the future. From the beginning the tensions and impulses of America's cities had given direction to the growth of the nation.

Suggestions for
Further Reading

This list of references is intended to be useful to the student who wishes to extend his knowledge of American urban history; it is also designed to suggest important secondary works upon which we have relied heavily in the preparation of the book. But the list is not intended to be comprehensive. We have, for example, included only a few of the vast number of scholarly articles relating to urban history—those in the main that we have quoted, or from which we have drawn extensive material.

BIBLIOGRAPHY: Blake McKelvey, "American Urban History Today," *American Historical Review* LVII (July, 1952), pp. 919–929; and Charles N. Glaab, "The Historian and the American City: a Bibliographic Survey," in Philip M. Hauser

309

and Leo F. Schnore (eds.), *The Study of Urbanization* (N.Y.: Wiley, 1965), are convenient and thorough guides.

DOCUMENTS: Primary sources are not included here. Many of our important sources—travelers' accounts, novels, census materials and other government documents, and contemporary writings on urban problems are suggested in the text. The following are useful documentary collections: Charles N. Glaab, *The American City: a Documentary History* (Homewood, Ill.: Dorsey, 1963); Wilson Smith, *Cities of Our Past and Present* (N.Y.: Wiley, 1964); David Weimer, *City and Country in America* (N.Y.: Appleton-Century-Crofts, 1962); Bessie L. Pierce, *As Others See Chicago* (Chicago: U. of Chicago, 1933); and Bayrd Still, *Mirror for Gotham* (N.Y.: N.Y.U., 1956).

THEORY: Contrasting theoretical approaches to urban history are offered in Arthur M. Schlesinger, "The City in American History," *Mississippi Valley Historical Review* XXVII (June, 1940), pp. 43–66, which appears also in Schlesinger's book, *Paths to the Present* (N.Y.: Macmillan, 1949); William Diamond, "On the Dangers of an Urban Interpretation of History," in Eric F. Goldman (ed.), *Historiography and Urbanization: Essays in American History in Honor of W. Stull Holt* (Baltimore: Johns Hopkins U., 1941); W. Stull Holt, "Some Consequences of the Urban Movement in American History," *Pacific Historical Review* XXII (November, 1953), pp. 337–351; R. Richard Wohl, "Urbanism, Urbanity, and the Historian," *University of Kansas City Review* XXII (Autumn, 1955), pp. 53–61; Eric E. Lampard, "American Historians and the Study of Urbanization," *American Historical Review* LXVII (October, 1961), pp. 49–61; Charles N. Glaab, "The Historian and the American Urban Tradition," *Wisconsin Magazine of History* XLVII (Autumn, 1963), pp. 12–25, reprinted in Abraham S. Eisenstadt (ed.), *The Craft of American History* (Harper Torchbook, N.Y.: Harper and Row, 1966); and Oscar Handlin and John

Burchard (eds.), *The Historian and the City* (Cambridge: M.I.T. and Harvard U., 1963).

STANDARD WORKS IN UNITED STATES HISTORY: Some of the series in American history contain useful material on urban development; see John B. McMaster, *A History of the People of the United States from the Revolution to the Civil War* (8 vols., N.Y.: Appleton, 1883–1913); Arthur M. Schlesinger and Dixon Ryan Fox (eds.), *The History of American Life* (13 vols., N.Y.: Macmillan, 1927–1948), fundamental for the subject, especially James T. Adams, *Provincial Society,* (1927), John Allen Krout and Dixon Ryan Fox, *The Completion of Independence* (1944), Arthur M. Cole, *The Irrepressible Conflict* (1934), Allan Nevins, *The Emergence of Modern America* (1927), Arthur M. Schlesinger, *The Rise of the City* (1933), and Dixon Wecter, *The Age of the Great Depression* (1948); Henry S. Commager and Richard B. Morris (eds.), *The New American Nation Series* (in progress, N.Y.: Harper and Row), especially Russel B. Nye, *The Cultural Life of the New Nation* (1960), Clement Eaton, *The Growth of Southern Civilization* (1961), Harold U. Faulkner, *Politics, Reform and Expansion* (1959), George R. Mowry, *The Era of Theodore Roosevelt* (1958), and John D. Hicks, *Republican Ascendancy: 1921–1933* (1960); Henry David *et al.,* (eds.), *The Economic History of the United States* (10 vols., in progress, N.Y.: Holt, Rinehart and Winston), especially George R. Taylor, *The Transportation Revolution* (1951), Harold U. Faulkner, *The Decline of Laissez Faire* (1951), and Edward C. Kirkland, *Industry Comes of Age* (1961).

SURVEYS: Constance McL. Green, *American Cities in the Growth of the Nation* (N.Y.: John DeGraff, 1957) contains valuable sketches of several cities' histories; her brief *The Rise of Urban America* (N.Y.: Harper and Row, 1965) is less successful. Adna Ferrin Weber, *The Growth of Cities in the Nineteenth Century* (Ithaca: Cornell, 1963, originally

311

published in 1899) is a pioneering statistical study that has never been superseded.

URBAN BIOGRAPHIES: The preparation of comprehensive histories of individual cities has been the most commonly pursued line of inquiry in American urban history. Urban biographies have been of obvious importance in this study but only a few of the more important and representative titles can be mentioned. Thomas J. Wertenbaker, *Norfolk: Historic Southern Port* (revised edition by Marvin W. Schlegel, Durham: Duke U., 1962): Constance McL. Green, *Washington: Village and Capital,* and *Washington: Capital City* (Princeton, N.J.: Princeton U., 1962 and 1963); Blake McKelvey, *Rochester* (3 vols., Cambridge: Harvard U., 1945–1956; 1 vol., Rochester: Christopher, 1961); Bessie L. Pierce, *A History of Chicago* (3 vols., N.Y.: Knopf, 1937–1957); Bayrd Still, *Milwaukee: the History of a City* (Madison: State Historical Society of Wisc., 1948, revised edition, 1965): Constance McL. Green, *Holyoke, Massachusetts* (New Haven: Yale U., 1939); Vera Shlakman, *Economic History of a Factory Town: A study of Chicopee, Massachusetts* (Northampton, Mass.: Smith College, 1954–55); Gerald M. Capers, *The Biography of a River Town: Memphis, Its Heroic Age* (Chapel Hill: U. of North Carolina, 1939); A. Theodore Brown, *Frontier Community: a History of Kansas City to 1870* (Columbia, Mo.: U. of Missouri, 1964); Powell A. Moore, *The Calumet Region, Indiana's Last Frontier* (Indianapolis: Indiana Historical Bureau, 1959). A sharply etched "urban vignette" is Bernard Mayo's essay on Lexington, "Frontier Metropolis," in Goldman (ed.), *Historiography and Urbanization,* cited above.

PERIOD STUDIES: Carl Bridenbaugh, *Cities in the Wilderness* (N.Y.: Ronald, 1938), and *Cities in Revolt* (N.Y.: Knopf, 1959), both major pieces of scholarship in American urban history; Carl and Jessica Bridenbaugh, *Rebels and Gentlemen: Philadelphia in the Age of Franklin* (N.Y.: Reynal and Hitchcock, 1942); Thomas J. Wertenbaker, *Father Knicker-*

bocker Rebels: New York During the Revolution (N.Y.: Scribners, 1948), and *The Golden Age of Colonial Culture* (Ithaca: Cornell U., 1942); Ralph Weld, *Brooklyn Village* (N.Y.: Columbia U., 1938); Sidney I. Pomerantz, *New York: an American City, 1783–1803* (N.Y.: Ira J. Friedman, 1965); Richard C. Wade, *The Urban Frontier 1790–1830* (Cambridge: Harvard U., 1959), a landmark, and *Slavery in the Cities: the South, 1820–1860* (N.Y.: Oxford, 1964); Robert G. Albion, *The Rise of New York Port,* (N.Y.: Scribners, 1939); Blake McKelvey, *The Urbanization of America, 1860–1915* (New Brunswick, N.J.: Rutgers U., 1963), contains a monumental bibliography; Ray Ginger, *Altgeld's America* (N.Y.: Funk and Wagnalls, 1958), a sensitive portrait of Chicago around the turn of the century.

URBAN RIVALRY AND PROMOTION: These themes from the nineteenth century have produced a considerable body of writing. The following are representative: James W. Livingood, *The Philadelphia-Baltimore Trade Rivalry* (Harrisburg: Pennsylvania Historical and Museum Commission, 1947); Wyatt W. Belcher, *The Economic Rivalry Between St. Louis and Chicago, 1850–1880* (N.Y.: Columbia U., 1947); Charles N. Glaab, *Kansas City and the Railroads* (Madison: State Historical Society of Wisc., 1962); Julius Rubin, *Canal or Railroad: Imitation and Innovation in Response to the Erie Canal in Philadelphia, Baltimore, and Boston* (Philadelphia: American Philosophical Society, 1961), important also for theoretical considerations; Glen Chesney Quiett, *They Built the West: an Epic of Rails and Cities* (N.Y.: Appleton-Century, 1934); Richard C. Overton, *Burlington West: a Colonization History of the Burlington Railroad* (Cambridge: Harvard U., 1941) and Paul W. Gates, *The Illinois Central Railroad and its Colonization Work* (Cambridge: Harvard U., 1934) are important for town promotion by railroads; Earl Pomeroy, *The Pacific Slope* (N.Y.: Knopf, 1965) and C. Vann Woodward, *The Origins of the New South* (New Orleans: La. State U., 1951), contain sections on urban development in the West and South respectively.

INTELLECTUAL HISTORY: Morton and Lucia White, *The Intellectual Versus the City* (Cambridge: Harvard U. and M.I.T., 1962), although we have frequently debated its conclusions, is a pioneering study; R. W. B. Lewis, *The American Adam* (Chicago: U. of Chicago, 1955); Anselm Strauss, *Images of the American City* (Glencoe, Ill.: Free Press, 1961); Daniel Horowitz, "The Meaning of City Biographies: New Haven in the Nineteenth and Early Twentieth Centuries," *Connecticut Historical Society Bulletin* XXIX (July, 1964), pp. 65–75; R. Richard Wohl and A. Theodore Brown, "The Usable Past: a Study of Historical Traditions in Kansas City," *The Huntington Library Quarterly* XXIII (May, 1960), pp. 237–259; Daniel Levine, *Varieties of Reform Thought* (Madison: State Historical Society of Wisc., 1964); George Dunlap, *The City in the American Novel, 1789–1900* (N.Y.: Russell and Russell, 1965); Blanche H. Gelfant, *The American City Novel* (Norman: U. of Oklahoma, 1954); Eugene Arden, "The Evil City in American Fiction," *New York History* XXXV (July, 1954), pp. 259–279.

GOVERNMENT AND POLITICS: A few citations must suffice to represent the large body of writing in these areas. On colonial cities, see Ernest S. Griffith, *History of American City Government: the Colonial Period,* (N.Y.: Oxford, 1938), and Richard B. Morris, *Government and Labor in Early America* (N.Y.: Columbia U., 1946). Useful surveys are John Fairlie, *Municipal Administration* (N.Y.: Macmillan, 1901) and Ernest S. Griffith, *The Modern Development of City Government* (London: Oxford U., 1927). Seymour Mandelbaum, *Boss Tweed's New York* (N.Y.: Wiley, 1965) makes interesting use of social science concepts. Harold Zink, *City Bosses in the United States* (Durham: Duke U., 1939) is a comparative study. The following articles will serve to introduce recent thinking on bossism and reform: Eric McKitrick,

"The Study of Corruption," *Political Science Quarterly* LXXII (December, 1957), pp. 502–514; James Weinstein, "Organized Business and the City Commission and Manager Movements," *Journal of Southern History* XXVIII (May, 1962), pp. 167–181; Samuel P. Hays, "The Politics of Reform in Municipal Government in the Progressive Era," *Pacific Northwest Quarterly* LV (October, 1964), pp. 157–159; Roy Lubove, "The Twentieth Century City: the Progressive as Municipal Reformer," *Mid-America* XXXI (October, 1959), pp. 195–209. Allen F. Davis, "Jane Addams vs. the Ward Boss," *Journal of the Illinois State Historical Society* LIII (Autumn, 1960), pp. 247–265, and Louis G. Geiger, "Joseph W. Folk v. Edward Butler: St. Louis, 1902," *Journal of Southern History* XXVIII (November, 1962), pp. 438–449, are analytical narratives.

SOCIAL HISTORY, WELFARE, THE URBAN IMMIGRANT: Many sources have been indicated in the text. The following should be specially noted: Roy Lubove, *The Progressive and the Slum* (Pittsburgh: Pittsburgh U., 1963); Robert Bremner, *From the Depths: the Discovery of Poverty in the United States* (N.Y.: New York U., 1956); Blanche D. Coll, "The Baltimore Society for the Prevention of Pauperism," *American Historical Review* LXI (October, 1955), pp. 77–87; Carroll S. Rosenberg, "Protestants and Five Pointers: the Five Points House of Industry, 1850–1870," *New York Historical Society Quarterly,* XLVIII (October, 1964), pp. 326–347; Miriam Z. Langsam, *Children West* (Madison: State Historical Society of Wisc., 1964); Charles Rosenberg, *The Cholera Years* (Chicago: U. of Chicago, 1962); James W. Cassedy, "The Flamboyant Colonel Waring," *Bulletin of the History of Medicine* XXXVI (March–April, 1962), pp. 163–176; Maldwyn Allen Jones, *American Immigration* (Chicago: U. of Chicago, 1960); Robert Ernst, *Immigrant Life in New York City* (N.Y.: King's Crown, 1949); Oscar Handlin, *Boston's Immigrants* (Cambridge: Harvard U., 1959); Moses Rischin, *The Promised City: New York's Jews* (Cambridge: Harvard U., 1962); Lewis E. Atherton, *Main*

Street on the Middle Border (Bloomington: Indiana U., 1954); Aaron Abell, *The Urban Impact on American Protestantism* (Cambridge: Harvard U., 1962); Allen F. Davis, "The Social Workers and the Progressive Party, 1912–1916," *American Historical Review* LXIX (April, 1964), pp. 671–688; Maurice R. Stein, *The Eclipse of Community* (Princeton: Princeton U., 1960); Almont Lindsay, *The Pullman Strike* (Chicago: U. of Chicago, 1942); St. Clair Drake and Horace R. Cayton, *Black Metropolis* (Harper Torchbook ed., N.Y.: Harper and Row, 1962).

ARCHITECTURE AND URBAN PLANNING: The writing on these subjects is voluminous but much of it is unhistorical. The following are important: John W. Reps, *The Making of Urban America: a History of City Planning in the United States* (Princeton: Princeton U., 1965), a magnificent piece of scholarship, beautifully illustrated; Christopher Tunnard and Henry Hope Reed, *American Skyline* (Boston: Houghton Mifflin, 1955), an incisive survey of American urban development with emphasis on building styles; John Burchard and Albert Bush-Brown, *The Architecture of America: A Social and Cultural History,* (Boston: Little, Brown, 1961); Wayne Andrews, *Architecture, Ambition, and Americans* (New York: Harper, 1955); Sigfried Giedion, *Space, Time, and Architecture* (Cambridge: Harvard U., 4th ed., 1962); several works by Lewis Mumford, especially *The Brown Decades* (N.Y.: Dover ed., 1955), *The Culture of Cities* (N.Y.: Harcourt Brace, 1938), and "The City," in Harold Stearns (ed.), *Civilization in the United States* (N.Y.: Harcourt Brace, 1922); John Coolidge, *Mill and Mansion: A Study of Architecture and Society in Lowell, Massachusetts* (N.Y.: Columbia U., 1942); Edmund H. Chapman, *Cleveland: Village to Metropolis* (Cleveland: Western Reserve U., 1965); William H. Wilson, *The City Beautiful Movement in Kansas City* (Columbia, Mo.: U. of Missouri, 1964); Roy Lubove, *Community Planning in the 1920's: The Contribution of the Regional Planning Association of America* (Pittsburgh: Pittsburgh U., 1965); Henry W. S. Cleveland, *Landscape Architecture as Applied to the Wants of the West,*

(Lubove, ed., Pittsburgh: Pittsburgh U., 1965); Paul A. Conkin, *Tomorrow a New World: The New Deal Community Program* (Ithaca: Cornell U., 1959).

TECHNOLOGY: This is a relatively undeveloped aspect of American urban history, but the following are valuable: Roger Burlingame, *Engines of Democracy: Inventions and Society in Mature America* (N.Y.: Scribners, 1940); Nelson M. Blake, *Water for the Cities* (Syracuse: Syracuse U., 1956); Harold C. Passer, *The Electrical Manufacturers* (Cambridge: Harvard U., 1953). Many of the works listed under architecture and planning contain material on building technology.

REAL ESTATE AND URBAN LAND USE: These subjects have not been studied historically to any extent but the following are useful: Aaron M. Sakolski, *The Great American Land Bubble* (N.Y.: Harper, 1932); Eugene Rachlis and John E. Marquesee, *The Landlords* (N.Y.: Random House, 1963), a good popular history; Glenn S. Dumke, *The Boom of the Eighties in Southern California* (San Marino: The Huntington Library, 1944); Sam B. Warner, Jr., *Streetcar Suburbs: The Process of Growth in Boston* (Cambridge: M.I.T. and Harvard U., 1962), an original study vital for understanding residential suburbanization; M. Mason Gaffney, *Urban Expansion—Will It Ever Stop?* (Yearbook Separate No. 2931, *Yearbook of Agriculture,* 1958) contributed to our understanding of historical urban land use, as did Homer Hoyt, *One Hundred Years of Land Values in Chicago* (Chicago: U. of Chicago, 1933).

RELATED SOCIAL SCIENCES: Social scientists in other disciplines have much to contribute to the study of urban history. Their work is voluminous, and only a few items can be cited here. Hauser and Schnore, *The Study of Urbanization,* previously cited, is a valuable guide; Paul K. Hatt and Albert Reiss, *Cities and Society: The Revised Reader in Urban Sociology* (Glencoe, Ill.: Free Press, 1957) contains excellent readings. See also Robert K. Merton, *Social Theory and Social Structure* (Glencoe: Free Press, 1949), especially for an approach to the subject of bossism; Leo F. Schnore, *The Urban Scene* (N.Y.: Free Press, 1959), a collection of Schnore's essays which has guided our thinking on metropolitan and suburban growth; Donald J. Bogue, *The Population of the United States* (Glencoe: Free Press, 1959); Rupert B. Vance and Nicholas J. Demerath (eds.), *The Urban South* (Chapel Hill: U. of North Carolina, 1954); N. S. B. Gras, *An Introduction to Economic History* (N.Y.: Harper, 1922); R. D. McKenzie, *The Metropolitan Community* (N.Y.: McGraw-Hill, 1933); Louis Wirth, "The Urban Society and Civilization," *American Journal of Sociology* XLV (March, 1940), pp. 743–755; Hope Tisdale, "The Process of Urbanization," *Social Forces* XX (March, 1942), pp. 311–316; Jean Gottman, *Megalopolis: the Urbanized Northeastern Seaboard of the United States* (N.Y.: Twentieth Century Fund, 1961).

Index

319